Praise for *The Devil Came on Horseback*

"*The Devil Came on Horseback* grabs the reader from page one, then takes us on a journey of Conradian intensity through a circle of hell, its horrors mitigated by moments of humanity amidst a tragedy in which we are all accessories. In every sense, the devil is indeed in the details."

—Karl E. Meyer, editor, *World Policy Journal*,
author of *The Dust of Empire*

"Nothing could be more necessary or timely . . . than Brian Steidle's *The Devil Came on Horseback*, a powerful first-hand account of the Darfur genocide. . . . Individuals like Steidle are achieving more for Darfur's victims than all the exertions of the U.N. Human Rights Council combined."

—*New York Post*

"The story is as compelling as it is devastating. What comes forth in the book are the feelings of despair and helplessness on the part of eyewitnesses in the face of human cruelty. . . . Mr. Steidle juxtaposes the government propaganda against the images of genocide, and he allows the reader to be the judge."

—*National Catholic Reporter*

"Brian Steidle's vivid, compelling account of the ongoing genocide in Darfur bears stark witness to the worst humanitarian crisis facing the world today. It pulls no punches as it begs the question: how can we sit idly by while thousands of innocent people continue to die? If you are at all concerned about your fellow man, *The Devil Came on Horseback* is not only a haunting must read; it is a call to action."

—David Freed, former *Los Angeles Times* reporter

The Devil Came on Horseback

The Devil Came on Horseback

BEARING WITNESS TO THE GENOCIDE IN DARFUR

Brian Steidle

and Gretchen Steidle Wallace

PublicAffairs

New York

Dedicated to the memory of Mihad Hamid.

She gave her life so that I could tell her story.

And to all those who have suffered

because of who they are.

PublicAffairs books are available at special discounts for bulk purchases in
the U.S. by corporations, institutions, and other organizations. For more
information, please contact the Special Markets Department at the Perseus
Books Group, 2300 Chestnut Street, Suite 200, Philadelphia, PA 19103, or
call (800) 255-1514, or e-mail special.markets@perseusbooks.com.

BOOK DESIGN AND COMPOSITION BY JENNY DOSSIN

Library of Congress Cataloging-in-Publication Data
Steidle, Brian.
The devil came on horseback : bearing witness to the genocide in Darfur /
Brian Steidle and Gretchen Steidle Wallace. — 1st ed.
p. cm.
HC: ISBN-13: 978-1-58648-474-3; ISBN-10: 1-58648-474-5
1. Sudan—History—Darfur Conflict, 2003- 2. Ethnic conflict—Sudan—
Darfur. 3. Genocide—Sudan—Darfur. I. Wallace, Gretchen Steidle. II. Title.
DT159.6.D27S74 2007
962.404'3—dc22
2007000116

1 3 5 7 9 10 8 6 4 2

PB: ISBN: 978-1-58648-569-6

Contents

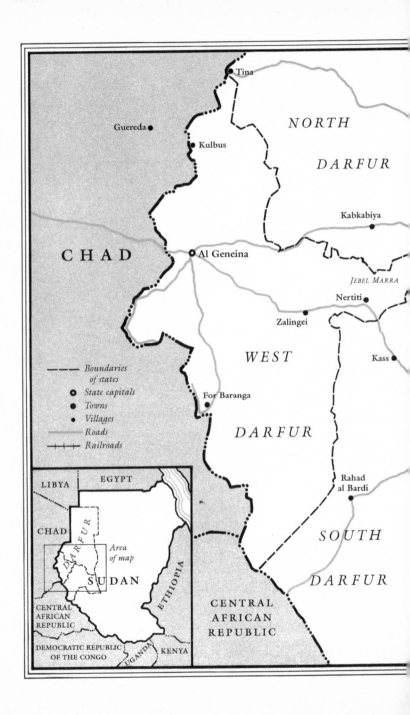

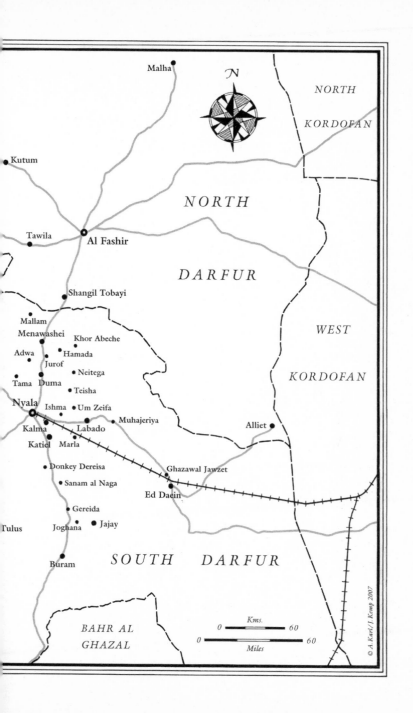

List of Abbreviations

AU	African Union
CARE	Cooperative Assistance and Relief Everywhere, Inc.
CFC	Ceasefire Commission
EU	European Union
GOS	Government of Sudan
ICRC	International Committee of the Red Cross, commonly known simply as the Red Cross; the Muslim affiliate is the Red Crescent
IDP	Internally displaced person, refers mainly to black Africans displaced from their villages in Darfur and gathered in camps within Sudan
JEM	Justice and Equality Movement, one of the main rebel groups in Darfur
JMC	Joint Military Commission, an independent monitoring group in the Nuba Mountains
MSF	Médecins Sans Frontières, a Paris-based NGO, known as Doctors Without Borders in the United States
NATO	North Atlantic Treaty Organization
NGO	Nongovernmental organization, groups such as Oxfam and CARE International
NMRD	National Movement for Reform and Development, a rebel group that broke off from the JEM in 2004
PDF	People's Defense Force, the formal militias of the GOS
SLA	Sudanese Liberation Army, one of the main rebel groups in Darfur
SPLM/A	Sudan People's Liberation Movement/Sudan People's Liberation Army, the political and military arms, respectively, of those seeking more autonomy during the twenty-year civil war in South Sudan
UNICEF	United Nations International Children's Emergency Fund
USAID	United States Agency for International Development
WFP	World Food Program, an organization of the United Nations

Prologue

The rains had already moved on, leaving a dry, oppressive heat that threatened to bake any creature moving too slowly beneath the sun. It was about 115 degrees Fahrenheit. As I disembarked from our helicopter, I breathed as deeply as I could without frying my lungs, steadied myself, and, blinking, took a look around. Camel-colored dust stretched before us as far as we could see.

Ahmed and I headed toward a large nim tree on the outskirts of Wash al Tool, where 250 homeless women and children had stopped earlier in the day to share in the small piece of shade. They had escaped the initial conflict in Alliet, a town of 15,000 we had just visited. The village was the most recent to fall prey to Government of Sudan troops in what was now described by Western diplomats—publicly, if belatedly—as genocide.

Had anyone been injured? We had to ask, even though we were all but certain of the answer. Expressionless, a woman slowly raised a one-year-old girl for me to examine, as if I were a doctor with miracle cures. I quickly took a photo to document the injury before motioning for her to put the child down. I examined the baby, gently directing the woman to move the child this way or that so we could understand her wounds. I realized my instructions only confirmed her presumption that I was a medical professional. I felt increasingly helpless.

The baby's breathing was labored, and she was wheezing noticeably. Upon closer inspection, I realized that this tiny human being had been shot in the back—the child had gaping entry and exit wounds that accentuated her struggle to breathe. Her guardian looked up at me with a blank gaze.

"What's her name?" I stammered, my sense of disbelief audible in my tone.

"Mihad Hamid," she said after a quick translation of my question. The woman, Mihad's aunt, explained that while the child's mother was running from the Government of Sudan troops, carrying the wrapped child on her back, Mihad had been wounded. Attempting to protect both Mihad and her three-year-old brother, Oman, their mother perished in the attack. I was shocked at the lack of emotion in this woman who had just lost her sister and who by default was now this infant's keeper.

Mihad also had received a shrapnel wound on the right side of her head. Round bloody gashes speckled the baby's scalp. Oman lay nestled in the lap of another woman, perhaps a relative or perhaps a mother who had lost her own children in this brutal assault. The woman carefully placed Oman on the ground on his stomach to show us his wounds. Someone had whipped him on the left side of his neck, and I could see a marble-sized shrapnel wound on his buttocks. Both children lay quietly despite their injuries—innocent victims of a ruthless conflict we still could not fully comprehend.

"Captain Brian! Now you see what they do here!" Ahmed screamed, full of rage at what we had just seen. Ahmed, the Chadian mediator for our African Union monitoring team, was a decorated soldier who had served as a rebel in his own country's civil war. Almost always smiling, he was a compact force of African muscle, confidence, and integrity. Ahmed fulfilled his official duties as a mediator with strict impartiality regardless of the situation, yet he had no fear of confrontation, if it was necessary, when we met up with the Arab nomad militias or their enablers—the soldiers and officials of the Government of Sudan.

I shook my head and swallowed with half-hearted acceptance that there was nothing I could say or do to change the situation. I took photos and made notes for my report. Silently fuming, I moved on, clutching my camera a little too fiercely.

I thought back to where I was a year before. I had just completed my term of service in the US Marine Corps, during which I'd served in Kosovo as part of the NATO mission policing villages and prohibiting arms trafficking from Macedonia. After leaving the Marine Corps, I was still eager to be involved somewhere in the field, using my military background. I thought it was a miracle when a civilian contracting company offered me a position in Sudan; it just didn't seem possible at the time that someone would pay me a six-figure salary to hang out in an exotic part of Africa, drive Land Cruisers around in the desert, and, as a civilian, advise a military operation. I accepted the mission with the enthusiasm of a boy invited to Disney World for the first time.

I wasn't completely naïve. I knew there would be conflict. Mass murder in the name of God or national and ethnic superiority had been an unfortunate reality of human life long before the birth of Jesus or Mohammed. Over centuries we have advanced technologically, and yet we still kill each other. It's something that never changes. In the last century alone, genocide was commonplace—Turks killing more than a million Armenians in 1915, the Nazi slaughter of 6 million Jews during the Holocaust, Indonesia's purge of hundreds of thousands of real and imagined Communists in the '60s, the massacres by the Khmer Rouge in Cambodia in the '70s and '80s, and tribe-on-tribe slaughter in Rwanda in 1994.

Now, a decade after Rwanda, it was happening again in Africa. Still, I never expected to see first-hand what I was now seeing in Darfur. Here was a country in the early twenty-first century run by a government that condoned slavery, that used rape as a weapon of war, and that was indiscriminate in its attacks on its enemies. American forces are trained to avoid civilian casualties at all costs. Here, before my eyes, civilians—men, women, and children—were equal targets of the Government of Sudan. This was genocide, up close and personal. I couldn't reconcile or even remotely justify what had happened in Alliet.

A limited African Union monitoring force of 300 and an additional 1,700 soldiers for protection had been assigned to the Darfur region of Sudan where fighting had broken out in early 2003. An initial uprising among black African tribes seeking greater rights had been quickly squelched by the oppressive, Arab-led Government of Sudan. The government took the occasion to dig deeper trenches between the African farming villages and the Arab nomadic herders of Darfur. By arming the Arab nomads, the Government of Sudan had orchestrated a bloody campaign of terror to wipe out the black ethnic groups and permanently alter the demography of the region. Civilians took up arms, often only using elephant spears and stolen weapons to protect their villages against the terrorists they called "the devil on a horse," or *Janjaweed*. By the time I arrived in Darfur, the conflict had reached the scale of civil war, and the United States had called it genocide.

Our mandate was to investigate and report on violations of the supposed ceasefire agreement between the GOS and the two "rebel" groups, the Justice and Equality Movement and the Sudanese Liberation Army. My particular monitoring team of eight was one of only two observer teams operating in South Darfur, an area one-third the size of Texas. Our cast of characters included two African Union members from other African states, a representative of each of the three parties of the Darfur Ceasefire Agreement, a Chadian mediator, an interpreter, and one representative from the European Union or the United States who provided impartial logistical and technical expertise. I was one of only three American monitors assigned to all of Darfur. As unarmed observers, our mandate prohibited us from taking any further action to protect civilians or arrest and discipline perpetrators of the chaos. Our only official task was to observe, inquire, and write reports. While world leaders applauded this "African solution to an African problem," it was slowly becoming apparent that any effort on our part to contain the expanding violence served merely as a facade for what was a relatively inexperienced, ill-equipped, and under-resourced mission. It was an ironic predicament: though my military background as a former US Marine gave me a unique perspective on the limitations of the monitoring force, it was obvious that I was standing on a battlefield where no American had ever been trained to fight.

It had taken me nearly a month to convince the African Union to allow me to take photographs for our team in the field. I was an amateur who had developed a love of photography and felt that a visual record could be useful to our team. I was exhilarated by the idea of playing a role akin to a war photojournalist.

The African Union's skepticism was grounded in a previous leak to *60 Minutes* of photographs shot during a bloody attack on Suleia, where a girls' primary school had been destroyed. Somehow I convinced African Union officials that I was qualified and also committed to what some might consider a gruesome task, but one that I thought was a vital contribution to the history of this conflict. The photos were to be used as supplements to each report we submitted following an investigation of a ceasefire violation.

Before heading to Darfur, I went online to research the best tools of photojournalism and wound up purchasing an expensive, ten-pound digital camera with a serious 16-inch lens. When I finally held it in my hands—after a carefully engineered journey to Sudan across three continents, carried by a colleague from home—I almost trembled with excitement at the thought of whipping this new weapon out of my reporter's arsenal. It somehow compensated for the fact that the only other things I carried with me, besides a darkening suntan, were desert survival accoutrements—all non-lethal—including a canvas hat, sunglasses, water in my Camelbak, a pen, and a waterproof notebook. But at first, I always reached for my smaller digital camera, which I considered less intrusive when faced with the crusted eyes of a wounded child or the downward glance of a woman recently assaulted by strangers.

.   .   .

Today in Wash al Tool, October 20, 2004, I lost my hesitation.

What kind of person can aim a gun at a one-year-old child?

If I wanted to capture evidence for whatever future cause, I was determined to make it the best damn evidence anyone had ever seen. And I would protect this photographic archive with my life. I swung my backpack around and retrieved my superior camera. It didn't feel quite like my old M–16, but somehow I felt more prepared for what I might uncover next.

We walked further into the village to speak with a few more wounded. Villagers directed us to two young girls, six-year-old Fatima Adouma Akhmed Ibrahim, who had been shot in the right foot, and eleven-year-old Salha Adouma Akhmed Ibrahim, who had been shot in her left thigh. Both were lying in makeshift cots, constructed of rough-cut logs and saw palmetto twine. One of the girl's legs had been placed in a wood splint and bandaged with fresh gauze—a rarity in these parts. I was struck by the remarkable resourcefulness of their guardians. I took the first few photographs for what would eventually evolve into a controversial campaign of evidence, espionage, advocacy, and threats to my career and my life.

Riding back in the helicopter that night, I felt shaken by what I had seen. It was still over 100 degrees, and we were sweating because no breeze came through the sealed windows. The stagnant air only added to the weight of my dismay. Sitting, stunned, in the backward-facing jump seat beside the latched door, I offered up my digital camera so my teammates could preview what I had just recorded.

At the sight of Mihad on the camera's screen, the Sudanese Liberation Army and Justice and Equality Movement representatives turned immediately to the Government of Sudan monitor and screamed at him in Arabic over the seats. Spittle sprayed from the Sudanese Liberation Army representative's lips as he gestured at my camera screen, shoving it into the Government of Sudan official's face so that he could see Mihad. Surprised, the government representative pressed himself back into his seat but said nothing. Ahmed jumped up to intervene. He shouted over the rebel monitors, bracing his arm against their chests, and retrieved my camera. The Government of Sudan representative turned away dismissively.

"We must handle this officially," Ahmed stated in English to the team as he handed me my camera. We rode the rest of the way in silence.

Back at home base in Nyala, we notified the International Committee of the Red Cross and other nongovernmental organizations of the fighting, casualties, medical and emergency needs, and location of the displaced so that they could respond appropriately. Coordinating with humanitarian aid groups to treat the injured was not part of our mandate, but it was one of our regular practices. I specifically mentioned the condition of Mihad Hamid so that they might find her.

We attempted to return for a follow up visit over the next two days, but the Sudanese Liberation Army had amassed several hundred troops to attack the Government of Sudan and push it out of Alliet. Our unarmed monitoring team was unable to gain access to the town. Instead, we remained in our helicopter, sitting on the tarmac 200 kilometers away in Nyala and awaiting word that the fighting had stopped. We received reports via satellite phone from our Sudanese Liberation Army contact on the ground that Antonov aircraft were dropping bombs and that helicopter gunships were firing on the village to eliminate the remaining residents.

Despite the heavy fighting in the surrounding areas, Red Cross medics traveled courageously to within 20 kilometers of Alliet, facing gunfire, to treat victims of the attack. But they were never able to locate Mihad.

The greatest regret of my entire time in Darfur—in fact, of my life to this day—is not taking Mihad Hamid and her brother back to our headquarters for medical care. The African Union had not authorized us to help civilians, and bringing those children back with us did not occur to me until we landed back in Nyala. But it would have been the right thing to do.

Instead, I can at least offer this account of what I witnessed in Mihad's homeland, a faraway place where a government, abetted by others incited to hatred, is attempting to "cleanse" an entire people—where Arab Muslims kill African Muslims because the Africans are "too black." Darfur is more than an occasional headline in the newspaper or 20 seconds on a forgotten nightly newscast. It is where genocide continues to happen while the rest of the world goes through the motions of concern but does nothing of substance to stop it. Will the world ever wake up?

As of this writing, I do not know if Mihad Hamid survived.

Author's Note

What follows is true. All the events described here actually happened. Details have been taken from audio journals I recorded on an MP3 player, e-mails sent home, recollections of conversations I had over the phone from Sudan, still photographs that were shot at the scene, and from notes, maps, descriptions, and sketches written in many notebooks at the time. Some descriptions are taken from memory. No actions have been invented.

Many of the conversations had no specific record that existed other than my knowledge of the conversation or in written notes to myself about the essence of what was said. I have tried to recreate those words and conversations honestly and accurately.

The actual names of my monitoring team members and my US embassy contacts involved in these events are not used within the book. Several of these individuals are currently still on the ground in Sudan, and to be associated with a book such as this one would endanger their lives. I apologize for any errors of fact, understanding, or omission.

PART ONE

Nuba Mountains

Chapter 1

It was 8:00 p.m. on a Saturday night, January 24, 2004, and I had been traveling for nearly twenty-four hours. As our plane descended into Khartoum, dim lights outlined the city limits below, and I wondered what lay in wait for me in this troubled country. I stretched my legs and followed the other passengers down the stairs and onto the tarmac. The smell of hot dust mingled with the body odor of my travel companions. Bleary-eyed, heart pumping with adrenalin, I stepped onto the parched soil of North Africa. I could see a few white aid workers in hiking boots and backpacks among the predominantly African crowd as we crammed onto the waiting buses.

.   .   .

Six months earlier, I had completed my four-and-a-half years of required service in the US Marine Corps. After a little travel and a brief woodworking apprenticeship, I was looking for more excitement. It was only two weeks before I first saw the lights of Khartoum that I had been exploring military contracting positions online. One of the jobs advertised had caught my eye: "Patrol Leader Sudan." I sent my résumé in by e-mail on Friday and received a call back from the contractor's project leader for the Joint Military Commission on Saturday. He offered me the job, explaining that the Joint Military Commission was a ceasefire monitoring mission created by an international body to oversee conflict in central Sudan. The job as a patrol leader would require a one-year contract, and they needed my answer within twenty-four hours. I knew very little about the situation on the ground and what "monitoring a ceasefire" would entail, but it seemed like too good an opportunity to pass up. The next day I called to accept.

On Tuesday, I received a FedEx package containing a contract and a plane ticket. The only other information provided was a phone number of someone on the ground whom I could call if necessary. Soon I was on a plane to Khartoum with no idea what I was getting into other than meeting a guy named Mohammed.

.   .   .

On the way to the terminal, we passed a warehouse of wrecked planes and scattered parts that was next to a long line of carefully parked military, United Nations, humanitarian aid, and commercial airplanes. The silence of our bus ride erupted into chaos as we entered the immigration hall. A haze of cigarette smoke hung beneath the already poor fluorescent lighting. Pushing toward the officials occupying two Plexiglas-encased booths, passengers stepped on each other's feet and propelled the crowd forward with their elbows. Hundreds of Arab and African Muslims swarmed on either side of the barrier in both Western clothing as well as white *jelabias*—thin one-piece cotton gowns. How the hell was I supposed to find a guy named Mohammed?

Just as I was cursing myself for not getting more details before my arrival, a towering, thin, black man approached me. I immediately noticed his official demeanor and clean clothes.

"Brian," he said, "hand me your passport."

"Who are you?" I asked guardedly.

"I'm Mohammed." Yeah, so is everyone else here, I thought to myself. "I'm with the Joint Military Commission," he added. "Come this way."

Reluctantly, I handed him my passport. He turned and disappeared into the crowd. A very long minute passed, and it dawned on me that I had just given my passport to a complete stranger in a developing country's airport halfway around the world from my home. What the hell was I thinking?

Just as I was preparing my escape from certain torture by local police, Mohammed returned with a form filled out in Arabic. I closed my eyes for a second and tried to appear relaxed. Mohammed instructed me to follow him as he pressed ahead, bypassing the impatient mob and rapping hard on the rear door of one of the Plexiglas booths. He shoved my passport and form at the official, who took it and, after a brief glance at me, stamped it. I had officially arrived in Khartoum.

My escort chatted with friends while I waited at the baggage claim. Mohammed seemed to know everyone. After identifying my luggage, we headed toward customs. I had crammed three months of supplies and clothing into one internal-frame backpack and a small day pack. One of the best lessons I had learned in the Marine Corps was to be prepared for anything, especially your own escape. My small day pack contained everything essential for ultimate mobility. I didn't know much about Sudan, but I knew the security situation was volatile. Despite my lack of sleep, I was on high alert.

The customs official smirked as I dropped my bags on his table. He began feeling the outside of the pack, asking me what I had in my bag. I heard him mention the word "Kalashnikov," even though my pack was obviously filled only with clothing. "Kalashnikov," I repeated with a nod. He seemed to get my joke, but he remained adamant about searching the contents of my luggage.

"Just give him his stickers!" Mohammed barked, and a shouting match ensued. Judging from their gestures, Mohammed was insisting that as a US contractor working for the Joint Military Commission, or JMC, I had immunity from such searches. This apparently disturbed the official. Finally, the guard slapped my pack with stickers and released me. Next to me were humanitarian aid workers, who were not as lucky; officials were confiscating their fashion magazines—considered pornography—and mouthwash—because it contained traces of alcohol, which was banned under Sudanese law.

As we left customs, we met up with another Westerner, a large, mustached Dutchman named Bert, who was returning to the JMC compound from vacation. Bert was a half-colonel (equivalent to a lieutenant colonel in the US Armed Forces), and he had recently retired from the Dutch Royal Marines after 34 years of service. The three of us edged our way through the confusion, with Mohammed alternating between greeting friends and shouting at people trying to carry our bags. We piled into a waiting Toyota Land Cruiser "Buffalo" and took off across town.

We sped through the city—no stoplights to worry about or street lights to guide us. The paved road from the airport rapidly deteriorated into a minefield of potholes. The dust-covered cement and mud-brick structures reflected our headlights poorly, giving everything a yellowish hue. Traffic jammed up at intersections as drivers turned and accelerated every which way regardless of their lane, giving the entire enterprise the flavor of a drag race and imminent demolition derby. I quickly learned that cars entering a main road from a secondary road have the right of way. Many drivers felt no need for headlights. Ignoring the pandemonium, people squatted and drank chai in front of curbside tea stands, while goats and donkeys meandered the alleyways sifting through the garbage. Looming mahogany trees helped mark the drop-off into sewer ditches that contributed to an overwhelming odor of burning trash, urine, and rotting vegetables. The scent was familiar, bringing me back to the Philippines where I'd lived as a child.

. . .

When I was seven years old, my father, a Navy test pilot, received orders to report to an aircraft carrier in the Indian Ocean. Our family would be able to join him overseas by moving to Subic Bay Naval Base in the Philippines. It was during this two-year tour of duty that I first discovered the Marine Corps. Each afternoon a pack of men in green camouflage or red and yellow gym clothes would jog by our house singing and marching in unison:

Why's that sergeant's face so green?
(Repeat.)
Somebody peed in his canteen.
(Repeat.)

My friends and I would laugh at the lyrics, dropping our bikes to watch the men pass by. Apparently, no Navy wives had yet complained about the chant. The Marines appeared so strong, so brave, so *mean*. Cars seemed to screech to a halt, pulling over to let them by almost the way trains stopped with a glance from Superman. That was it. I immediately *had* to have my own camo outfit. Soon my friends and I were wearing our uniforms, hiding among the saw palmetto and hibiscus shrubs, and ambushing each other with broomstick rifles and damp dirt clods. There in the jungles of the Philippines, I knew I wanted to grow up and someday be part of a real military operation in an exotic location. Well, here I was.

.   .   .

We came to a stop outside the Joint Military Commission compound, a three story house surrounded by a relatively secure wall topped with barbed wire. The guards buzzed us through the first entry to check our identity from behind a glass wall and then buzzed us through a second entry to the front of the building. I noted the security cameras. We walked along an alleyway and up some stairs into a confusing series of rooms. Bert said, "Find a rack, the head's there, I'll meet you up on the third floor." I explored the labyrinth of hastily constructed rooms, some containing up to four or five twin beds. I chose a relatively private space instead of a large bunk-bedded room that had an air-conditioning unit. Fighting off the urge to collapse on my bed, I decided to investigate level three.

I walked up the stairs to find a party in full swing, attended by a rowdy group of 25 to 30 expatriate men and women who, I later learned, came from various missions, aid groups, and embassies. Someone had hooked up their iPod to the speaker system. I helped myself to a serving of orange jungle juice from the 25-gallon cooler and introduced myself to my new colleagues. Before long, I found myself sitting with Bert in wicker chairs and sharing a bottle of twelve-year-old scotch. I still had no idea what I was doing there, but I knew I could get used to this.

It could have been the scotch, my anticipation, or the 90-degree heat—I should have picked the room with the AC unit—but I slept fitfully that first night in Sudan. The next morning I met with Frank, the Deputy Chief Administration Officer, for a briefing on JMC operations in the Nuba Mountains region. As I prepared for my departure from Khartoum, I felt the rush of embarking on a new and exotic assignment.

Chapter 2

Two days after my arrival in Khartoum, Bert and I headed back to the airport. We clambered up a small ladder behind the pilots' seats into a rickety, twin-propeller charter plane. I took the seat closest to the emergency exit and tried to get comfortable. Later, the United States would forbid any of its personnel from flying this local company's charters because of its crash record. About twenty aid workers and civilian contractors filled those seats not already crammed with cargo, and I wondered about our allowable weight limit. As we sat on the tarmac waiting to take off, I battled a squadron of flies that had been excited by the fragrance of overripe fruit and raw meat that saturated the cabin. The supply flights transported meat in coolers, but apparently they were not always sealed completely.

As we soared over the arid plains of central Sudan, the two-and-a-half hour flight to the Nuba Mountains revealed nothing below but sand and scrub brush. The rains had stopped in September or October, and the region was now at the height of the dry season.

The Nuba Mountains region in northern and central Sudan is about the size of Maine, and it consists of a fertile highland plain with scattered mountain ranges. For roughly 20 years, a civil war had been raging between the Government of Sudan (GOS), a military dictatorship led by wealthy Arab Muslims who populated the North, and the opposing "rebel" group, the Sudan People's Liberation Movement/Army (SPLM/A). The SPLA forces were fighting on behalf of hundreds of black African tribes in the South, including those in the Nuba Mountains region, who were mostly poor, rural, Christian or animist farmers. The rebels sought political representation, equitable investment in the region's development, oil rights, and an end to civil-government-enforced Islamic law. More than 2 million people had perished, and about 4 million had been displaced by the conflict—the longest-lasting civil war in African history to date.

About 150 unique tribes with different languages occupied the Nuba Mountains. These Mountains were basically divided into three areas: the Western Jebels, the Eastern Jebels, and the Central Plains and Miri Hills region. *Jebel* means "mountain" in Arabic. Most of the Jebels were controlled by the SPLM/A. However, the Miri Hills, though sympathetic to the SPLA, were under the administrative control of the government. Forming a pocket of fierce resistance, the Nuba people consistently ambushed GOS forces, preventing the government from infiltrating their mountainous stronghold.

In January 2002, with the help of the international community, the two sides had reached a ceasefire. An international body made up of around twelve countries in the European Union, the United States, and Canada, called the Friends of the Nuba Mountains, was established to oversee the ceasefire. The Friends then created the Joint Military Commission to monitor the ceasefire on the ground while protracted peace negotiations ensued. I would soon learn firsthand that the JMC mission in the Nuba Mountains was extremely successful owing to the transparency of its information, the efficiency of its communication, and the effectiveness of its leadership. The mission had made the crucial difference in helping to establish peace in the Nuba and, thus, in all of South Sudan.

The JMC officers in command were deeply committed to the mission. Each of these exceptional leaders had been hand-picked by their governments to represent their countries on this English-speaking mission to Sudan. The JMC divided the Nuba region into five sectors, each with a sector commander and several teams. Each team consisted of a representative from each of the warring parties—the SPLA and the GOS—and each was led either by an international active-duty military officer or a civilian contractor with military experience, like me.

Our mission was to investigate complaints of ceasefire violations. Disputes over land, wives, cattle, camels, the right to carry a weapon, and the right to bring goods to certain markets were typical ceasefire violations that had the potential to explode and send the country back into civil war. In response to each complaint, our unarmed monitoring team would travel out into the field on one- to six-day-long patrols to investigate. Our transportation options included helicopters, turbo-diesel SUVs, 4-wheelers, mountain bikes, and our own two feet. Each multi-day patrol would require that we camp in local villages and interact with the indigenous population. I couldn't believe I was going to be paid to do this. It sounded like an exotic adventure vacation.

During my first briefing in Khartoum about the JMC's Nuba Mountains mission, Frank, the Deputy Chief Administration Officer, mentioned that the GOS had resumed bombing a different set of rebel forces in a western province of Sudan, called Darfur, killing hundreds and forcing thousands to flee to neighboring Chad. He gave me an overview of the 2003 uprising and the government's brutal response. But Frank's references to Darfur in his brief were minimal, and I knew little else of the increasing deterioration of the situation in that part of Sudan.

.　　.　　.

We landed safely in the town of Kadugli—7,000 feet above sea level—on an airstrip the town had just paved for the first time the previous week. It was an anomaly in this area, since all other paved roads ended about 150 miles north of where we now were. Bert and I gathered our luggage and exited the airport area toward a scattering of tractor trailers that served as a JMC outpost for incoming flight inspections. The JMC had constructed its field head-quarters, which we called "Tillo," on the outskirts of the village of Kadugli.

A JMC truck waited to take us to the base camp over what could have been the worst road in Africa. We drove by sparse markets that would barely pass for a lemonade stand back home, fragile grass huts, mud-brick houses capped in corrugated tin, and ancient farmland. Thirty minutes later we arrived at base camp. Dropping my bags at the JMC offices, I barely had a chance to realign my spine after the jostling ride before Bert grabbed me to take another drive up to Sector 4, about an hour away. Bert drove like a kamikaze in a rally race. The potholes melted beneath our tires at that speed.

.　　.　　.

The JMC had assigned me to Sector 1, which was based in the village of Kauda about 100 kilometers, or a six-hour drive, to the east of Kadugli in SPLA-controlled territory. Bert, it turned out, would be my sector commander, and he assured me that I would not get bored. He had initially planned to fly by helicopter to our assigned area, but since two of our trucks were in Kadugli getting fixed, we decided to convoy in the morning when the maintenance was complete. Plan B sounded like much more fun to me, and I salivated at the chance to drive on the mountainous terrain. A few years earlier, I had looked into Land Rover driving school, but I changed my mind because of the outrageous cost. Here in the Nuba Mountains, extreme off-road excursions would be a daily part of my job. The trucks that the JMC used for patrols were Toyota Hiluxes—four-door pickups with a five-speed, four-wheel drive, turbo diesel engine. Added to the package were big knobby tires, a stiff suspension, full brush guard, and a winch to get us out of heavy sand or mud. I made a mental note to look into shipping vehicles back to the US.

That night in Kadugli, I settled into a large bunk room for transients. Temporary walls that stopped five feet below the twelve foot ceilings offered some privacy around each bed. I walked into the first room and assembled my mosquito net over my bed. Having not yet adjusted to the time change, I located my headlamp so that I could read for a while and flopped down on my stomach with my book.

Thwap. I heard the sound in front of me. Then I heard it again. The noise sounded like someone was lightly smacking their hands together, yet it was coming from between my bed and the wall closest to my head. I sat up and turned toward the wall, my headlamp catching the net. Lifting the net, I searched around for the sound. Nothing. I returned to reading my book. *Thawp, thwap.* I couldn't figure out what was making that noise.

When I heard the sound again, it was accompanied by the sensation of some object about four to six inches long attaching itself to the right side of my face. I cursed and dropped my book, smacking the creature off my cheek. Throwing open the net, I jumped out of my bunk. I was being attacked by something in my own bed under what was supposed to be my net of safety.

My eyes took in the scene. Several large locusts hovered near my bed and inside my mosquito net, clearly attracted by the headlamp strapped to my forehead. I shook the mosquito net vigorously. Grabbing my book to swat the creatures away from my covers, I shivered with disgust. I quickly learned that securing the net under my mattress would ensure no large insects would cuddle up with me during the night. Tucking the net tighter than the sheet on one of my Marine Corps racks, I tried to get to sleep. All night I had nightmares about being attacked, and I kept turning on my light to find nothing. Another night of fitful sleep. Welcome to Sudan, I thought, hoping my more permanent lodging in Sector 1 might be better.

The next morning, Bert and I drove two vehicles out to Sector 1. Slamming the door of the Toyota Hilux, I gave Bert a thumbs-up that I was ready. It was nearly impossible to follow him as he flew through dry stream beds and swerved along mountain passes. I wondered how long this six-hour trip would take most drivers. Women and children walked single file and barefoot along the roadside carrying large clay pots or jerry cans on their heads. They looked at us with wonder for a split second before we lost them in a cloud of dust. I was almost embarrassed, but I kept up with Bert out of fear that I might lose him completely in the middle of nowhere. By early afternoon, we were pulling into the camp for Sector 1.

Chapter 3

A 1920s British school served as our camp in Kauda. We had access to electricity via two huge generators, satellite TV, phone, and internet. A canopy of hearty mahogany trees provided visual relief from the broad expanse of red dust and protection from the harsh sun. Various mud-brick buildings housed our offices, bunkhouses, bathhouse, storage, and gym. Under a flimsy metal roof, a huge plastic bladder that could have contained a swimming pool stored our drinking water. My assigned bedroom was a fifteen-by-fifteen-foot cell with thick cement walls. The metal-frame windows contained no glass, yet, absurdly, one window housed a small AC unit that blew somewhat cooler air through the room. I was given a single bed with mosquito netting and a wall locker for my personal belongings. The ambience was not too far removed from the Marine Corps barracks I knew so well. In other words, it was tolerable.

I met our monitoring team that first evening at chowtime. I felt welcomed and easily at home despite the fact that I was the youngest on the mission. Our team included four Europeans, a South African medic, two GOS monitors, three SPLA monitors, an interpreter, and a driver. The camp also employed nine local staff who cooked, cleaned, repaired the vehicles, watered the flowers, and chased the goats, chickens, cows, and wild dogs away. I felt confident with Bert at the helm. Shortly after my arrival he appointed me the operations officer for our sector, and I began planning the schedule for the first two weeks.

Our sector was the largest in the Nuba Mountains, covering about 40,000 square kilometers. At the time I arrived, there were about 10,000 square kilometers that still had not been visited by the mission, and they were represented by a big blank spot on our map. Not many white people had ever set foot in that area of Sudan, and those who had explored the region had last done so in the 1920s. Africa, of course, had been a rich target of European explorers for centuries, and with their "discoveries" had come colonial outposts. Eventually these outposts evolved into colonial empires that, by design or accident, were built on the notion of conquering and "enlightening" the indigenous people of these lands. I knew that this was a murky and often ugly legacy, and yet the idea that there were places on this earth that might not have been completely investigated—and that I could do some of that exploring—gave me a rush of energy.

.　　.　　.

My daily schedule embodied the Arabic term *inshallah*, literally meaning "God willing" but usually used to mean "whatever" or "whenever." It could not have been more different from the Marine Corps. If we expected a plane to arrive at 1500 hours, it really meant that it could land anytime between 1400 and 1600. Each day one of us conducted flight inspections while the others would manage special tasks. Each week we visited at least one military site controlled either by the GOS or the SPLA.

If we did not have anything scheduled we were free to do whatever we wanted. We loved to visit the local markets, usually held weekly in each village. Therefore, if a market were to be held on a Wednesday, we would plan a patrol to that particular village on that day. We could also take the four-wheelers, motorcycle, or truck for a drive, go for a walk, sun bathe, or sit and watch a movie. Even though this area had been a war zone in the past, it was relatively safe now. I expected to really enjoy my time in the Nuba Mountains.

Our work enabled us to interact daily with the more than thirty international NGOs (nongovernmental organizations) conducting aid work and other miscellaneous research in the area. We would visit their operations and invite them over to our compound for cookouts. Our cook was very good, and there was always plenty to eat.

Our responsibility for flight inspections included examining the humanitarian supply flights arriving in the Nuba Mountains. Kauda's airfield was a small dirt strip about 200 meters long in the middle of nowhere. Shipments could contain pipes and drilling supplies for water wells, books for the local school, and food aid. People would come out of the woodwork to unload the plane onto trucks for delivery to the NGOs' headquarters. One characteristic of Africa that continued to baffle me was that, despite the emptiness of the surrounding landscape stretching for hundreds of miles between towns, people always seemed to appear from nowhere without any advance notice at the exact moment of a food distribution or a possible job opportunity.

.   .   .

Despite a strong NGO presence in our sector, food aid was often restricted to certain areas by the government. In fact, the ongoing civil war was not the only difficulty facing the Nuba tribes. Famine was widespread due to drought or the government's denial of food aid. Disease was also prevalent: polio, hepatitis—A, B, C, and E—rabies, malaria, typhoid, yellow fever, meningitis, leprosy, tuberculosis, and HIV/AIDS, though HIV was reportedly not as pervasive in Sudan as in other African countries.

There were few jobs in the Nuba Mountains and virtually no economy beyond barter. Most inhabitants were subsistence farmers or nomads who lived off the land. Their most valued possessions were goats and donkeys or, if they were rich, a pig or a cow. Their staple crops included peanuts, referred to as "groundnuts," and sorghum, a grain similar to barley that was eaten most often as a porridge. There were some shops in the villages we toured, but they consisted of little more than a shack constructed out of branches and twine with an open front selling as many wares as a single traveling salesman could carry. A woman would sit on a grass mat with maybe three onions, a pile of beans, and two toothbrushes. The onions were likely all she had left from harvesting her crops, while the remainder of the items she probably traded for along the way. Markets were held periodically where villagers from many surrounding towns would travel for miles to sell or barter whatever they could spare.

There was little infrastructure in the Nuba Mountains, if any—certainly no public transportation, electricity, or telecommunication capability. The Shanablas, an Arab tribe of nomads, tended to use camels to travel. As for the rest of the indigenous population, they would be lucky if they had a Chinese-made bicycle. Mostly, they walked or rode a donkey.

Basic education was also nearly nonexistent. Some youngsters went to schools run by NGOs operating in their area, but they might have to walk five or more hours to get there. Occasionally, we would come across a "bush" school, usually run by volunteers from the local community. Each student paid about $10 per school year to attend, and the money allowed the village to purchase supplies and food for the teacher. But few families could afford the fee. Some traded crops for their children's education. Others appealed to the community to allow their children to attend for free. Education was very important to the tribes of the Nuba Mountains. All classes were taught in English, and villages usually chose their teachers based on their ability to speak English. I eventually discovered that the tribes of the south were intent on learning English to separate themselves from the Arabs of the north.

Despite the poverty, it was very surprising to me that crime was almost nonexistent. The Nuba people would tell me that it was their tradition not to lie or steal. I could leave $1,000—about twice the average annual wage—in my pants pocket when I sent my clothes to be washed, and the pants would come back clean with the money returned to the same pocket. The north was also relatively safe from crime, perhaps due to the strong Muslim culture. But I saw no evidence of these traditions among the Shanablas, whose actions continued to aggravate the ceasefire.

As far as I could tell, for women life was extremely difficult. Sudan was primarily a patriarchal society, yet the women were the laborers. They might walk five or six hours with huge bundles of firewood or five-gallon buckets on their heads to collect their daily water. Girls could be sold by their fathers into marriage for as little as two cows—roughly $400—and human trafficking was not uncommon. Women were stoned to death in some places if they cheated on their husbands, but men were legally allowed to take up to four wives. In almost all circumstances, men would not even stand next to a woman. The men would sit, and the women would stand behind them. I had heard that approximately 90 percent of Sudanese women still undergo female genital mutilation, and I learned that there are two methods. The first removes only the clitoris, but the second procedure involves sewing the vagina closed, often using thorns. As a result, women experience many complications with urination and menstruation, not to mention the pain and tearing during sex and child birth.

.   .   .

One of the ways I kept myself from feeling totally cut off from the rest of the world was by talking with my older sister, Gretchen. We had grown up in a military family, and our parents had instilled in us a commitment to public service from day one. While I joined the US military, Gretchen worked to effect social change in developing countries. Gretchen and I, along with our younger brother, Eric, were typical "Navy brats": I think we knew how to salute before we knew how to walk.

Looking back, it sometimes seemed that the three of us were the only kids that really existed on the planet. Every two years my father was stationed at a different base around the country and then overseas. Each move brought us closer together because we had to rely on each other as playmates as well as for moral support; it wasn't always easy being the new kid in school.

Once when I was in sixth grade, my dad came to school in his test pilot's flight suit as a part of career day. Kids in my class began asking him for his autograph when they found out he had gone to Top Gun. Having recently moved for the seventh time, I smiled proudly as my fears of being the new kid slowly melted away. I had always admired my father's career in the Navy and anticipated that I, too, might wear a US military uniform.

Gretchen and I were only two years apart and had remained close through our teens and twenties. By the time I was heading off to Sudan, Gretchen was already in South Africa on a self-designed investigation of AIDS issues.

We began a correspondence by e-mail immediately after I had landed in Khartoum and she had returned to the United States. Gretchen had seen chilling cases of sexual violence in South Africa. In one orphanage, she was told of a tiny girl who had died after being raped at her own mother's funeral; there was a broadly believed myth that having sex with a virgin would cure you of AIDS. In another case, a young man arranged for a gang rape of his girlfriend to teach her a lesson. Gretchen had been deeply affected by these cases. She grew more and more curious about the culture in which I was embedded, especially the lives of women.

She prodded me with questions in her emails:

How much freedom do the women have? Can they vote? Go to school? Work? How prevalent is HIV/AIDS? I heard Sudan is the one of the last places on earth where slavery is still active. Can you tell me more?

Gretchen, [I wrote back] I am vaguely aware that there is a slave trade, but I don't know much. The people who are kidnapped by the nomadic tribes of the north are kept and sold as slaves. But even here, without official slavery, there is serious inequality. Among some Nuba tribes, if I were to ask a woman if she was married or how many children she had, her husband would have to challenge me. They fight with sticks, like swords. I don't know the rules. But if I were to win, then I would get his wife. Just like that.

Slavery, in particular, is kind of kept down-low. The government certainly doesn't say much about it. I know that there are some NGOs, mainly church-affiliated groups, that are working to free these people. People rarely talk about it, though, because within each NGO there are local staff who report back to the GOS. We never know for sure which staff members are embedded by the GOS, but it is understood and assumed that they are there to help the government keep tabs on what the NGOs are doing.

By February 4, 2004, barely a week after my arrival, violence had erupted in most of the regions bordering the Nuba Mountains. This instability threatened to extinguish what remained of the ceasefire in our area. In the north, our monitoring team had been trying to arrange a meeting between the Shanablas and the SPLA. The Shanablas had traveled south for centuries to graze their cattle and camels, and they were the group predominately responsible for kidnapping people and taking them back up north to the slave markets. Those Shanablas who had been armed by the GOS were also known as the People's Defense Force (PDF). The government used the Shanablas to raid, pillage, rape, and burn throughout the Nuba Mountains.

During my first week, three Shanablas riding camels and armed with AK–47s entered SPLA territory. The SPLA arrested the Shanablas, seized their weapons and camels, and then released the nomads. The nomads were furious and attempted to negotiate for their weapons and animals, to no avail. Mysteriously, a Sudanese man of African descent turned up dead the next day with hands and head cut off. In response, the SPLA ordered armed men to hunt down Shanablas. Luckily, they could not find any. As the second recourse, the SPLA set a steep fine the Shanablas would have to pay in order to get their camels back, though they still refused to return the weapons. The fine—300,000 Sudanese dinars, or $1,153—was more money than the Shanablas earned in two years. The Shanablas retaliated by smashing water barrels and burning local crops. A meeting was set for Sunday, but within an hour it had been called off. The Shanablas wanted the meeting place changed.

This was typical of the posturing and political wrangling the two sides engaged in. One of the primary obstacles to peace was that the PDF had a number of high-ranking officers who were well paid by the GOS. If the war were to end, they would have no jobs, so they did everything they could to delay the reconciliation process, even attempting to incite war again.

To the west of us in a town called Eyre in SPLA territory, armed GOS troops had shown up to retaliate against members of the Attoro tribe over a dispute concerning settlers' rights. The Attoro once occupied the land before the war but had been driven out during the fighting. They had returned to claim their land only to find other people living in their houses and cultivating their fields.

The fighting had resumed about 120 miles to our south as well, just north of Malakal. We were expecting to see refugees from the fighting reach us within twenty-four to forty-eight hours. My JMC colleagues were visibly anxious.

I wrote home to Gretchen, Eric, and my parents:

> The situation here is tense. Two weeks ago the SPLA soldiers would wave at us when we drove by. Now they just stare. I asked one of our local monitors if there was going to be peace. He just shook his head and said, "I don't know." Two weeks ago the answer would have been, "I think so."

I packed all of my essential belongings into one bag and prepared an evacuation strategy should the fighting move farther north. The Sudanese monitors from the SPLA and the GOS were waiting to get called back by their respective parties. I could see dread in their eyes, anticipating a return to a war that had already claimed 2 million of their countrymen. It was equally possible that things could settle down in a day or two. The only constant was the instability.

· · ·

A few days later, I departed on my first overnight patrol to the village of Tungoli in the northern area of our operations. Despite the instability that threatened the region, going out on patrol was fascinating. This would be my first opportunity to experience the essence of rural culture in Sudan and my first look at the impact of this long war on village life. We drove for about four hours through the mountains, where fleeing tribes had sought refuge from the conflict for decades. These mountains were essentially huge piles of boulders between which the soil had eroded, leaving dozens of caves. Naturally-occurring springs provided water for drinking and irrigation. From our vehicles, we could see small terraces speckled with old sorghum stocks throughout the mountainside. I was astounded by the living conditions these tribes had endured for so long—they were still living in open caves.

People had now started to move out of the mountains to reclaim their fields for planting. There was nothing left of most of their old towns except for a few desolate foundations. Yet, along the way, we visited several new villages under construction. Elsewhere, people stood on the rocks looking down at our convoy, not yet ready to leave the safety of their mountain dwellings.

We brought our vehicles to a halt next to a series of grass huts. A rocky shelf rose up steeply before us. The chief of Tungoli lived in one of the homes at the base of the mountain, near which other new structures were being built. I guessed that the villagers were rebuilding in close proximity to the hills so they could seek protection if they faced another attack. Disputes were now frequent with Shanablas who had been grazing their camels in these same vacated fields over the last few years.

We sat down to talk with the chief outside his hut. As we finished our introductions, the chief took a moment to whisper to a man who then rose and left the circle. The team resumed the discussion, asking about the new village and seeking information on any conflicts in their area.

"You see," the chief explained through our interpreter, "the well that we have been digging has just collapsed again. We have made several attempts to salvage it but have not yet been successful." We knew that villagers returning from the mountains usually needed to locate a new source of water for their settlements. Their choices were either to dig a well by hand or, if they were lucky, with a drilling rig provided by an NGO. Otherwise, they would have to hike two hours back into the mountains to get water from the natural springs.

"We now have only twenty liters of water for our entire village of 450 people," the chief added. At that moment, the man who had left returned, bringing a single glass of water for me to drink.

"For me?" I stammered with surprise. I looked at the glass and sucked in my breath. Even if they were to give it half an hour to settle, I was certain it would still be half-full with dirt. I took the glass with a plastic smile on my face, catching a whiff of livestock. How could they be surviving on this? Did they really want me to drink it? I waited to see if other glasses would be produced for the other two white monitors with me. No other such offerings emerged, and everyone looked at me in anticipation. Maybe this was their only glass and a similar gift would await the rest of our team after I was through.

Despite my increasing dehydration, there was no way I could drink that muddy water.

"I really wish I could, but I just cannot accept their gesture," I gently told our interpreter. "First, I know that they certainly need it more than I do; second, I know I will spend the rest of our drive back with my head out the window."

Without translating my remarks, he explained, "They will be extremely offended if you do not drink that glass—immediately."

Forcing a smile, I tipped the greasy vessel, avoiding floating insects, and drank as much as possible without chewing the sediment on the bottom. I might as well have licked a goat. I tried to keep my composure as we continued our meeting. We discussed the usual incursions and other conflicts. They told us that an increasing number of Shanablas had been entering their area and allowing their camels to feast on the local crops. We offered to do what we could to look into the matter. Sweat dripped down my face as I waited for my stomach to begin churning. But when the meeting ended, I was fine.

"Thanks for taking one for the team," my colleague slapped me on the back as I spit the remaining grit from my teeth.

The Tungoli villagers were extremely hospitable. We were invited to stay overnight by the omda, the village chief. The community brought us cots made by weaving twine from saw palmetto leaves between wooden frames. Mine was about seven inches too short, and my feet kept falling asleep because they were hanging off the end. I wound up sleeping on the ground, which felt like a slab of cement with a dusting of rocks and sand on top. All of the dogs, goats, chickens, and pigs wanted to know what this thing on the ground was. When I woke up in the morning, there was a clear area all around me because I had thrown all of the rocks at my frequent visitors. By the early hours of the morning, I had ended up resorting to throwing handfuls of sand just so they would leave me alone. It was another long night in Sudan, but this time with an extraordinary view above me. With no generator within a six-hour drive, there was no ambient light; that, and a late-rising moon, left a night sky exploding with a billion stars.

In the morning, our hosts served us some tea made from the same water I had barely mastered the previous evening. Our female monitor could still not bring herself to drink it. The other male monitor and I smiled like men taking on a necessary duty and drank it all. It was foul. The tea smelled and tasted like the water even though it was warm and had lots of sugar.

Later that day we visited two more new villages and a market. The market was filled with all kinds of products brought in on trucks as well as on the heads of women from all of the surrounding villages: cots, clothing, bicycle parts, pots, ten-kilo blocks of hashish, and all kinds of food. One of the most amazing items I discovered was a potion made from hibiscus flowers. The locals would soak them in water for days and then add sugar to make a beverage that tasted like sweetened pomegranate juice. It was said to be good for fighting urinary tract infections and diarrhea, and serving as a poultice for skin problems. Our local cook served this juice with every meal. I also discovered what I first thought was a bean pod with sticky, fuzzy hairs called *al arab*. Prepared the same way as the hibiscus flowers, it was used as a malaria preventative. I had decided early on to stop taking my malaria medicine because its long-term use was damaging to the liver, so I was delighted with this local concoction. Luckily, there were no mosquitoes during the dry season and few in the mountains during the rainy season.

That afternoon, I tried my first dried locust. My interpreter instructed me to peel off the wings and the back legs and pop it into my mouth. It was very dry and surprisingly fishy. It could have been a dried shrimp. Not my idea of an afternoon snack, but really not that bad.

A few days later, we toured a mahogany forest with one of the local tribes. This tribe was eager to protect the forest against the other tribes in the area. The trees were spectacular, with thick trunks, expansive branches, and small oval leaves, towering at least 75 feet overhead. As we walked, one of the villagers explained, "In Sudan, no one person owns the forest. For years, anyone could go cut a tree down and sell it. Now we are trying to stop this practice." They spoke passionately about using the forest for the good of the community, seeming to understand the importance of protecting their valuable resource.

Omar, our interpreter, was an elder and a highly respected member of this village. At one time, he had to flee to Ethiopia because of his preaching against the government. When the JMC was established, we needed to hire interpreters from both sides to avoid any actual or perceived bias. We had an SPLA interpreter for SPLA-controlled areas and a GOS interpreter for the GOS-controlled areas. Omar, previously an English professor, was recruited back to the Nuba Mountains for the SPLA position. He also had an interest in botany and for some time had been growing hundreds of mahogany seedlings. He understood both their importance in terms of forest preservation and their potential as income. Omar was particularly interested in the possibility of US investment in the region following the conflict. He and I would spend long hours discussing his interest in plants and my background in forestry and wildlife.

Omar had invited me to speak to his village about good forest practices, allowing me for the first time to tap into my college degree in natural resources from Virginia Tech. The tribe members seemed to hang on my every word, or at least on Omar's translation. After my talk, the villagers came up to me: "We're so happy to have someone from such a great country come to speak with us in our village." They asked me to take their stories back to the people of the United States. It was always amazing to me how the local Sudanese looked up to Americans.

This was particularly gratifying right now. It had been nearly a year since the US government had led the invasion in Iraq to bring down Saddam Hussein. Since then, according to international polls, public attitudes toward America had hardened in many countries in Europe and the Middle East. Our government wasn't as popular as it had been before the war, even though most people distinguished between their feelings for the administration and their opinions of individual American citizens.

Perhaps the growing concern about US foreign policy hadn't taken hold in rural Sudan. I felt a sense of pride as well as a great sense of responsibility.

Chapter 4

By mid-February, the general situation had still not improved. The fighting to the south of us in the Blue Nile Region continued. An artillery barrage a few days earlier had reportedly leveled Malakal. I heard rumors that fighting to our west in Darfur was intensifying. Apparently, thousands had been killed and hundreds of thousands had fled to neighboring Chad. If fighting were to resume in the Nuba Mountains, it would likely start in Sector 1, home to SPLA headquarters. Meanwhile, we went about our business as usual; flight and military inspections and village visits continued. It seemed the only thing we could do was to look over our shoulders a little more often and never travel alone.

In mid-March, we embarked on a four-day patrol to the east of our sector to inspect all of the GOS military positions and units. Bert and I, each with our respective teams, with national monitors and interpreters, headed out. It was fascinating. Suddenly, crossing the border from the SPLA region to GOS-controlled territory, I felt as if I had entered an entirely separate country. We drove through larger, more developed towns that had running water, electricity, and telephones. Cars roamed dusty streets alongside mud-brick buildings with actual storefronts. This level of established commerce couldn't have been more different from the road-side stalls of the SPLA-controlled villages, where bundles of sickly produce sat displayed on grass mats beneath poorly constructed stick shelters. There was still no pavement here, and simple grass huts populated the outskirts of the towns. But the government had plainly invested in development that the rest of the Nuba Mountains had yet to enjoy.

Unlike the SPLA areas, where there was a substantial level of NGO activity, there was little international presence in those controlled by the GOS. Still, I was caught by surprise to discover that most of the people in these towns had never seen a white person before. We stopped our truck in the market square of one village and got out to stretch our legs and look around. People immediately stared at me, pointing and shouting *"Khawajah,"* which literally means "foreigner" but was most commonly applied to whites. Soon, a horde of children gathered around me, all of them too afraid to shake my hand. I politely reached toward them with a cheerful *"Salam alaikum"* ("Peace be unto you," a common Arabic greeting), and the children shuffled backward, peering around one another in a huddle. I stepped toward them again and they chattered at each other shyly. One brave little boy offered a limp hand and giggled when I shook it. That seemed to give others in the group enough confidence to begin to poke and prod me like an alien. One grabbed my wrist and turned it over, pointing at the veins that they could see through my skin. The Transparent Man, I thought to myself, laughing. The children asked me a question, and the GOS interpreter responded with a chuckle. He turned toward me and said the kids had asked how I got to be that color. I smiled and replied that my mother had scrubbed me too hard. He laughed loudly and interpreted. The children's eyes grew wide, and a few ran in terror back into the village. Out of the corner of my eye, I saw a man farther down the road fall off his bicycle while staring at me. Our team moved on, the children following us like American paparazzi, as we ordered chai from a tea shop and wandered among the stores.

Stopping at an old man's store that contained beautiful hand-dyed cloths, I asked about a gift or two I thought I would bring home on my next leave. Startled, the old man rose to his feet, bowed, and, with a deep sweep of his arm, presented his merchandise. As I started to inspect the cloths, he immediately responded with offerings of others I might prefer. I finally made my selections, haggling a bit with the help of my interpreter out of respect. We agreed on a price and I paid him. He took the dinars I offered in both hands and gestured at me in praise, muttering an exclamation I could not understand. As we returned to our vehicle, I asked my interpreter what was said.

He replied, "The shop keeper is praising God that a white man has shopped at his store. The villagers will now consider him the luckiest man in town."

.   .   .

I was continually impressed not only by the warmth and generosity of the Sudanese people, but also by the resilience and persistence of the local staff with whom we worked. A week or so after our trip to GOS territory, William, the new UK monitor, and I took separate vehicles and escorted a convoy of fourteen World Food Program (WFP) 18-wheelers, each with about 35 tons of food, over the same treacherous path Bert and I had driven on my first trip to Sector 1. It reminded me of the tank tracks at Camp Lejeune, the Marine Corps base in North Carolina where I had once been stationed. The WFP had requested our escort to ensure that the nearly 500 tons of food aid arrived where it needed to go. These convoys were sometimes hijacked or "taxed" by local officials—taxed to the point that when they arrived at their final destination, if they arrived at all, there would no longer be enough aid available for the people who needed it.

The journey lasted eleven hours, and I loved every minute of the scenic drive through the mountains of Sudan. I listened to a tape of local Sudanese music left in the cassette player by the last monitor as I followed the monstrous trucks slowly dipping this way and that between rocks and potholes. As we maneuvered across a dry stream bed above what would become a waterfall during the rains, the convoy came to a halt. I wondered if this was number nineteen or twenty in flat tires that needed to be changed. I put my vehicle in gear, killed the engine and got out to see what the problem was. Looking beyond the dozen trucks ahead of me, I was astounded to see our path blocked by a boulder the size of a pick-up truck. To the left, our rocky path disintegrated into loose sand. White-painted rocks lined the roadside, indicating the roadway itself had been cleared of mines. Beyond the white rocks set into the soft sand, it was not safe to travel. To the right of our trail, the stream bed dropped off a 45-foot ledge. The turn was simply too tight to maneuver past the boulder without venturing into a minefield.

The various Sudanese drivers were gathering around the rock, lighting cigarettes and pacing to and fro with heads tilted as they considered their options. I was convinced we would have to back up the entire convoy and find an alternative route through the hills, which might not be possible and at best would delay us for hours.

But instead of getting back into their trucks, the men began pulling sledge hammers and crow bars out of their cabs. All truck drivers in Sudan were prepared to have to repair and rebuild a truck in the middle of the desert rather than waiting for spare parts. I watched with growing admiration as a group of nearly thirty drivers and their crews began chipping away at the boulder. They were going to remove the rock no matter how long it took them. I thought I'd better help and jumped in to lend a hand. But they refused to let the international monitors work, so we simply sat in the shade and watched. Within ninety minutes, the entire rock was broken up and removed from the roadway.

I was humbled watching how hard the local crew had worked. These drivers had put their hearts into a difficult task because they knew how desperately people needed this food aid. It was remarkable. Most days it was hard to measure what we'd accomplished as monitors. I knew I was somehow helping to uphold the ceasefire, but so few disputes that we mediated ended with a definitive solution. We mostly went on patrol, asked how people were doing, and filed reports. Today's convoy, though, was a concrete success. It felt great to have been a part of it.

By early April, the word from the peace talks in Nairobi, Kenya, was not good. The talks, now two years old, had regressed. The United States was no longer imposing a deadline for signing a treaty, and the United Nations had postponed deployment of peacekeeping troops to the Nuba Mountains and South Sudan indefinitely. The six-month mandate that defined my work with the JMC was to end in July and would only be renewed if the GOS and the SPLM/A decided to sign an extension of the ceasefire. If the peace treaty were signed soon, the UN would still have time to deploy during the current calendar year. If the UN did not deploy, there was a promise of armed troops to take over the mission or assist us. The JMC mission had been successful thus far without weapons; I was not sure how long I would stick around if and when the armed troops arrived.

I had also heard that fighting was continuing in western Darfur along the border with Chad and that the violence in the south had moved further north—to within 50 kilometers of our base camp. Rumors told of some of the worst human rights violations ever seen in Africa. The GOS was apparently supporting a campaign of ethnic cleansing, and yet the US was negotiating the removal of sanctions and the reopening of trade relations.

I was beginning to feel frustrated by the general responsibilities of a military observer. I wrote home to Gretchen:

You know, we don't have any authority here. We're only reporters. It's kind of disappointing. There was this one village meeting last week where we were sitting with a man making a complaint about how his wife was stolen. He pointed across the hut and said, "That is the man who stole her." The guy who was being accused just shrugged and admitted it. What could we do? Nothing. Did I mention that there were local police that attended this meeting? They refused to do anything either because the man who stole the woman was the brother of the police chief. It was grassroots corruption at its finest. It's really too bad we can't help these people more. We simply wrote our report and thanked the parties for their time. I didn't realize we would have so little power.

Gretchen wrote back,

Brian, that's awful. I know corruption exists, but so blatantly? It must be really hard when situations like this totally undermine any chance you have of influencing the way these groups resolve conflicts. What can you do?

I didn't know. It was a strange position to be in. On the one hand, my JMC colleagues respected my expertise as an American military–trained professional, and many local villagers looked up to me as a Westerner. On the other hand, if the international community was wavering in its commitment to achieving peace, and the warring parties had no interest in adhering to the Ceasefire Agreement, the JMC had absolutely no authority to enforce it.

· · ·

My assignment in Kauda was drawing to a close. I was to leave my mountain paradise to relocate to the Miri Hills, about 100 kilometers to the west. I had hoped to stay in Kauda longer than three months, because I felt like I had just started to learn about the area. I knew where to go, who to seek for information, where roads would be flooded, and which towns had markets on which days. It seemed to me that monitors should be allowed to stay at least six months in one place to maximize their contacts and resulting intelligence. I suppose the JMC was afraid people would get complacent.

As I prepared to depart for the Miri Hills, the rains arrived. The wind switched from the north to the south, and in two days it rained for several hours. Sunshine visited briefly between showers that cooled the searing temperatures. The average temperature for the previous two weeks had been 116 degrees. The rainy season, knocking the temperature down to 80–90 degrees, would bring rain every day until October, and then it would not rain again for several months. A light green covering would appear on every inch of soil. It was beautiful, and no one was complaining.

Chapter 5

By mid-April, I had settled into my new home. Our camp sat on a large hill from which I could see for miles. A rocky area with few trees and a single lake, the Miri Hills were just as big as the mountains surrounding our base in Kauda and just as beautiful. We heard baboons at night and knew a family of hyenas lurked nearby. Ostrich were an occasional sighting along the hillside pastures. We loved being surrounded by wildlife, but its very existence was due to a darker circumstance. There was more animal life here in the Miri Hills because most of the tribes had been driven out of the area by war and, thus, there were significantly fewer people hunting animals for food.

Our sector commander, Johan, was Swiss. Though he had no formal military background, he had extensive field experience from other missions he had conducted, mainly in Palestine and Israel. I really respected him. Nevertheless, due to his lack of official military training, we affectionately called him the Swiss Hippie. Besides me and Johan, there was only one other international monitor for the whole sector. The entire Miri Hills territory for which we were responsible was controlled by the GOS, and our area of operations stretched another 100 kilometers west of the Miri Hills, close to the border with southern Darfur. It was a large territory for two small monitoring teams totaling ten people.

The Miri Hills housed a demilitarized zone of about 100 square kilometers. This "box" was the site of the most horrible atrocities since the beginning of fighting in Sudan. Some said that the worst human rights violations ever committed in the world happened there. In fact, the demilitarized zone was established out of fear that the GOS would completely wipe out the indigenous populations. They were now like an endangered species.

Gretchen always wanted to know more about life in the Miri Hills and the impact of the violence on women. She wrote to me about her desire to interview the women and help them advance their own ideas. I really appreciated our e-mail conversations because there was no one in the mission I confided in and because she made me notice things I wasn't naturally focused on. I wrote to her:

Gretchen, this is still a very closed country. The women in this GOS-controlled area are really silenced. I spoke with some of the NGOs. I have told them about what you want to do and they said there is no shortage of women who want to talk in the SPLA areas. In the GOS areas, though, most women are afraid. They are stoned to death in some places, if they cheat on their husbands. Women's rights issues are very sensitive here, especially among government officials who want to enact Islamic law.

It had not rained in about a week, and the humidity had started to rise, intensifying the heat. Nevertheless, I attempted to exercise, setting out on a jog one afternoon. I lasted about ten minutes before I turned around, not even certain I would make it back. I felt like I had been running on a treadmill in a sauna under a heat lamp with a hair dryer blowing in my face. It was still so dry that the sweat evaporated out of my pores before it even got to the surface of my skin. Staggering back to my room, I looked forward to running at home in a few days when I returned to the US for a visit.

In late May, I went on leave to attend Eric's graduation from the Naval Academy. It was great to see my family, but after six months in Sudan, life in the States besieged me with activity. I felt out of place, overstimulated. The pace of life in Africa had been so slow and simple—I almost needed to go back to Sudan to get a break from the intensity of my vacation home. I spent some time sailing on my 50-foot wooden sailboat, traveling from Maine to Maryland, which provided some relief from the materialism and rush of American life.

While I was home, the warring parties extended the North-South Cease-fire Agreement for three months and signed three peace protocols. We expected that they would sign a comprehensive peace agreement based on these protocols by the beginning of August. That meant that within 30 days the UN would begin to take over for the JMC mission. This agreement excluded the murky conflict in Darfur. The JMC bosses said that they might move our operations over to Darfur when the Nuba mission concluded, possibly by November. I did not anticipate staying past that time in Sudan, and flew back after vacation with some expectation that my one-year assignment might be drawing to an early close.

.   .   .

The Miri Hills region was less dangerous than Sector 1, but it was more exciting in other ways. Ever since the JMC had been operating in the Nuba Mountains it had mainly concentrated on the trouble spots of intense fighting during the civil war. As things had progressively calmed over a period of two years, the teams had been able to spread out to the far reaches of our mission's area of responsibility as defined by the Ceasefire Agreement. But our monitoring team had still not explored an extensive portion of this terrain. Within this region stretched one of Sudan's oil pipelines—from the oil fields in the Lagawa province, about 200 kilometers to our south, all the way to Port Sudan on the Red Sea. These pipelines and oil fields comprised one of the central reasons for the continuing violence and disagreements over the peace treaty.

It also was a symbol of Sudan. The country's economy was growing by leaps and bounds, according to traditional measurements, and the driving force was oil. Sudan was pumping about half a million barrels of crude oil a day. That wasn't much when you stacked it up against the big producers in the Persian Gulf, but it was enough to keep the ruling class in Khartoum wealthy and the military well armed. The West, led by the United States, had imposed sanctions on the Khartoum government, but other countries—China in particular—weren't playing; instead, they eagerly traded with and invested in Sudan. The big losers in these deals were the people in central Sudan, where I was now stationed with the JMC—the people in the south and the people in Darfur.

Our primary interest in patrolling the pipeline region was to find out whether there were large numbers of GOS troops stationed in the area that could take offensive action against the SPLA if the peace talks turned sour. Second, we wanted to determine the accuracy of reports stating that there were Chinese soldiers working along the pipeline. Third, we wanted to learn if financial and logistical support from the GOS was traveling along the pipeline roads to the conflict in Darfur. In the area between the pipeline road and the border with Darfur, Osama bin Laden had reportedly once conducted training operations. While old Al Qaeda camps in the Nuba Mountains were now used as GOS military training facilities, rumor had it that Al Qaeda still had active training camps in the pipeline area as well as Darfur. SPLA supporters did not hesitate to claim that Osama bin Laden might be present in the area to encourage more international attention. Given GOS sensitivity about the pipeline, we could only gradually push our patrols farther and farther southwest into the Lagawa province to explore the region for intelligence that could confirm or deny these reports.

.   .   .

On July 4, I led a patrol to visit the commander of the Pipeline Security Battalion. We met him in his office, a nondescript cement structure at a military outpost that was home to about 300 GOS soldiers. Chinese furniture adorned the entrance, above which hung a single picture of the Sudanese president next to an outdated wall calendar of scenes of Sudan from 2002. The commander, a fat Arab in his middle forties, greeted us warmly. He was extremely charming, and he graciously invited us to have chai with him. We emerged from the stifling, dark office and sat down in a circle of plastic lawn chairs arranged in the sand under a grass roof. The commander's chai was absent the usual grit, but heavy as always with sugar.

After the GOS monitor and the commander exchanged extended pleasantries concerning their health, the weather, and their families, I started the official conversation, asking him about his operations in the region. We invited any concerns or complaints and offered our support for peace. I explained that we would begin periodic long-distance patrols along the pipeline in our expanded area of operation.

He smiled and set down his cup. Looking me in the eye, the commander said through our interpreter, "I am, of course, entirely supportive of the JMC and your mission. However, I am afraid that you are forbidden to drive on the pipeline road, visit any unit or village, or talk to any omda, sheikh, or nomad in this region." In essence, he was prohibiting us from operating anywhere in the Lagawa province.

I shook my head, "To forbid the JMC's movement in this region would be a clear violation of the Ceasefire Agreement."

He looked at me stoically. "I have my orders from the Commanding General of the 15th Division. You are a former military officer, are you not? I'm sure you understand then. Orders are orders." He sat back in his chair with a satisfied expression on his face.

The guy was certainly arrogant. "I have a Ceasefire Agreement right here with the Vice President's signature on it," I said. I flipped through my little booklet and pointed to the last page. "Your Vice President's signature is right here."

It made no difference to him. "My orders are my orders."

I turned to my GOS monitor to ask him to explain that this was a requirement of the international agreement. He refused to translate and reiterated the commander's statement.

Irritated, I got up. "I hope you understand that we will have to report this to our higher command." He nodded and thanked us for our visit. There was nothing we could do.

The peace talks had resumed in late June, yet the people of Sudan seemed scared. They feared that they could be imprisoned if they spoke out against the government or even looked the wrong way at the many security officers who roamed the markets and downtown areas. They had good reason to worry. A day or so later, I was called to the GOS State Security Agency to investigate the arrest of an individual who had returned to the region after years of living in hiding. After three "round up" patrols throughout his village, the GOS had arrested him. He likely would be held for at least a week, tortured and beaten until he confessed something he did not do. This was how the GOS worked.

During our next long-range patrol, I spoke in depth with two other men who had been jailed because they were Africans, not Arabs. Both were interpreters from other JMC monitoring teams, so I could speak with them openly in English. The first man had filled out a job application that had asked for his tribe. Upon submitting his application, he was immediately jailed and deported because his tribe originated in Nigeria, even though he had been born in Sudan and had lived there for 30 years. The government considered him an outsider, as an African, and it was easy to deport him for not being Sudanese. He had only just returned to Sudan after fifteen years of fearful exile in Nigeria.

The other man was from Darfur. He told me that he had been in the Nuba Mountains seeking work when his family's village had been attacked by Arab nomads. He had heard that most of his family had escaped by fleeing through the desert to get to Chad, but they had given up everything to get out. They had no clothes, no food, no house, no cows, no donkeys, and no chickens. They did not even have a plastic milk jug to carry water. They were seeking registration in a newly established camp for refugees, and he was hopeful that humanitarian aid groups would care for them.

I wanted to know more even though I was essentially asking them to put at risk the last thing they had—their lives—to tell me what they thought about the government, the peace process in the south and the situation in Darfur.

"Do you think there will be peace in the Nuba Mountains after the peace treaty is signed?" I asked.

They looked over their shoulders and, after a moment, continued.

"No," they stated in unison. The man who had returned from Nigeria added in a hushed voice: "There will only be peace in all of Sudan when it is divided up into five different regions that rule themselves."

I asked them to tell me more about Darfur. Again, they peered about and proceeded only when they were certain there were no other passersby who might overhear them.

"The government is supplying arms to Arab nomads, who have formed militias to attack and destroy our villages. These are the ones we call *Janjaweed*, 'the devil on a horse.' The Janjaweed travel on horses and camels and often enter villages in the early hours of the morning. They shoot anyone they see, even the elderly and children. They rape our women, steal our livestock and food, and then burn our homes."

"Why are they doing this? Is it because the nomads want to graze their animals on your farmland?" I asked.

"Not at all," the Darfurian replied. "We have been able to coexist for centuries on the same land. Now that the government is supplying them with weapons and allowing them to take our property as loot, it is easy for them to comply. The government wants us dead because we are African, not Arab. We are too black. They hate us and hope we will leave this country." He looked around quickly, then dropped his head and lit a cigarette nervously.

"Are you the exception? Is this just your opinion of why this war is happening in Darfur?" I asked cautiously.

"Everyone knows these things, everyone."

I wrote home to my family about my conversation:

These men told me that the Sudanese government and its leaders have backed Arab militias to force the Africans out of their country. This is exactly what they have tried to do in the south, and now it is what they are doing in Darfur. Only in Darfur, there is no religious difference. In the south, we thought it was about religion, as most of the tribes are animist or Christian. In Darfur, they are almost all Muslim. How can a Muslim country justify killing its Muslim brothers? The Arab hatred of Africans appears to transcend even religious boundaries. What I don't understand is how the international community seems content with establishing peace in only one region in Sudan while letting another fall prey to the same hatred. Why don't we open our eyes?!

Within days, I had heard that Colin Powell and Kofi Annan had visited Darfur. From my vantage point, I could not be sure whether Darfur itself was actually of interest to the international community or just an annoyance that threatened its hard work in the south. We heard that Annan was scheduled to visit an IDP (internally displaced person) camp housing approximately 1,000 people, but when he arrived, the camp was gone. The people were reportedly moved overnight to a new location by government trucks.

Here we had the first black African secretary-general of the United Nations and the first African American secretary of state—a former general and fourth in the line of succession to the presidency—coming together in a place too long neglected. Before he left for Sudan, Annan had acknowledged the "terrible crimes" in Darfur. He declined to call them acts of genocide, but also said, "we don't need a label to propel us to act."

That was heartening. But where was the follow-up? Where was the pressure? Why wasn't there more international attention given to what was really happening? That late June 2004 visit to Darfur by Annan and Powell should have been a turning point, but in reality it was a lost opportunity.

.   .   .

While the conflict in Darfur loomed, the facade of peace celebrated in the south seemed to be deteriorating. The SPLM/A eventually gave up the Nuba Mountains to GOS control. When the peace agreement was finally signed, the mountains were included in the area above the border delineating the north from the south. The Nuba Mountains, an SPLA stronghold and one of the keys to their success, would now be excluded from the south's right to secede in six years. When word of the arrangement reached our sector, one of our SLPA representatives screamed in despair: "My whole family is dead! Everyone I know is dead! I have been fighting for 20 years and what do I have now? Nothing! I have nothing, not even my own freedom!" I was certain that we would be hearing about Sudan for a long time to come.

Gretchen and I were e-mailing frequently. There was so much I wanted to say, but I had a hard time writing every day. Instead, she suggested I start dictating notes into my MP3 player so I would be able to write it all down when I returned. At the same time, there was a lot I really should not have been writing in my e-mails home. The JMC, like a peace-keeping mission, was supposed to be impartial, but when I wrote home, I was undeniably biased. In order to conduct any type of monitoring or mediating mission, both sides of the dispute have to believe that you are completely neutral or the mission will not succeed. Yet the longer I was in Sudan and the more I learned about the government, the guise of impartiality was increasingly the most difficult part of my job each day. Luckily, the GOS representatives I worked with had no idea how I felt.

.   .   .

Shortly after the Fourth of July, the JMC presented me with a new position that would require me to move yet again. They offered me a promotion to Senior Operations Officer for the entire JMC mission. It was an important career opportunity that could certainly challenge me. But most of the work would be conducted in the operations room at headquarters. That made it less appealing because I really wanted to remain in the field. This kind of office job was the reason I had decided to get out of the Marine Corps. I began to consider volunteering to work as a monitor in Darfur. At least then, I thought, I would get to sleep under the stars.

I spoke with my father to get his take on the situation. I often solicited his advice, especially where my professional career was concerned. He was a retired admiral now, working as the Associate Administrator of Exploration Programs at NASA. In his opinion, Senior Operations Officer was a strong leadership position that would look good on my résumé. Dad had always pushed us to excel, to become the best at whatever we did. He encouraged me to take the promotion.

I respected my father's advice, but I still hadn't made up my mind. One day the general came to me and said, "I know you want to be in the field and not work in an office, but I need you." When I realized that out of 35 professional military officers from around the world working for the JMC the general's list for the position included only me, I finally accepted. I felt a sense of duty to the mission, but I was also honored by the general's confidence in me. There had been only two senior operations officers since the JMC was created, and I would be taking over from a highly qualified individual. The general expected me to report to headquarters in Tillo by the end of July.

On July 13, my team set out on a patrol toward the village of Miri Juwa. We passed through destroyed areas littered with what appeared to be remnants of a thriving village. Rusted pieces of oil lamps, pots and pans, old hoes and axe heads, a spring mount from a bus once used as an anvil, and several broken grinding stones were scattered among charred foundations. I guessed there could easily have been 500 people who had lived there.

Arriving in Miri Juwa, we came across a woman who was making chai on her charcoal stove in the shade of a large nim tree. We ordered a few teas and had a look around. Behind the tree there was a traditional mud-brick stove fashioned like a bee hive where several villagers were baking bread. Local Sudanese bread was better than anything I'd ever tasted back home. I imagined it was a very simple recipe, but the secret was that wood was used to fire the oven, which gave the bread a smoky, earthy flavor. I took in the warm toast scent and nodded a greeting toward the villagers.

Several of the residents left their bread-making to gather with us under the central meeting tree. Someone sent for representatives of the local police. We sat on stools in the shade, and the discussions began normally. We asked how many people lived in the village, how many police there were, what weapons they had, and whether they had recently encountered any problems. The conversation quickly turned to the various tribes and traditions of the Nuba. We learned for the first time that each of the tribes was named after the closest mountain, had its own dialect, and at one time could not even communicate with another tribe as close as 5 kilometers away. Out of necessity as well as the long-term Arabization imposed by the North, all of the tribes could now communicate using Arabic. Yet the Nuba people were concerned about losing the last of their traditions.

Traditional customs of 50 years ago, such as body painting; Nuba wrestling, piercing, scarring, dancing; and tribal dress were now rarely found in the Nuba Mountains; many were forbidden under Islamic law. A few traditions were still practiced, such as the drinking of local wine. Sudanese Islamic law strictly forbade drinking alcohol, but the tribes of the Nuba overlooked the law, brewing their own drink by fermenting sorghum. They carried the wine in hollowed-out gourds to the fields to accompany them during their work. It looked to me more like flat beer than a fine wine, but it contained vital carbohydrates that allowed them to work all day in the brutal sun. One time when I was in the market, my fellow monitors bought me one of these gourds. I figured I'd give it a try. I lifted it up to my mouth to have a sip and stopped abruptly. It smelled like the armpits of a man who had been working in the sun of Sudan all week without a shower. I noticed a drunk leaning contentedly against a tree watching me. I handed him the gourd,and he gave me a wide smile with toothless gums.

As we sat under the tree, I felt completely relaxed. We so rarely got to speak with the local populations about issues unrelated to our monitoring mission. The Nuba were aware that their lifestyle was changing, but the concept of protecting their own traditions seemed somewhat foreign to them. I found their customs absolutely fascinating and felt disappointed that they had lost so much of their culture under the current regime. Johan and I felt compelled to encourage them to preserve and celebrate their traditions so that they weren't forgotten. We explained how Christianity had eventually merged with pagan culture in the West: the Christmas tree had originated in a pagan tradition of bringing new life into the house during the winter. Now, the tree was brought into the house and decorated as a symbol of Christmas, celebrating Jesus' birth. I also shared with them that many Native American traditions were nearly lost with the arrival and movement west of American settlers. The villagers seemed genuinely interested in what we had to say and invited us to attend their harvest dance after the rains ended in the fall.

Chapter 6

On July 22, I moved to my new position at Tillo, on the outskirts of Kadugli. The transition to my position as Senior Operations Officer kept me extremely busy my first week. Once again, a converted British school served as our headquarters camp, this one consisting of two long mud-brick buildings separated by a courtyard. The only disadvantage of this new location was that most of our living quarters were created by adding a door and punching two small windows into opposing ends of a tractor trailer. We did have air conditioning, though, to keep the temperature inside from rising above 90 degrees.

Shortly after arriving in the operations office one night for watch I heard a familiar buzzing by my ear. Now that the rains had arrived, so too had the mosquitoes. I had stopped taking my malaria medicine because I knew the threat of liver damage was real. I knew I would be in the area for about a year, and I wasn't cavalier about the dangers of the disease, so I was always careful to wear long pants, a long-sleeved shirt, and bug repellent after dark.

This particular night I was wearing long pants, but not long sleeves. Still, I was certain that I would be okay because I was working inside with the door closed.

I settled in at my desk and turned on my computer to go online when I felt a sharp sting on my left forearm. There it was: a mosquito had somehow snuck into my office. It was feasting. Damn! I had been so careful.

The next day everything was fine, though I felt a little tired by evening. It was our weekly barbeque night so we had steaks on the grill, and we each had a few beers. The day after that I woke up with what felt like a terrible hangover. I knew it was possible to get dehydrated, but I certainly hadn't had enough beer to warrant this. I went to work sucking on a large bottle of water.

Later in the day one of the medics stopped by, and I mentioned to him that I still felt lousy. He immediately insisted I take a blood test. I went to the clinic down in the village to get my finger pricked and then headed back to work at the camp to await my results. A few hours later, one of the medics came by to deliver the bad news: I had malaria. And the good news: We caught it early. The medics quickly started me on a series of shots and other drugs to try to get the parasite out of my system.

That first night was one of the worst nights of my life. It started with the most vivid dreams I have ever experienced. Colors, sounds, smells, and even emotions were intensified beyond reality. Next the dreams shifted to nightmares. Accompanying the horrifying delusions were chills, cold sweats, and shaking. I would wake up suddenly freezing, grasping at my blanket. Minutes later, I would be swimming in a pool of my own sweat, swearing my skin was on fire. Suddenly, I was ice-cold again. The torment was repeated again and again. I was shaking so severely the whole time that I would not have been able to rub my own eye for fear I'd poke it out.

The next morning began with a frantic scramble to the bathroom followed by a pathetic trudge back to bed, where I collapsed for a few minutes only to repeat the trip again and again. I seriously considered moving my cot into the latrines. Several times I simply passed out on the toilet, having a nightmare with a side of shakes and waking up later merely grateful that I hadn't fallen off the seat.

The only part of the experience that was somewhat entertaining was the sensation that my brain was loose in my head, as if I had an inch of space separating it from the edge of my skull. When I turned my head to one side, I knew that I was looking in that direction, but it took a very noticeable second for my vision to catch up. I had to be careful not to turn my head too fast or I would fall down. I was lucky on one count: I didn't experience the intense vomiting that accompanies most cases of malaria.

After four or five days of feeling alternatively crazed and exhausted, my body slowly returned to normal. Now I felt like I had been officially initiated into the club of African aid workers and contractors, many of whom had experienced malaria several times. I was somewhat weak and had lost quite a bit of weight, but I gradually regained my strength and resumed work in the operations room.

.   .   .

The security situation continued to deteriorate as the peace talks stalled. Fighting had broken out again to the southeast, and there was rising friction between Arab nomads and the SPLA in the north. One of our investigations involved some shooting at civilians by GOS troops. No one had been hurt, but the Sudanese government had claimed to be hunting down SPLA supporters for spreading propaganda. We began to observe GOS troops massing ammunition as we conducted our inspections. Thousands of machine-gun and mortar rounds that did not exist in February suddenly began to appear in GOS stockpiles.

The SPLA was busy, too. One night a few Red Crescent trucks attempting to deliver food aid were robbed just a few miles down the road from us; the six armed robbers were suspected to be SPLA soldiers.

If the UN imposed sanctions, all commercial airline traffic would be canceled. There were so many unknowns. We also were aware that the Darfur conflict was spreading farther east and threatening to enter our area of operations. I did not see how there could be peace in the south when in the west the government-backed militias were killing civilians. I had just received a report that several contractors working with the African Union in Darfur were taken hostage by the Janjaweed Arab militias the day before. They had since been released, but the expatriate community was nervous.

On July 29, 2004, another contractor from our camp returned from a trip to Darfur, where he was helping the military observers with the African Union set-up. He seemed shaken.

"How is it over there, what's really going on?" I asked him.

"Brian," he said in a hushed tone, "you have to see something."

Curious, I followed him into his office. He hesitated, then went to his bag and pulled out a laptop. "This is what's happening in Darfur."

As he handed me his computer, a series of the most disturbing images I had ever seen came across the screen. I saw the charred remains of tiny schoolgirls who had been shackled with makeshift handcuffs and had crouched together while they were set afire and burned alive outside their elementary school. Family members that likely tried to save them were shot dead or burned elsewhere in the village. Rings of ashes indicated where grass huts once stood. I was horrified.

I gulped. "What the hell is going on over there? These are children!"

We had heard that villages had been torched, and we had heard that people were being killed in the fighting. But I never imagined atrocities on this scale. Looking at these photos—photos of children—this was unbelievable! This was no longer war, this was definitely genocide. Even though the word was floating around in the international community, people could not truly understand what that meant until they saw it with their own eyes.

My colleague explained that the African Union had assembled this confidential report to condemn the Janjaweed militias for the slaughter in this village called Suleia. Because the report was classified, it could not be distributed. Nevertheless, he felt compelled to bring it back to the JMC mission to show us what was happening in Darfur. But he refused to share the files with me for fear of risking his career.

"If these photos were released to the public, there would be troops in Sudan in a matter of days!" I exclaimed. "How can anyone ignore this?"

"You'd be surprised," he said, and shut his computer.

Why was the US letting this happen? I had such faith that the United States government would put an end to the violence if only it had accurate and complete information.

I couldn't get Darfur out of my head, day or night. Images and voices of young girls haunted my dreams. And I was hardly alone: everyone in the operations room who looked at the horrendous photos felt helpless. We had our mission, and there were others in Darfur handling that region. What could I do, what could I do? Nothing had ever rocked me like this. I e-mailed home to my family and friends about what I had seen:

I have to write to you to get this out of my mind. I don't know whether or not you are aware of the African Union's recent statements. They have released a report that states that they have evidence that individuals have been chained and burned alive by the Janjaweed. This is from a confidential AU report, and it included photos. I am not permitted to send them nor do I wish on you the same nightmares that I have had as a result of these photos. The individuals that were burned were children—from a girls' school—and their family members who tried to save them. I have never seen anything more disturbing. I saw girls who had their hands bound by make-shift cuffs huddled together and burned alive. Men strewn all over the village, burned alive—this because they were trying to protect their families. The entire village was in ashes. If these photos were released to the public there would be troops in here in no time. What is going on here is most definitely a "crime against humanity" and most definitely "genocide." There is no question about that. These people have been burned alive because they are "too dark." This is what the women are told when they are raped in front of their families. They are told to leave behind their child born of rape, because they will not be "too dark"—but for the mother to leave this country now or she will die. Why is the world so slow to act? Why are we sitting here letting this happen? This is not the doing of humans; this is the work of the devil. We as human beings have to stand up for what is right. There is no group of people in any place in the world that I have ever heard of, that can condone these atrocities. If we fail to act, I fear for the future of humankind. Please feel free to forward this to whomever you want. The world must know what is happening here.

Gretchen immediately wrote back:

Brian, did you say the AU report was CONFIDENTIAL? Are you serious? What authority has the right to keep such atrocities—genocide—confidential?!! Who are they hiding this information from? Why should the world not know about these things? How could any parent anywhere possibly stand aside and let this happen if they really knew what was going on there?

The fact was that no one had the right to hold genocide in confidence. The fact was that the entire world had a right to know.

It was hardly surprising, then, that these same photos from Suleia ended up on a *60 Minutes* special about Darfur a few months later. Despite the risk represented by this leak and despite the hard work by the production team that created a powerful televised report on the crisis, CBS aired the segment during the final game of the historic seven-game American League Championship Series between the New York Yankees and the Boston Red Sox. Was anyone on the East Coast even watching *60 Minutes*?

I immediately put in a request to transfer to the African Union mission in Darfur and received notice within weeks that I would move there at the end of August. I had to see what was happening for myself.

Chapter 7

"*Inshallah,*" I thought to myself. Time seemed constantly suspended in Sudan. Though I could have anticipated the delay, I was nonetheless disappointed to find that I would have to wait a few weeks into September to transfer from the Nuba Mountains to Darfur. The African Union operated in all of South Sudan, but it was slowly relocating its limited forces to concentrate on the growing crisis in Darfur. The AU mission would deploy across five sectors in eight-person monitoring teams protected by Rwandan and Nigerian troops. I would be one of only three American monitors to operate in all of Darfur, a territory roughly the size of France. Like JMC monitors, the AU monitors were not armed, although the US embassy indicated that it might be possible for us to carry weapons if we felt that we were in imminent danger.

I was, frankly, unconvinced that I would be well protected by Nigerians and, especially, Rwandans. William, the UK monitor who worked with me back in Kauda, had told me how he had once been taken hostage by Rwandan "peacekeepers" in Sierra Leone. He barely succeeded in convincing them that he was worth more alive than dead. It would have been bad PR to kill a British monitor. So I was a bit uneasy about having Rwandan troops as our protectors, regardless of their military qualifications. I was also concerned that entering a war zone with armed troops could threaten the irrational militias who had no sense of the rules of war, ultimately jeopardizing the entire mission.

I spent a few days in Khartoum taking care of some administrative chores before departing for Darfur. The AU had no housing for personnel in transit, so I had to stay at the familiar and comfortable JMC headquarters even though I was no longer officially working for the JMC.

The most urgent task on my list was to get a wisdom tooth pulled. After sitting contentedly in my jaw for all these years, this particular tooth decided to emerge at the precise moment when I could not possibly expect Western-quality dental care. Yet, facing an impending infection and another few months before I could head home, I knew I had to make an appointment with a Khartoum dentist to have it pulled. I asked the staff at the JMC for a recommendation and placed the call.

My appointment was scheduled for September 11. The Irish, superstitious side of me immediately kicked into gear. This might just be the perfect celebratory day for my dentist to have an evil infidel drugged up in his chair, with all forms of sharp tools and drills within easy reach. I was plagued by all sorts of visions, such as waking up in a ditch with only one kidney or having the wrong tooth pulled because it looked like a good match for a set of partials.

Nevertheless, I nervously found a driver to take me over to the dental office. We parked in a dirt lot filled with trash behind a five-story cement building. I peered around for a professional-looking office, but could not recognize one. The driver nodded and said, "This way." We stepped over piles of cigarette boxes and plastic bags and climbed through an open hole in the crumbling wall where a door may once have been. A shoddy staircase without railings emerged from the scattered garbage. As we ascended, we passed boarded-shut doors that had yet more debris crammed against them.

On the third floor, the driver hammered on a door and pried it open. I relaxed slightly when I discovered that the office waiting room was much cleaner than the staircase. Gradually, I began to notice a strange yet familiar odor. An image of frogs popped into my head. It took a few minutes to figure it out, but I suddenly realized I was smelling formaldehyde. Now I was really worried. I pictured myself floating around in a little jar. The smooth twanging of Sudanese music on the radio offered absolutely nothing to calm me down.

I sat down for a moment in one of three chairs in the waiting room. A water cooler—the only one I had ever seen outside JMC headquarters—was propped against the wall as a sign of certain prestige. It almost looked as if it had been placed there today just for my benefit. But as it bubbled furiously, a steady stream of precious purified water leaked into an eight-foot puddle on the cement floor.

Finally, the dentist appeared and invited me into his practice area. He sat down at a makeshift desk on one side of the room, across from the chair. I could see all of the pretty tools laid out on the table, though I failed to notice an autoclave or any other sterilizing device. The music, which now seemed to be blaring, was beginning to get to me. The dentist jumped up to take an x-ray and then asked me if I was ready. I kept telling myself to be very nice and maybe I would leave with both kidneys.

I sat down in the chair reluctantly. The dentist gave me one shot of Novocain, then another, and then a third. My jaw, neck, and ear began to numb. When he was satisfied that I could not feel a thing, to my horror, he pulled out a mini crowbar. Placing one foot on the seat of the chair and squeezing my bottom jaw with his hand, he began prying. My eyes watered as scraping and cracking sounds shivered through my body and infiltrated the droning music.

As the dentist pried on my tooth with two hands filling my mouth, he suddenly looked me in the eye and asked in English with a big smile, "Are you lucky?"

Was I lucky?!! I didn't feel lucky. I shook my head, hoping he would have pity on me. I felt like I was going to faint. As tunnel vision closed in on me and the room started to spin, I fought with everything I had to stay awake.

A tremendous crack shook me into full consciousness as the tooth popped right out, followed by a geyser of blood. As the dentist stuffed my mouth with gauze, he nodded and repeated with a chuckle that I was indeed lucky. I wondered if anyone had died in his chair. I thanked him, quickly paid my $30.77 bill, and offered a brief prayer that I would never require any further dental or medical treatment in Sudan.

.   .   .

After a few days of healing, and once I was able to eat solid food again, I set to work obtaining my African Union ID card and the supplies necessary to depart for Darfur. I wandered over to the AU compound just down the road. The Imams were calling the devout to their afternoon prayers from the loudspeakers affixed to the mosques. Men squatted on the curb with tiny plastic tea pots of water to wash before praying. I walked carefully past rows of men facing east and moving between positions of standing, kneeling, and bowing to place their heads on the ground. Having worked in Morocco, Turkey, Egypt, Kosovo, and the Nuba Mountains, this religious practice was becoming a comfortable standard.

Given that the AU was still only establishing its operations in Sudan, I was not surprised to find its building under construction and the compound without a gate. I was truly astonished, however, to find not even the smallest measure of security. I opened the unlocked front door, walked right in without passing through any checkpoint, and found myself standing in a small office with computers everywhere and no one at work. I returned later that evening to find the offices deserted again. The next day I went in early in the morning, in mid-afternoon, and late in the evening. Still deserted. It took two entire days before I finally surprised someone and attempted to check in and get my ID card.

A tall African man sat before a desk piled high with papers spilling over onto the floor. A fan standing in the corner threatened to send the entire mess airborne. I told him my name and that I was one of the US monitors checking in for my assigned mission in Darfur. "Who?" he asked. I offered my information again. He seemed confused but scribbled my details on a piece of paper and nodded that he would look into it. He placed the paper on one of his piles and bid me good day. I returned to the JMC compound without much confidence in the efficiency of the AU bureaucracy, at least in Khartoum.

During my temporary residence in the capital, I began working on logistics. We were charged with ensuring that fuel could reach Darfur for the new AU mission. In only a few short days, I dealt with stolen trucks, a refusal from the AU to escort the fuel shipments, a lack of storage tanks, and logistical breakdowns during attempts to airlift tanks into rural areas. Compared to the Marine Corps, it was a mess.

Three days later I visited the African Union offices again. My Joint Military Commission ID card would not work with Government of Sudan border patrols in the Darfur region because the JMC mission was unique to the Nuba Mountains. I luckily found the same administrator busy at work moving his piles around. He squinted at me and asked me who I was again. I could not imagine too many white men from America were making requests for African Union ID cards.

"Oh," he responded. "I am sorry to say that we have lost your information."

I took a deep breath and gave it to him again, stating firmly that I would be there the next day to pick up my ID. When I arrived the next day, I happily received my ID card, but the AU representative told me that I was not approved to work with the AU as a monitor. I was surprised: how could they tell me this after I'd already been assigned? Frustrated and confused, I decided to head to my contracting company's compound to discuss the situation and evaluate my options.

My colleagues explained that the AU was afraid that the West would take over its mission. Darfur represented the first time the AU had ever conducted a full scale operation, and its leaders felt strongly that they had to demonstrate their own success without UN, NATO, EU, or US interference or, even worse, dominance. But the US, for its part, was funding the majority of the AU mission in Darfur, and it wanted more US monitors on the ground.

I was caught in the middle. The State Department and the African Union would have to reach agreement before I would be approved to serve as a military observer. My contracting company's director for Africa suggested that I go down to the AU's headquarters in Darfur, located within the city of El Fashir, to help with logistics support. El Fashir, the capital of Darfur, was the first location the rebels attacked when the conflict began as a civilian uprising. A large city with a decent airport, huge market, and even a soccer stadium, El Fashir now hosted the GOS military headquarters for Darfur and thus was chosen as the regional headquarters for the African Union's mission as well. There was a plane leaving the next morning at 0800. As I got ready to depart, I packed a large supply of water purification tablets and made sure that I had a pocket full of Sudanese dinar.

.   .   .

I felt a surge of energy as I looked down on Darfur for the first time. I squinted out the airplane window, surveying the horizon for burned villages or pillars of smoke, but I could see nothing except rocky terrain between the occasional tree and spiky bush. It was the end of the rainy season, but the land appeared crisp, without any hint of new life; the landscape reminded me of Baja California's high desert. As we approached El Fashir, I was surprised by the size of the sprawling city. Buildings rose up from dry sand where the imposing volcanic range of the Jebel Marra melted northward into the Sahara.

El Fashir's airport rivaled Khartoum's, offering evidence of infrastructure investment made in Darfur, if only in this location. Touching down, I noticed a line of waiting trucks begin to move toward the plane. Contractors disembarked and lined up beside the cargo hold to unload pipes, barbed wire, food, water pumps, and other supplies.

I caught a ride into El Fashir with the AU medic. Sudanese life flickered by like an ancient newsreel. Under grass roofs, a market area swarmed with women arguing fiercely over wilting produce, their hands dancing among flies. Little children waved from a gateway, running beside us with arms outstretched until their bare feet could no longer manage and they doubled over, trying to catch their breath.

I was set to stay at my contracting company's compound until the AU mission approved my role as a monitor. Our contracting company was responsible for providing logistics and medical support for the AU. While I waited for my approval papers, I spent the next two weeks overseeing the building of a medical clinic and accommodations for the medics, and working with operations and fuel-supply logistics.

Though the town of El Fashir was generally safe, it was not difficult to feel the oppression of the military presence that surrounded us. One day, while exploring the area, I wandered with a few other civilian contractors beyond the invisible GOS boundary. As we crested a large sandy hillside, we confronted a checkpoint of military troops who told us to turn back. They were adamant that we not go any farther, forcing us to return to the city limits. An eerie feeling flooded me, and I wondered what was happening beyond the confines of the city. I began to notice helicopters flying around every day: GOS Mi–24 Hind attack helicopters. They went out fully loaded with weapons and returned, hours later, with empty missile pods.

It was early October when I finally received word that my approval had come through—after a visit to El Fashir by US embassy personnel. I would be stationed in Nyala in South Darfur, one of the AU's most active sectors. Attacks on civilians and NGOs were a regular occurrence in this region. I could barely wait to be part of the action.

Chapter 8

Flying south over rural Darfur, I spotted a few camels and their herders following a path into nowhere. Every so often I could distinguish a cluster of sunburned grass huts from the dusty earth upon which they were built. What could anyone want with this torched soil? What the hell were they fighting over?

Nearing Nyala, a vast IDP camp suddenly rose up before us. Tens of thousands of tiny white structures glimmered below. As we began to descend, I thought it looked almost as if this sea of tents were buffered by an expansive sand beach—all trees and bushes for about 500 meters surrounding the camp were missing.

Our Mi–8 transport helicopter touched down at Nyala airport. Jumping from the aircraft, I ducked to avoid the rushing winds of the propellers. I was met by retired US Army Colonel John Anderson, the senior US representative to the mission, whose position I was taking on the monitoring team so that he could move over to the operations department. Thin and in shape, John was probably in his late 50s, but he had the energy of a 13-year-old boy. He greeted me and immediately began talking, interrupting himself to point at something or switch subjects. I tried to pay attention while I searched for my bags. He was intense, but I quickly drew energy from his animated chatter. Identifying my luggage, I tossed a couple bags to him. Clutching the handles, he yelled, "Welcome to hell."

"What?" I figured he was joking, but I waited for more.

"You just missed it!" he screamed.

"What do you mean? What did I miss?"

We hurried away from the tarmac, John taking fast, solid strides. He shouted over the helicopter, "I just came from an investigation where there was a Hind hovering above the road just mowing people down in this market place! There were 20 millimeter shells from the guns piled knee-high."

I thought that I must have gotten off the wrong helicopter. I turned around, but the helicopter was already revving up to take off.

.   .   .

Like most of the other African Union encampments, the base camp on the outskirts of Nyala was still under construction. John and I stopped by briefly to have a look at where we both would soon reside, once the camp was complete. The massive tent camp formed a large rectangle with a center courtyard that was protected by barbed wire. Rows of huge canvas tents—some of them as large as circus pavilions, roughly 50 feet by 20 feet—spread to the left and right for what seemed miles. I was happy enough to think I no longer had to operate out of or sleep in the back of a metal tractor trailer. The Nyala base camp would house up to 500 troops when it was completed in a few weeks. The necessary size of the operation here gave me a sense of dread.

We drove north through Nyala. A single paved road provided a gateway for the movement of goods on all forms of transport including people's heads, donkeys, carts, and vehicles. Walled compounds with high-frequency antennae defined the more official establishments where NGO and UN agency logos marked gates behind armed guards. We passed the compounds of Oxfam, the World Food Program, and CARE.

Nyala was a smaller town, and it was not uncommon to see cylindrical grass huts mingling with cement structures. Conical reed roofs, corrugated metal, and flapping tarp covers formed a skyline that shifted slightly with the wind. Men sat in what looked like children's plastic play chairs at small card tables drinking chai. There was no pleasant fragrance in the mild breeze; instead, the scent of a dead animal or donkey feces occasionally permeated the air.

The temporary location where we were to be situated for the next few weeks was on the main road to Zallingi, within the town of Nyala. The AU offices and living quarters were contained in three separate compounds. Fifty or so Rwandan troops took up residence in the growing tent camp, rotating to stand guard at our compounds each night.

While I unpacked, John checked in with me periodically as he tended to his office duties. As members of the AU teams returned from the field, I introduced myself to them individually. Major Joseph, a Kenyan soldier and leader of Team C, glanced at me with disinterest. I said with enthusiasm that I expected I most likely would join his team. Aloof, he looked ahead and offered an equivocal, "We'll see," apparently expecting to be responsible for making that decision himself.

The team's interpreter came up to me after Major Joseph left. "My name is Ibrahim," he said, and his eyes were bright and a smile spread across his face. A small, thin Sudanese man, Ibrahim pumped my hand excitedly. "It is so nice to meet you, Captain Brian. I hope you will be on our team. I am really working hard to get better at my English. Please, if I ever say something wrong or backwards, please correct me."

"Sure," I said. "No problem. Nice to meet you too."

The Chadian mediator for Team C introduced himself warmly as Major Ahmed. He was of medium height, with a thick neck of solid muscle. Slapping me on the back, Ahmed announced, "Come with me, Captain Brian." We toured all areas of the two compounds, finishing with a small celebration of my arrival—a round, juicy watermelon. "Ah," he said, satisfied with his refreshment, "let us go to the meat market." I accepted his invitation and we drove into town.

The meat market consisted of five long rows of charcoal grills that backed up to an island of goats both grazing and at various stages of becoming a kabob. Some were in the process of being slaughtered and others were hanging from posts under the grass roof. Most prices at every grill were fixed, and it was up to the consumer to pick which leg they might find tastiest, inspecting the offerings raised in turn by each chef. We selected our legs and found a table in the eating area off to the side where we joined a group of men seated on low plastic stools devouring their meals. The women in a nearby tea shack immediately brought out sweet, syrupy chai while we waited. The chef chopped our leg meat into bite-sized morsels and delivered our platters. Except for dishes of red pepper and salt, there was nothing—no sauces, no vegetables, no bread. Just meat. I laughed to myself wondering what Gretchen, a vegetarian, would think of this dining experience.

.　　.　　.

I settled into my bunk that night and tried to get to sleep. It was quieter here than in El Fashir. I listened carefully and could pick out some distant birds and the occasional high shriek of a donkey. The donkeys made such a desperate effort for their voices to be heard, their vocal cords cracking painfully as they revved up to a blaring honk. Every few minutes a motorcycle buzzed in the distance. I tossed and turned restlessly as the monitor in the next bunk snored.

I knew I was scheduled for briefings tomorrow, but I couldn't wait to get into the field again. It had been more than a month since I had left the monitoring team in the Nuba Mountains. I felt so alive when I was out on an investigation, exploring towns, talking with villagers, learning about the cultures and the conflict. I treasured my time in the Nuba Mountains, though it had been relatively calm. I had investigated only one killing in my entire seven months there. I certainly had not witnessed the violence that I knew from the Suleia photos was happening here in Darfur. But at the moment, I was less concerned about what I might experience than I was about just getting out there. I hardly slept all night.

.　　.　　.

The next day my briefings, led by Dave, a Major from South Africa, began in our operations office. Dave, somewhere in his early to mid-30s, towered over me when he stood up to greet me.

"Hey, come on in. Good to have you here." He shook my hand and jumped immediately into the briefing. "Let me tell you how everything works." Since I had been doing monitoring work in Sudan for the last seven months, Dave started with procedural matters. I liked his calm, professional manner.

"Alright, each of our sector's two teams consists of two AU military officers, who serve as team leader and deputy team leader. In addition, you'll have a Chadian mediator, an interpreter, and one representative from each of the warring parties—the JEM, SLA, and GOS. Finally, each team has either an EU or US representative. That, of course, is you. You'll spend some time with each team before reporting permanently to Major Joseph's team."

"Now, take a look at this," Dave pointed to what looked like a map. The cement walls of the tiny operations room were decorated with what initially looked like maps, directives, and reports. On closer inspection, I determined that what I'd thought was a map was actually a photocopy of a British colonial diagram that denoted water holes, nomad communities, and *wadis* (dry riverbeds) with black scribbles and other marks added over time. I looked around the room again. The office had only one computer and radio, no logistics information on the status of AU supplies and equipment, no diagrams of the warring parties' command structures or military positions and no detailed data on the region to reference. This seemed to me to be a reflection of both a lack of resources and the fact that this was just a start-up operation.

"The SLA controls roughly 75 to 85 percent of South Darfur at this time. The majority of the violence that has affected civilians has been mostly in North and West Darfur. Though villages in our area have also been attacked, most of the ceasefire violations have been smaller skirmishes between SLA/JEM forces and the GOS." I waited for more, but he simply gave me a binder on AU procedures to read and went back to work.

·　　·　　·

That afternoon, while I was still getting up to speed on our operations, the GOS carried out an attack on a local village. It was Friday, the Muslim holy day, which was usually a day off for the teams. Since there was no scheduled investigation that day, Team C was able to move quickly in response to the news, arriving at the village just as the Hind attack helicopters were leaving. When Colonel John returned from this preliminary investigation, I caught up with him on his way into the operations office. He was delivering some evidence that could help educate other monitors about what weapons were being used in the conflict.

"How are you?" I asked. "How did it go?"

"Take a look at this," he said and handed me a tiny, spiraling nail with a fin on it. I held it in my hand, examining it. I immediately identified it as a *flechette* or "dart" in French, the contents of an anti-personnel rocket. In other words, this small dart and hundreds like it were fired at people with the sole purpose of killing or maiming them.

"Where did you find it?"

"There were tons of them used on this civilian village."

"Seriously?" I shook my head. "They're using these on civilians?" My stomach sank as I connected this nail with the helicopters I had seen taking off daily from El Fashir armed with rockets. I had assumed that the attack helicopters were going after bigger military targets, such as rebel vehicles. I never expected the GOS to use anti-personnel rockets containing flechettes to attack civilians.

PART TWO

Into Darfur

Chapter 9

Two days later I went out on my first patrol. There had been reports of attacks on three villages by Janjaweed and GOS forces. We headed first to the expansive IDP camp I had seen from the airplane, Kalma Camp, to find any new arrivals who had come from these attacked villages. Besides interviewing them about the attack, we would need the villagers to take us to their homes.

Simple geography and logistics were problems. In the Marine Corps, the very first thing we would acquire was a map. But the AU had no maps. Instead, we had to rely on the knowledge of our SLA and JEM representatives to guide us, and when all else failed, we asked a local where to go. When we inquired exactly how long it would take to get to our destination, it was never clear whether the estimate corresponded to a journey by foot, donkey, or truck. I decided I would start to build my own map by taking GPS positions and incorporating them into a mapping program on my laptop.

As we crested a large sand dune, Kalma Camp suddenly loomed before us, a massive settlement for between 150,000 and 175,000 homeless men, women, and children. Makeshift tents stretched for miles in all directions before vanishing into the rippling heat. Chills ran up my spine. I was astounded at the camp's size and the sudden realization of the sheer number of people already displaced by this conflict. What had looked like sparkling white structures from above were really mere shanties: the residents had bent sticks into dome-shaped frames, which they covered with plastic sheeting, tarps, trash bags, and old clothing. A few long-time residents had tried to establish crude walls for privacy by mixing sand and some of their water rations together to make mud bricks. These walls would likely crumble or melt with strong dust or rain storms. As we drove through, I could see that a single shelter, the size of a six-person US tent, often housed up to a dozen people. Given the cramped quarters, all activities besides sleeping seemed to take place outside.

It took nearly twenty minutes to drive across the camp. Ahmed and John skillfully maneuvered between the shelters, wandering dogs, and children in rags playing in the dust. Women peeked guardedly from behind colorful yet dingy robes—perhaps the only clothes they owned. Pathways led every which way between the shelters; occasionally, our road came to a dead end, and we had to turn around and drive in another direction. As we moved farther into the camp, the proportion of garbage to permanent structure increased. There were no trees, and only a few woven grass ceilings on stick posts provided some respite from the burning sun. Any trees that had once existed had already fallen victim to cooking fires.

We drove past a funeral ceremony in process. About 15 men in crystal-clean, white jelabias stood with heads bowed in a line alongside a few bodies wrapped in white sheets. A single shallow grave gaped open nearby. I wondered whether it had been injuries, disease, age, starvation, or something else that killed those people. Here in Darfur, life had many enemies.

We passed by women sitting on grass mats hoping to trade or sell their few belongings for extra food. There was no cafeteria line and no meal tent. Instead, John explained that families received the bare minimum on a monthly basis and had to cook each meal using whatever fuel source they could find. The camp's residents had to walk for miles, risking rape or murder, to find some lone tree in the barren landscape with which to heat their meals. A typical monthly ration from the World Food Program contained foods indigenous to the region but grown elsewhere, including a sack of sorghum, some beans, a jerry can of oil, salt, and a bag of flour. There were no vegetables or milk or meat for growing children. I noticed women gathering in groups to take turns hammering away at a huge mortar and pestle, in which they pounded sorghum into a fine grain to serve as a porridge. They would eat this porridge as their staple dish at every meal for the uncertain future. People all around us looked resigned and fatigued. How could they survive like this?

At one point, we drove by a very large plastic object that reminded me of a deflated bounce house at a child's birthday party. I asked what it was, and John explained that it was an empty water bladder. He did not know when they would receive more water, which had to be trucked in by an NGO.

As we neared the far reaches of the camp, we began to come across new arrivals who were sitting on the ground with their few belongings. They had no shelters and likely had not yet been able to register with the UN so that they could receive food in the next distribution. They would have to rely on the generosity of other refugees who were trying to survive on so little as it was. I wondered how many more were already on their way here.

By this time, estimates of those displaced ranged around 2 million. That would mean that there could be fifteen more camps of this size somewhere in Darfur. The shear scale of the crisis shocked me. How could it get so massive so quickly? This was a catastrophe caused by people, not natural disaster. The Indian Ocean tsunami of December 2004 got 24-7 cable news coverage in the US and around the world. I wondered what kind of coverage the conflict in Darfur was getting on TV back home. Did people know that places like this existed?

.   .   .

After asking for directions a few times, we found several witnesses from the village of Angarta, one of the settlements that had been most recently attacked, and pulled to a stop to begin our interviews. But someone accidentally left the back door of one of our trucks open, and before we knew it, 12 people had squeezed inside.

Ahmed, our Chadian mediator, confronted them. "Okay, what do you think you're doing?"

"We're going with you," one of them offered.

"Right. Everyone out," he demanded.

During the scramble, John snickered. "How many Sudanese can you fit in a Land Cruiser?" Without pause, he answered his own joke. "Always one more," he chuckled under his breath. I thought to myself that if I were facing the possibility of waiting another few days for a passing vehicle, I would manage to squeeze in, too. I was too new to realize that making jokes was one of the only ways to make the daily misery that permeated life in Darfur manageable.

Standing in a circle in the heat, the elders stepped forward while other IDPs gathered around, curious about us and what was being said. Following careful protocol, our team leader, Major Joseph, a proud but cautious soldier from Kenya, asked all investigative questions. A true officer in the colonial tradition, he took his position of leadership extremely seriously. Every day he had the enlisted soldiers clean his tent and shine his boots. Though he treated our monitoring team of professionals and officers with slightly more respect, he maintained a level of aloof detachment that ensured his ability to delegate as necessary. I flipped open my military-style, waterproof notebook and prepared to scribble notes onto the shiny pages.

"Tell us what happened," Major Joseph began.

The group looked with deference toward a bent old man in a torn jelabia. His toes were as weathered as the crusted leather of his sandals. He leaned forward on his walking stick and scratched the side of his nose. He suddenly jerked the same finger into the air, announcing with disdain, "The attackers were Arab. The first we saw were on foot, but others soon followed on horseback and camel."

"Were they soldiers? What were they wearing?" Major Joseph asked.

"Some men had uniforms, others were dressed like us. Except they were shooting at us."

"How many people were killed or injured in this attack?"

"I cannot know. We had to escape very quickly into our fields. No one has returned, but we have heard that they burned our homes and took our animals."

I was eager to participate in the investigation, but I was unfamiliar with the typical aspects of an attack, so I hung back to observe. Major Joseph paused, turned toward us, and asked if we had any questions. Our SLA representative, Anour, leaned forward and whispered a question in his ear. I wondered why he was whispering and strained to hear what he had said.

"Ah, yes, from what direction did the attackers come?" Major Joseph repeated aloud.

"We don't know. We were in our huts when we heard the first gunfire," the elder replied.

Anour leaned forward again to whisper in Major Joseph's ear. I was surprised at what was apparently the team's modus operandi.

Major Joseph nodded and then asked, "Did you see where they went?"

Shaking his head, another elder replied, "The men were still in our village as we were fleeing. We had to hide so that they could not kill us or steal our children." A fly buzzed in the broadening silence. The crowed looked at us expectantly, but Major Joseph offered no further questions.

Our Congolese deputy commander was very friendly and eager to be engaged. A short man with great pride in his round belly—a symbol of stature and good health in his part of Africa—the deputy had a poor command of both English and Arabic. Frowning to try to comprehend the discussion, he asked toward Major Joseph, "What were the attackers wearing?"

Ahmed politely explained that we had just asked that question and repeated the witness's reply to make sure he understood. Major Joseph looked annoyed.

I jumped in, neglecting to direct my questions through Major Joseph: "What time was the attack? Can you estimate how many attackers there were and what type of weapons they were using?" Ibrahim hesitated, looking at our team leader for a cue as to how to proceed before he translated. He was not really a member of the team; he did not ask questions. He only translated whatever we said, usually following Major Joseph's lead.

Major Joseph glared at me and rephrased my question to Ibrahim, "Ask this man what time the attackers arrived and how many men had weapons."

I grumbled under my breath. I knew I was the new kid and needed to give it some time before Major Joseph knew and trusted me, but I did not like his attitude toward me. I gritted my teeth and said nothing more.

The IDPs conferred among themselves in Arabic, trying to compile an estimate from various witnesses, but were unable to provide any meaningful details. John explained to me that we would usually get a more precise overview from the SLA once we made it to the villages.

Our GOS representative, Lieutenant Colonel Mohammed, a soldier in his mid-30s with Arab features, sat silently, disengaged. He did not speak English and did not care to ask questions, but he understood the conversations as they went on in Arabic. Mohammed rarely obstructed our work, but he did not help us either.

After recruiting a guide to join us, we traveled to the village of Angarta to seek out other survivors we could interview and to survey the destruction. Our guide pointed into the distance. It was only a short drive along dusty tracks before we could see conical grass rooftops clustered near a set of baobab trees. Pulling into the village of Angarta, my curiosity turned into unease about what we would find. We turned off our engines under a large meeting tree and got out to explore. I could still smell the acrid scent of charred wood.

Angarta was deserted and looted. There had always been at least a few people, donkeys, goats, or kids running around or watching us whenever I visited a Sudanese village. Now, for the first time, I confronted doors gaping open, cooking utensils and pots abandoned amid an interrupted task, and sacks of grain torn open and spilling onto the ground. The few things that these poor farmers actually owned had been tossed out of their huts to be inspected for their value, divvied up, and taken away. All of the livestock except a few chickens were missing—likely stolen, as fleeing villagers could scarcely afford to be held back by a few animals, despite the fact that they represented a family's only store of wealth.

We walked around in silence, listening to our boots crunch on the course sand. A few grass huts stood intact; elsewhere only round mud foundations remained. Crumbling and blackened, the hand-made bricks had surprisingly withstood the blaze, offering testimony to what had once been a beloved home. I stepped inside one charred cylinder, wondering how a family could sleep, cook, and otherwise exist in such a small, single space. A feeling of sadness at this injustice briefly overwhelmed me—that a people with so little should have everything taken from them. I tried to clear the weight of this emotion quickly and return to the business of my investigation. I would not get very far in this work if I allowed each incident to affect me. I searched through the debris until I identified tracks leading away from the village.

After a few minutes of exploring, Major Joseph called us to return to the vehicle, which John had left running. Ahmed had not even gotten out of his car.

"Captain Brian, we're leaving," Major Joseph called. I was still on the edge of the village following a set of tire tracks that led away from the scene.

"Look at these tire tracks and boot marks," I pointed towards the sand. Deep into my analysis, I said, "It looks to me like they dismounted from their vehicles here, having come from the north. I bet we can find a few shell casings to help us identify their weapons if we move outward from these tracks."

Major Joseph cleared his throat with annoyance, catching my attention.

I looked up and realized that he was impatiently waiting for me; the rest of the team had already loaded into the vehicles. I was perplexed by his apparent indifference. I paused, feeling frustrated that I couldn't take the investigation further. We hadn't yet found any valuable information. But, I relented. I walked toward the vehicles. It was too soon to pick a fight with my team leader. I was willing to observe more objectively on this first patrol, but I wasn't sure how long I would tolerate this arrangement.

. . .

Our last task was to conduct interviews with people injured in the attack who were now receiving treatment in the civilian hospital in Nyala. We passed through the hospital gates into the open compound where a number of clinic buildings and medical tents sat in the dirt between sickened trees. I looked around slowly, taking in the site.

Dozens of patients lay lifelessly on stretchers and thin mats lined up on the ground outside the clinic buildings. Others were slumped against walls. Many were children, including infants, held in the arms of crying mothers who were trying to shade them from the sun. It was not clear to me how many were waiting to be seen and how many had already been treated. A few nurses ducked in and out of rooms, but there was no apparent triage system. I knew most of these patients would have had to travel for days on foot to get here. Did they even have any water to drink? People were moaning in pain, some missing their limbs, others with round stains of blood seeping through their bandages. None of the victims seemed to notice our official presence, their dull eyes stuck somewhere in the past. Though it was late afternoon, the sun hung oppressively above us. I felt dizzy.

I motioned to Ibrahim. "Ask this man what happened to him," I said. We squatted next to a man lying on a mat on his stomach with a bloody cloth wrapped around his buttocks and waist.

"Gunshot wound. They usually dive into the fields but often get hit from behind," the interpreter explained.

"Ask this woman what happened to her." I pointed toward a small, elderly woman wrapped in a blue cloth. She was sitting against a tree with a large bandage over her elbow.

"Gunshot wound."

"And what happened to this child?" I gestured almost frantically at a small boy, no more than eight years old, his leg disappearing into a tightly wound, bulky dressing.

"Gunshot wound."

These casualties of war were not soldiers. I looked around the compound courtyard. These women, children, and other civilians packed together along the clinic walls were all unnecessary victims of this growing crisis. What were their chances of survival in this environment?

Anour, our SLA representative, located the room of the patient we'd been seeking. We stepped toward a dark hole in the long cement structure. Blinking, I strained to see into the blackness. Seven people hooked to IVs were crammed into a tiny room. It felt like a cage. I stumbled on an old syringe and struggled to keep from falling onto other medical waste on the floor. The room smelled of rot and excrement. I squinted to check if all the patients were alive. I could see from the light of the doorway that the sheets were far from white. Our team crowded inside to interview a victim from Angarta. I stood in the doorway two beds away from our subject, holding my stomach.

The man was weary, his lips still wrinkled with dehydration. When he first noticed us—and our military uniforms—his eyes widened with fear. Ahmed quickly introduced us as the African Union monitoring team. The victim lay back but appeared to remain on guard with the little energy he had.

"I did not see my attacker," he explained cautiously. "Suddenly I was shot in the leg and I fell to the ground. My brother carried me to safety." He offered little additional detail but let us inspect his leg, which was wrapped in bloody gauze below his single sheet.

The attack on Angarta had taken place a few days prior to our interviews, making it difficult to locate enough witnesses to construct a reliable picture of the event. As I quickly learned, either the AU would not receive information in a timely manner or our investigation would be late due to a significant backlog. At any time, we could have a backlog of up to 50 complaints—some of them repetitive, from more than one source. In such circumstances, it could take days before we had the chance to visit the scene of an alleged crime. Also, the local population did not understand the Ceasefire Commission's function, and therefore many of their complaints were unrelated to ceasefire issues. Making matters worse, the police in Nyala routinely refered any and all police matters to the AU whether they had something to do with the ceasefire or not. I viewed this as a byproduct of an inefficient, inexperienced, and ill-equipped AU operation.

.　　.　　.

"Ok, here is how we do it." John was walking me through my first report so that I would understand the procedure. In fact, the drill was probably more bureaucratic than it needed to be. "After returning from an attack investigation, Joseph will handwrite the majority of the report's observations, interviews and conclusions, then hand it off to you for typing and proofreading. Because English is your first language, this task will fall to you. Now, wherever possible, we add photographs and sketch out how we think the attack happened and then pull everything together into a PowerPoint presentation. I'm the designated photographer for the team right now, but when I move over to Operations, I'm assuming you'll take that on as well."

"Gladly," I said. We needed to document evidence accurately and thoroughly, and I was happy for this to be my responsibility.

"Next, we make recommendations of what can be done to prevent the violation in the future—as if there is anything that would keep the Janjaweed or GOS from attacking—and then bring the report to the team for their signatures."

"What do you do if someone disagrees with the report or recommendations?" I asked.

"We exclude anything we can't reach consensus on," John replied.

"You just omit it?" I asked. "How do you create any accurate picture of an event when all the warring parties on the team probably disagree entirely about what happened?"

"Well, we get to some version of the truth that the majority can agree with. If a monitor still contests the final report, he still has to sign it to acknowledge that he's read the document. But, he can write an addendum with his comments. Our GOS rep does that a lot."

"Where do the reports go?"

"Well, we turn over each report to the sector commander for comments and then on to the AU regional headquarters in El Fashir. Next it passes through the Ceasefire Commission and then on to Addis Ababa, the AU international headquarters in Ethiopia. Finally they're supposed to be disseminated to all of the donor countries through their embassies, but I doubt that actually happens. We never get any feedback on our reports. But, we go through the motions," John shrugged.

At the JMC, we frequently got feedback on our reports from Friends of the Nuba Mountains member countries. In Darfur, we would hear absolutely nothing.

Chapter 10

From the helicopter, the village of Adeila looked small. Miniature conical huts surrounded a central marketplace canopied with an uneven trellis of woven grass. It was October 11, and we were investigating an alleged attack on September 25 by the SLA on Abu Karinka, another village not too far away. The GOS had initiated the report, alleging ten civilians had been killed in the incident. Adelia housed a GOS military base. We touched down near the outpost and walked toward the village to talk with the GOS. We saw fresh mounds of dirt covered with thorny bushes to prevent animals from disturbing the new graves. Could these have been GOS casualties?

As we approached the GOS outpost, the officials rose to meet us and called their staff to bring over orange Fanta soda for us. It was a Sudanese custom to offer a beverage during any meeting. After an extended greeting, we sat down outside to conduct the investigation, asking the GOS to explain the story behind their complaint.

"Rebel attackers hiding in the village market area assaulted our troops," the GOS leader said. "The rebels had three vehicles, Kalashnikovs, and grenade launchers. So we retaliated and returned fire into the civilian market area."

"Using what?" Joseph asked.

"One hundred and twenty millimeter mortars," he said in a calm voice.

Our SLA representative, Anour, who was easily outraged, repeated calmly but firmly, "You did what? You fired mortars into a village marketplace?"

"We fired into the market to defend ourselves from the rebel attackers," the GOS leader said, looking right at us.

Now, a 120mm mortar round is the size of a football. The mortar, which requires a truck to carry it, is usually lowered to the ground and fired from a specific military position, but it can also be fired from a trailer. Assuming that the SLA had attacked, the GOS would have had a right to retaliate and defend its position. But it was obvious to me that if what they were saying was true, the GOS soldiers had blatantly endangered civilians—mortar rounds of this size would blow huge holes in the ground and easily take out huts. Why would the GOS actually admit to firing mortars into a civilian market in a ceasefire violation report they had initiated against the SLA? This story did not add up.

Lieutenant Colonel Mohammed, our GOS monitor, asked a few leading questions about the SLA, seeking emphasis on retaliation and defensive measures by GOS soldiers. While we listened to the GOS soldiers, I noticed two police Land Cruisers pass by with machine guns mounted on the hood. As the policemen got out of their vehicles, I saw that they were wearing new uniforms and boots. It struck me that there was no real difference between the police and the GOS. They interacted as if they were the same unit, and both groups seemed well equipped and well trained.

I shouldn't have been surprised. Sudan was effectively a military dictatorship. One of the features of such grim enterprises—like Iraq under Saddam Hussein—is the consolidation of firepower. The police force in Iraq was an extension of the military, which itself was organized as much for internal suppression as it was for fighting wars against other nation-states. So in Sudan too, the police were, in a sense, an arm of the GOS military. They simply wore a slightly different uniform, which meant that we had to be wary of what we said to them because they weren't neutral in this conflict. We were the only genuine neutrals on the battlefield.

From Adeila, we headed to Muhajeriya, the SLA South Darfur headquarters, to talk to SLA representatives about the incident in Abu Karinka. As our helicopter touched down, hordes of villagers surrounded us. We estimated later that there were about 2,000 people. The SLA soldiers emerged from their protected position in the bush. I learned quickly that this was standard operating procedure: The rebel forces—guarding their location, capabilities, and weaponry—never met us in the bush where their military positions were located. Instead, they came to a village when they saw our helicopter land.

The SLA guys knew our team and spoke excellent English. I was introduced as a new monitor, and the SLA members each shook my hand, saying that they were happy to meet another American. At first I was surprised that these rural farmers who had picked up arms against the Government of Sudan spoke English so well. I soon learned that most of the SLA leaders were actually educated professionals, such as doctors or lawyers. On our team, for instance, our JEM representative, Ali, was a lawyer; Anour was finishing up his law degree. Where Anour tended to be more confrontational, Ali was much more even-handed in his responses. But both men were professional.

Our interview with the SLA members was brief.

"The SLA did not order this attack you speak of, so we did not conduct such an attack," the SLA commander stated plainly. I could not read his tone. He did not sound upset about the accusation; he did not sound defensive, as if he were hiding something. It was nearly impossible to tell if he was speaking the truth, and he did not seem to care what we thought.

"Were the fresh graves on the outskirts of town from the skirmish?"

He frowned. "I know nothing about such graves. As I have said, my men were not there." We continued to look at him, like he had more to offer. "There is nothing else to say," he finished.

We left, somewhat reluctantly. Except for the fresh graves in Adeila, which could easily have housed people who had recently died of starvation, we had no proof to support the GOS claim. Over the subsequent three weeks, we could still find no concrete evidence of the GOS report—no refugees, no injured, no looting—nothing. This would be the first in a series of GOS complaints that, despite extensive investigations, never resulted in any solid substantiation.

.   .   .

When we arrived back at our compound, we heard that an attack had just occurred in an IDP camp—a particularly shocking example of GOS brutality if it proved to be true. A headquarters team had gone out for a quick evaluation, and our monitoring team would investigate tomorrow.

I took a moment to sit up on our roof, read a magazine, and record my thoughts on my MP3 player. I was shocked at how brazenly the GOS soldiers had reported their attack on villages in Abu Karinka and how minimally the team had questioned them. I was amazed that they would admit so readily that they fired mortars into a civilian marketplace. Apparently, this was viewed as a normal and acceptable tactic. They could have been lying, but why in the world would they choose to make up such a story? They seemed to think nothing of it. The casual comments of the GOS officers alone confirmed that in Darfur, civilians were no longer sacred citizens of Sudan—they were hunted down like military targets. What was even more disturbing was that my team did not even appear surprised. Sure, Anour and Ali were angered, but they too seemed to accept the GOS account as within the range of possibility.

And I was supposed to just stand there and listen? The reality was that I was being paid to watch. It was not my job to prevent, protect, aid, or fight against but simply to watch the violence unfold. On top of all this, the African Union didn't trust me enough to let me take pictures yet. They thought my professional camera was too *imposing*. How can a camera be too imposing when we are talking about armed forces mowing down women and children?! I dreaded what we would find tomorrow in the IDP camp.

Chapter 11

The next day we drove out to Bashum Camp, home to 500 displaced people. The conditions at Kalma Camp had been horrible enough—now an IDP camp had become a GOS target. The attack had taken place the previous afternoon on what happened to have been a market day.

After an hour-long drive we pulled into the most disheartening collection of shelters I had ever seen. Each hut was constructed completely of recycled trash: plastic bags, cardboard, metal, and scrap wood. A bloated donkey and a few dead dogs attracted flies nearby. Though the initial reports had been provided by Norwegian Church Aid, there was no immediate evidence of NGO emergency operations here. These people had suffered greatly, and now they were living in what an unknowing stranger could reasonably believe was a garbage dump. The residents looked weary and extremely dirty. For many weeks to come I would see their faces as I lay in my bunk at night.

We were greeted by 50 SLA members with weapons. The men from the village—wearing dingy pants, T-shirts, and flip flops, and propping themselves up by a club or spear—gathered around us. A number of them had been wounded and had bandages wrapped around various parts of their bodies.

One witness stepped forward and began. "On the day before the attack, 50 to 60 Janajweed arrived on horses and camels."

"What time was it and what were they wearing?" Joseph interrupted.

"It was about 1600. Some were in normal clothing and others were in green camouflage and police uniforms," the witness responded. He continued. "They began to set up camp nearby. The next day was our market day. We had a bad feeling about their arriving the day before our weekly market."

The witness grew visibly agitated, waving his arms and pacing about, but Ibrahim continued his translation in a monotone. "The Janjaweed rushed into the marketplace. They whipped several people and then stabbed one man who tried to stop them. They came in two groups—one would move toward us while the other held back, almost protecting them while they shot at us. Then the other group would move forward while the other would stand back firing at us. We wanted to fight, but we had nothing to defend ourselves with."

He paused, looking down for a moment. Then he pointed to a set of fresh graves, saying nothing.

A minute later, the witness identified the Janjaweed leader by name and told us that his militia came from Mirrel and Nitega. I was stunned.

"These victims know who is in charge among the Janjaweed groups?" I whispered to Ahmed.

"The nomads attacking their families are people these villagers used to trade with on a regular basis. They know each other—well, *thought* that they knew each other—like brothers," Ahmed explained.

An SLA commander spoke up. "When we received news of the attack, we immediately responded." The hand he was waving around in the air as he spoke was wrapped heavily with bandages, yet blood was seeping through from his palm. Nevertheless, the leader participated in our discussion without any hint of pain from what was obviously a gunshot wound. "Our men arrived while the Janjaweed were still in the IDP camp looting, but the attackers were still able to steal 31 cartons of biscuits and most of the camp's medicine. We chased them for an hour after driving them out of the camp. The Janjaweed killed ten civilians and wounded seventeen others." Like the SPLA in the Nuba Mountains, I expected the SLA was committed to protecting the people, and this story was certain confirmation.

Our first witness offered one more piece of testimony. "I have information that suggests the villages of Ishma, Labado, and Um Zaifa will be attacked in the coming days." He looked at us expectantly. The rest of the team did not seem very interested. I made a brief entry in my notebook, considering this potentially valuable intelligence, though I was not yet sure how reliable it might be.

Two things about this attack were particularly significant for me. First, the IDP camp residents had anticipated an assault since they had seen the Janjaweed arriving the previous afternoon. These Janjaweed had attacked the IDP camp specifically because they knew it was a market day and there would be swarms of people and plenty of goods to steal. The IDPs wanted to fight back but did not have the capacity to do so. Still, despite their anticipation of the attack they refused to leave because this camp was their last home and possible safe haven. They had nowhere else to go. It is one thing to attack people in their village; it is another thing entirely to attack an IDP camp. These people had already been driven out of their homes violently and had established a camp of last resort—an act of desperation as they sought to meet their basic needs and find safety. But even that was to be denied them by the GOS and the Janjaweed militias. I was convinced: This was systematic ethnic cleansing. This was genocide. There was no other way to describe it.

The second thing was the assault itself. From the way witnesses described it, the attack appeared to be a well-coordinated military offensive, using a technique called "bounding over watch." In this leapfrogging maneuver, one small unit fires while another unit moves forward under another's protection. This meant that the Janjaweed nomads had been well trained and were using a system of command and control in their attacks. These Arab militias appeared to enjoy a much deeper relationship with the GOS than I first realized.

It was inexcusable that we did not know of the anticipated attack at Bashum prior to its occurrence. All of the witnesses saw the fires of Janjaweed encampments the previous night. If we had known ahead of time, we could have been there to stop the attack. Even though we didn't have a mandate to protect civilians, driving through the area or even flying over in a helicopter might have been enough to dissuade the Janjaweed from attacking.

We hadn't even heard about the attack directly from the IDP. The Bashum Camp incident was first referred to us by Norwegian Church Aid. In general, we had an amicable relationship with the NGOs, exchanging information with them almost on a daily basis. The NGOs would inform us of the movements of troops they observed in the field and report any incidents that occurred. The AU did not officially allow us to pass information to the NGOs, but we felt it important to provide general security information on an informal basis whenever NGO staff visited our compound. When possible, we would escort their convoys if we had a patrol going to a certain place and the NGOs were headed in the same direction. These informal relationships were more effective than our established protocol.

. . .

The next day, I traveled with Team D to the village of Donkey Deressa to investigate the October 2 rape and murder of a 75-year-old woman named Halima Anour Adam, allegedly by a GOS soldier. On our drive, we passed a new IDP settlement where 400 homeless people had been gathering over the last week or so. Children squatted under thorny trees while women cooked over small fires. As we drove by, they gazed at us with resignation that seemed to me a complete absence of hope. I thought their eyes looked hollow and felt what was becoming a familiar pain—the emptiness of knowing that I could do nothing, right then and there, to make their lives any better.

When we arrived in Donkey Deressa, the whole community gathered around us to lend its assistance to our investigation. The omda, or chief of the village, called to someone who brought out the customary chai in tiny glasses. It was so hot I could hardly hold it and had to place it on the ground while we spoke.

The crowd allowed the woman's brother to step forward. An elderly man, likely also in his seventies or eighties, looked down before he began. I could not tell whether his face reflected shame or sadness. He began quietly.

"I found her body. She was," he hesitated, "naked. When I touched her, she did not move." I was pained to think of a 75-year-old woman left with such disregard in the sand. "Someone had beaten her with sticks." He shook his head. "Then they shot her in the head." He looked up, catching my gaze briefly. I felt a chill run through my body.

"Who would want to kill Halima?" His voice wavered. I looked at this man's withered frame, only guessing that the body of his sister—a woman who probably carried nearly half her weight on her head every day since she was six—would have visibly born the marks of her long and difficult existence.

The omda took over. "Halima's brother found footsteps in the sand leading away from her body to the military base. It is less than one kilometer away. On the edge of the base, a soldier's uniform was found. We took Halima's body to the hospital." Reports we later obtained from untrained doctors announced that she had died of heart failure, though it was obvious to everyone that she had died from the gunshot wound to her head.

Not long after our arrival, a GOS military commander showed up in a police truck with a Dushka mounted on top. The Dushka is an old Russian anti-aircraft machine gun that fires 12.7 millimeter rounds—600 rounds a minute. Several soldiers got out. The whole circle of villagers grew silent, and Halima's brother disappeared back into the mass of people.

Lieutenant Commander James, a timid Ghanaian naval officer with glasses, was the patrol leader of Team D. He nudged the team's GOS monitor. "Go tell them to leave." The soldiers were intentionally intimidating the villagers. Emboldened, the group of witnesses pointed out a security person in civilian clothes standing among them in the crowd. We insisted he leave as well.

The police harassment to keep people in line was remarkable. We had heard reports of police beating people who spoke out. These poor villagers had to live in constant fear for their safety and had virtually no one they could turn to. I wondered what would happen to Halima's brother now.

After speaking with the civilians, it was time to talk to the GOS. Its encampment of 250 soldiers a short distance from the village was fairly large and surrounded by deep trenches in which soldiers sat armed with machine guns. We got out of our vehicles and walked over to the grass shelter under which the commander sat in a plastic chair watching us. The claim that soldier's clothing was found at the edge of the encampment could not be substantiated. There was really no way to prove a soldier committed the crime. All of the accusations were hearsay, and unfortunately we had no ability to investigate further. There would be no justice, accountability, or closure for the family of Halima, their sister, their mother, their wife, their grandmother.

Our inquiry was over. Our Sudanese and Chadian team members asked for water with which to wash and a mat on which to pray. The Muslim members of our team did their best to pray five times a day. They looked for certain breaks in our patrols rather than sticking to a rigid schedule. The series of prayers they conducted while we were out in the field usually only took about five minutes, but it seemed to me they were always praying whenever we had a few minutes to spare. This commitment awed me. It was difficult for me to stick to doing even one thing a day consistently, writing in my journal for example. At the same time, other practitioners of Islam were committing horrible crimes against the black population. I wondered how people in any radical group, so close to prayer, so constantly conscious of God, could reconcile the act of murder and other violence in their religion's name. The complexity of the conflict—and its relationship to religion—baffled me.

.　　.　　.

Finding a villager to guide us, we departed for Ketil, another village that had recently been attacked. We were stopped by the SLA before we even arrived. SLA fighters were set up in a defensive position facing GOS troops who were located on the other side of town. They hustled us over to the wadi so we could hunker down with them to talk. Apparently, the village had been attacked again that morning. Some of the SLA members had been treated with fresh bandages. Smoke rose from the town beyond the tree line.

We spoke with the SLA commander, named Ahmed Ibrahim, who reported that the attackers had arrived from the east in three or four Toyota Hiluxes and one military truck. Beginning at 10:00 a.m. and lasting until 4:00 p.m., the soldiers fired rocket-propelled grenades and mortars on the village.

"They fired into our village and caused some type of gas cloud that made our families ill. Everyone was coughing violently, and their eyes were tearing and burning."

"How many rounds did they fire?" Lieutenant Commander James, Team D's patrol leader, asked.

The SLA commander thought for a moment. "Nine," he said.

"Let's see one of those rounds," I inserted. The SLA brought over an RPG round, which did not seem normal. I turned it over in my hands. It had a screw cap on top and looked to me like it could contain a chemical or biological agent, possibly CS gas, commonly called tear gas. I had no idea the GOS had the capability to use chemical or biological weapons or that it would use them on civilian villagers. It just kept getting worse.

As I held the RPG round in my hand, the witness added that the soldiers had then set fire to the area. From our vantage point, we could still see smoking huts, and I was eager to advance into the village to collect more evidence of a possible chemical weapons attack. I noticed Lieutenant

Commander James glancing at his watch and looking skyward. James was nice enough, but often he seemed to be simply going through the motions.

"We have to get going," he said, cutting off the SLA member who was speaking. "We can come back another day."

I saw the men's faces drop. We had only been there about five minutes. The SLA member tried to continue, quickly describing the effects of the gas clouds.

"Yep, we need to get going," James cut him off again, pointing toward the western sky. "It's getting dark and we don't know these roads well enough."

An SLA soldier stood up and walked away without a word. Here we were with the likelihood of a chemical weapons attack by the GOS on a civilian village and James did not even seem to acknowledge the significance of the information or the evidence we could obtain. He started walking to the car. I felt the need to apologize to the SLA soldiers, and yet I was still a visitor on this team and new to the operation.

I hurried up to James and suggested that we at least investigate the village, understand what happened, and document the attack in detail.

"We will come back another day," he said to the crowd over my shoulder. "Let's go," he said to me.

"But we haven't even asked how many people were wounded!"

He sighed, "Fine, go ask and then let's go."

There had been four villagers wounded, two of whom had been affected significantly by the gas clouds. I was fuming on our ride back. We arrived at our compound at 6:00 p.m. It would not be dark for at least another hour. I called Gretchen to vent.

"This is our job," I argued. "If we have to stay out past dark, so what?— we have to stay out past dark. We are traveling in safe vehicles and we have no curfew for the precise reason that we need the freedom to conduct these investigations. We are here to support the people of Darfur in achieving peace. We will never succeed in our mission if we don't even listen to them."

"That's unbelievable," she said. "How on earth are you supposed to look like a legitimate monitoring mission if you don't appear interested in what the people have to say?"

"I was so damn pissed when he said we would come back another day.

I just wanted to scream at him, 'If we have to stay out until 2100, 2200, 2300, and spend the night because we can't get back, then THAT IS OUR JOB!' Gretchen, I *cannot believe* the incompetence that I saw today."

.   .   .

The next morning, on October 14, I awoke as usual just before sunrise to the daily chant calling the faithful to prayer. We checked in first with sector headquarters. The sector commander ordered us to go back to the village. Before I had even said anything, he asked the team, "How do you know the village was even attacked?" James made some meek excuses for our hasty return but accepted his orders obediently.

We headed out. I was not yet an official driver, but Team D invited me to drive that day. We decided to approach Ketil through the GOS military position this time. We stopped and announced our intentions to the GOS soldiers, who agreed to escort us. The GOS left us at the edge of a hill and pointed in the direction we needed to go to access the village. Given the route we had taken, the entire team was worried that the SLA would shoot at us, confusing us with GOS troops. We drove a short distance up the hill. James concluded that the village must be "over there," where it was unsafe to venture, and then announced we could go.

Stubbornly, I took my vehicle in a different direction. Rounding another knoll, I could finally identify a village by a few huts that appeared from my vantage point to have been burned. Clearly, the attack had occurred. I was ready to go down into the village, but James insisted that we leave. I had already proceeded farther than I was authorized to go by the team leader. I had to turn back. I clenched the steering wheel tightly and bit my lip. How the hell were we supposed to investigate an attack if we couldn't get closer than 300 meters to the village?

Returning to camp, James and I met in the operations room to write up our report. He gave me his handwritten notes to type up. I glanced over his scribbles and found absolutely no mention of chemical weapons. I looked up at him. Watching him move on to his next task, I decided not to say anything. Later, as I typed up the report on my computer, I carefully detailed the evidence of chemical weapons myself.

But where would the report end up? It seemed that important information wasn't making it all the way through official channels. I decided to take matters into my own hands just to be safe. Members of the US embassy staff were always at our contracting company's compound because the US funded our mission and wanted to oversee the effectiveness of our operations. But they did not have their own "eyes" on the ground, nor did they have an independent view of what was happening in the field. I began to talk them up and pass along information from our reports. The US embassy staff was hungry for this information and asked me to keep it up. It felt good to be doing something. Hopefully, with enough intelligence, the US would use its influence to stop the conflict. The AU should have been reporting to them eventually, and yet I could tell from talking to the embassy personnel that it wasn't happening.

I never heard whether the AU decided to investigate the chemical weapons any further.

Chapter 12

Walking into Suleia gave me a feeling of déjà vu. I was standing on the soil where those little girls had been shackled and burned to death. Officially assigned to Team C, I listened while Major Joseph described to me what had happened here prior to our arrival—the villagers had been driven out by a brutal militia attack. But I pretended that I was hearing it for the first time. Now, standing in the same village, I easily recognized some of the surrounding areas from the confidential photographs I had seen less than 3 months earlier. The children's bodies were no longer there, of course. But somehow I felt strangely connected to them. They had been partly responsible for bringing me here.

Now here I was. I wandered around slowly, trying to imagine the terror these families experienced while they watched their loved ones murdered. What would I have done if Gretchen or my mom were being attacked? I noticed grass mats and beds tossed on their sides, apparently shoved from homes in a hasty looting session. The entire town was deserted except for these small remnants of a former life. One of those girls might have slept on one of these small grass mats. I bent down to touch the crisp, slightly rolled end. These farmers had so few belongings that a grass mat would have been treated with great care. Ash piles suggested a wooden fence had surrounded each torched compound. Long grasses indicated the village had been abandoned for months. No one was going to return here, to the site where their kids had been chained, raped, and burned alive. I could not comprehend the fear and pain of their last few minutes on earth.

I had been desensitized to violence in the Marine Corps, to a certain extent. Standing in Suleia, I felt empty, but not shocked. It was more like a cognitive recognition that a great horror had taken place. In the Marine Corps,

we talk about killing in a straightforward way, compared with the eu-
phemisms—"servicing the target"—used by our Army, Navy, and Air Force
friends. The truth of the matter is that we teach kids that killing is okay,
undoing everything they have learned up until then that says killing is wrong.
In our Infantry Officers Course, we spent weekends hanging out in scrubs
in the trauma centers of southeast DC. I remember one guy who came in after
a motorcycle accident. The emergency-room doctor let me put my finger in
his head wound and touch his exposed skull. I was never grossed out by death
or blood in the ER. And it didn't bother me when I went hunting, either. Now
I stood in Suleia, where that horrible act had occurred last July, and again I felt
numb. Things were terribly wrong here. But I had already accepted that evil
existed in the world—and that here, in this place, it was manifest.

Suleia had once been SLA-controlled territory, but the villagers had been
driven out by the July attack. The GOS had established a military base in
Suleia on September 22 in direct violation of the ceasefire. The ceasefire
required that the borders of the territory controlled by the SLA/JEM and
the GOS remained fixed to where they were at the time of the signing and
strictly prohibited any and all advancements or new outposts. We met with
the outpost commander, who seemed annoyed that we were there. This time
they did not offer us drinks. I pulled Ahmed aside as people were situating
themselves.

"What do you think the ethnic background is of the GOS leadership
here?" I asked.

"The lieutenant, his deputy, and his plainclothes security-officer are definitely of Arab descent."

"Okay, that's what I thought, but the rest of the soldiers look more
African."

"I agree," Ahmed confirmed. "They are definitely from African tribes."

"Then why," I asked him, "are the GOS soldiers from African tribes if
they are specifically fighting other Africans?"

Ahmed signed, shaking his head. "It is a shame," he said. "You see, the
GOS will typically take conscripts from different tribes in other areas of
Sudan to fight in Darfur. In Sudan, the people are more tightly associated
with their tribe than with their religion or nationality. In fact, Anour was
once a corporal in the GOS and was conscripted to fight against other

Africans in the long civil war in the south. We hear he defected to the SLA once he saw what was happening here."

The story just seemed to get more complicated. I joined the circle as the inquiry began.

The GOS lieutenant told us that his higher command unit was the 16th Division, but he would not reveal any further information on his own unit of approximately 50 to 75 GOS military troops. The lieutenant explained that his orders were to protect the local population of the area and even went so far as to suggest that the civilians would come to him and ask for protection in the fields. Not only did we not see any civilians, we saw no cultivated fields either.

As our helicopter took off, I tried to get a shot from the air with my little camera, but the foggy windows prevented me from capturing anything clearly. I desperately wanted to use my professional digital camera. I shook my head with regret, imagining myself hanging in the helicopter doors in a harness capturing high-resolution photos of the scene below. I needed real evidence to show the atrocities clearly taking place here.

.   .   .

On the same day we were in Suleia, Team D left for an investigation in the town of Baraka, south of Donkey Deressa. In Baraka, 10 villagers had been tortured and brutally murdered by the Janjaweed. When the members of Team D returned, they shared their photos with us in the operations room. I did not think anything could shock me at this point. I was wrong.

Several bloody corpses filled a shallow grave. They were lined up in a row and covered with grass mats. Images from the Holocaust and Rwanda filled my mind. I looked closer. Every single man in this countless row of African civilians had had his eyes plucked out and his ears cut off. I closed my eyes and shuddered to think of the pain of having your ears sawed off—maybe ripped off—and your eyes speared from your face while you were living.

It got worse. Another photo revealed a man lying in the dirt, blood streaming away from his groin. He had been castrated and left to bleed to death. A third photo showed a man stripped naked, likely sexually assaulted and executed after the humiliation.

I experienced the same rage I felt when I first saw the photos of the girls in Suleia. We would probably have to go back to that village to track down the Janjaweed, since it was our responsibility to speak to both sides. I would welcome the opportunity to look these murderers in the eyes. Usually, the cowards would attack and then run. But, it would not take long to find a group of Arab nomads who normally traveled the barren landscape with 300 or more camels. I was ready to fill up our vehicle with 3 to 5 days of food or take a helicopter to go look for the bastards.

But in reality, the AU never went back. Team D wrote a report and closed the case.

.　　.　　.

On some level, I knew the situation was absurd. But it was hard to break out of the cage of our monitoring mission. Every day we went out to investigate, to try to get a grip on what was happening around us. But the details of our investigations so occupied us that sometimes it was hard to step back and see the situation for what it was—one ethnic group wiping out the other.

Meanwhile, I did not have any real power to influence the process. As a civilian contractor on loan to the AU from the US, I did not really have any superiors I could go to for support; not to mention the fact that this was a military operation, and you could not just go around the chain of command. But every day there were more and more attacks and atrocities to investigate, so we had to move on, for better or for worse. I told myself that the best I could do was to focus on documenting everything I saw. Maybe later it would be useful.

.　　.　　.

I had been in Darfur, I suddenly realized, only one week. What had John said? "Welcome to hell." I had only investigated one report of a killing in seven months in the Nuba Mountains. What I experienced this first week in Darfur was a nightmare that repeated itself day after day. As far as I knew, I would be in Darfur for a year. I would have to keep my composure if I was going to investigate these attacks on a daily basis. If I allowed myself to get sucked in, I would be dragged down too quickly. I had been trained for war. I had never been in active combat, but I was trained to know what to expect.

In conflict between nations, between professional militaries, there is supposed to be a boundary, a set of rules agreed to that prevent torture and such barbaric treatment of human beings. Furthermore, there is a process of justice that holds accountable any abusers of this code. Here in Darfur, all bets were off. There were no rules of war—somehow I had to accept that. If I allowed myself to get emotionally involved, I would not be able to do my job for very long.

The incompetence of the AU mission made each day of violence that much worse. As I sat outside my tent making notes in my MP3 player, I heard a plane take off. I checked my watch. It was 2000; the airport closed at 1900. My bet was that it was a GOS Antonov 26, armed and dangerous. Somewhere, an attack was taking place. I guessed I would find out tomorrow.

Chapter 13

October 20, 2004. The day is tattooed permanently in my memory. Anour had received word from an SLA contact on the ground that the GOS had attacked civilians in the village of Alliet. It was midday when we soared in our helicopter over Alliet, a town of 10,000 to 15,000 inhabitants, for the first time. From above, I squinted through the haze, identifying the smoldering ash outlines of huts and former fences. It appeared from the air that the equivalent of one city block in the northeast area of the village had been burned to the ground, extinguishing up to four family compounds of around a dozen grass huts. We touched down in the center of the town, an open courtyard framed on one end by a large gathering tree that disappeared briefly into our dust cloud.

It was already too hot to breathe comfortably. As we disembarked, the dust settled gently around us. We found the village eerily silent. No curious children ran towards us, no mothers peered from their huts. The only village life we spotted was a group of male village elders, a few of whom rose stiffly from their crouched position under the tree. Others remained, as if attached to the nearby cement wall, eyeing us with cautious fatigue. They wore dingy jelabias and either plastic penny-loafers or worn-out flip flops. We walked towards them, offering a greeting in Arabic, identifying ourselves as the African Union but skipping over individual introductions.

"We understand there was an attack here. Can you tell us what happened?" Major Joseph opened.

One of the men blinked, considered our question, looked around and offered almost in a whisper, "The government troops entered over there and started firing," he said, pointing to the northeast. "Some were on foot;

others had vehicles and just started shooting everyone and everywhere. Some people were shot and killed and the rest have fled."

"How many were killed and injured?"

The man pressed his palms together, frowning. After thinking for a moment, he responded with a word and a shrug. Ibrahim replied, "He says there were at least 50 wounded."

I wondered how these old, decrepit men had survived since they could never have fled. It seemed, in contrast to Janjaweed attacks, that when attacks were carried out by the government, elders who would not fight back were left hiding under a bush or crouching with their arms up in the air.

We hadn't been in Alliet for more than five minutes before a dozen GOS officials tore into town in two camouflaged and heavily armed Toyota pickup trucks. Each vehicle sported Dushkas or 12.7 mm machine guns mounted on tripods in each truck bed. A brief tornado of dust flung sand into our eyes as they circled us and skidded to a halt.

The old men immediately fell silent and shuffled quickly back into the shade. The commander stepped out of one truck as his team, armed with Kalashnikovs, formed a protective semicircle around him. After dusting the settling sand off his uniform, the commander charged towards us, followed by a soldier with a gun.

"Do you not intend to speak with the government in this investigation?" he demanded.

Major Joseph looked at us. Ahmed nodded at him and we turned to face the commander.

"Fine, let us speak," Major Joseph replied and gestured toward the tree indicating that we would continue our interview of the villagers after the officials had left and could no longer intimidate them. We squatted around the commander as the old men dispersed. One soldier remained with us at all times, holding his weapon with a look alternately hostile and disinterested. The remaining soldiers took up guard positions around the square. Over the next hour I noticed them gradually make their way to the trees and walls for shade, later slinking down into relaxed positions, some of them dozing off and on while we spoke to their commander.

After we introduced the team members, Major Joseph led the way, asking all investigative questions. That helped to guarantee diplomatic leader-to-leader contact and underscored Joseph's authority when dealing with GOS officials.

"Okay, what happened here?" Major Joseph invited him to begin.

"I am Lieutenant Colonel Badris Alden Yuossef Altaib. I command the Peace Protection Forces, based out of El Fashir. We were just on a routine patrol, making sure this road was secure from bandits to allow for commercial trade."

"What time did your unit approach Alliet?"

The commander shrugged, "I estimate it was around 1530 hours when we were provoked by bandits. We counterattacked to defend ourselves until . . . 1700 hours or so, when it got dark."

I jotted details in my small notebook. By now I knew that clearing a road of bandits was a fairly common excuse used by GOS troops to defend their attacks on civilian villages. *Mistake number one in his story*, I wrote: *It doesn't get dark here until around 1900*. Southern Darfur was only twelve degrees north of the equator. Without a major seasonal influence, days were relatively the same length as nights through the year. There would never be a time when it got dark at 1700.

"Could you identify your attackers?" Major Joseph asked.

"JEM," he responded disdainfully. Mistake number two: We had received our initial report from the SLA.

"The attackers were hiding among civilians, using them as shields."

Mistake number three. I knew that the SLA and JEM were committed to protecting civilians, one of the only reasons they existed and fought back against the government. A more appropriate term for them would be "freedom fighters." They would never even consider using their fellow civilians and tribe members as shields.

"Were there helicopters here?"

"Oh, yes." He replied with little concern. "I had to call in for air support. The helicopters arrived about ninety minutes after the fighting began. But, they didn't fire," he added innocently.

"Did you have any casualties?" Joseph moved on, running quickly through our usual line of questioning.

The commander hesitated. "Well, four of my men were wounded."

"Were any killed?"

Refusing to answer our question, the commander instead announced, "My forces will remain in Alliet until I receive word from my superiors to move."

"Okay," Major Joseph concluded with a sigh, "let us see the village."

.　　.　　.

We rose to walk toward the torched part of town. The GOS commander, Major Joseph, Mohammed, and Ibrahim led the tour, while the rest of us and four of the commander's soldiers followed behind. I took pictures as we walked, asking Anour to catch me up on the discussion when I missed something. The group came to a stop and the commander waited for all of us to give him our attention before continuing.

"Here is where they viciously attacked us." The commander drew his arm across the landscape. "We had to fire back, and some of the bullets unfortunately caught these huts on fire."

A few paces farther, we stopped again before a partially dismantled, burned-out pick-up truck, its tires cracked and peeling. "This here is one of the bandits' vehicles that we were able to destroy in the firefight," he declared, smacking its fender. As he paraded on, mimicking his troop's defense, one of my team members motioned to me, then pointed at the vehicle. I peered into the rusted-out hood and saw straight through to the sand below where an engine once was housed. This truck likely sat as a store of parts for its village mechanics over the last few years. It obviously took no part in the supposed attack, except falling victim to the fires that surrounded it.

As we entered the still-smoldering portion of the village, Anour called me over to see a poor donkey that had remained tied to a center tree as a compound around him burned to the ground. "Can you believe this?!" he said. Two-thirds of the hair and skin on his entire left side was burned as if someone had sanded it off, leaving a raw, open wound. I walked over and cut his strap loose from the tree with my hunting knife. I looked around me, asking someone with a gun to put him out of his misery. A GOS soldier responded by snatching the strap from me and retying him to the tree.

I winced and turned away. I hung back from the team for a moment at the edge of the village, my stomach churning with anger. Looking across the surrounding fields, I could see the stubble of sorghum stocks remaining after the recent fall harvest. They seemed unusually thin compared to the corn stocks that I was used to seeing late summer in Virginia, where my family lived. The lack of rains and the insecurity of the fighting must have made it nearly impossible to plant the previous spring. But it was now the beginning of watermelon season, and patches of tiny green globes lay tangled in spiky brush. I found it amazing that this hard, sandy earth could produce a fruit comprised mostly of liquid.

Behind me, the commander was pointing to a spot perhaps two kilometers away. "That is where my forces dismounted from their vehicles to enter the town."

As a Marine, I had undergone extensive training in urban combat. A convoy entering a village had no reason to disembark and walk with weapons drawn unless an imminent attack was expected or the convoy was preparing its own attack.

I whispered a question in Major Joseph's ear and he repeated it: "Why did you expect a threat from rebels? What initially caused your troops to dismount?"

"Well, naturally, we saw vehicles moving in the town," he responded.

I looked him in the eye but said nothing. I knew that the GOS did not use binoculars. Even if they had seen vehicles moving in a village of this size, it would not automatically signify rebels. Certainly, a farming village would use carts, wagons, and the occasional truck to move goods and supplies.

Perhaps the commander read disbelief in our body language because he promptly corrected himself, "I meant to say, we did not *see*, but *heard* the movement of vehicles."

Another lie: There was no way he could hear the movement of vehicles a couple kilometers away from the village while he was in a vehicle that also was running. This was absurd. Did the GOS really think we were that stupid? Were we really that stupid? I looked around the team wondering if the rest of the members also knew that this could not happen. I didn't know what kind of military training they had gone through, or whether they were familiar with convoy operations and dismounting procedures, but I hoped that they were only remaining silent to avoid looking biased.

We walked a short distance farther before the commander pointed and said, "Here is where we were ambushed. My troops fired back solely to defend themselves."

We surveyed the area but saw no evidence of spent round casings on the ground. I spoke to Ahmed in English, assuming the commander standing nearby could not understand me, "Ahmed, there aren't any rounds here, no grass matted down. There was definitely no firefight." The thin, dry grass surrounding us would easily be crushed or folded down when someone stood on it. And any spent brass rounds would reflect the bright sun. The GOS official must have sensed my skepticism; he smiled in my direction, but I could feel his eyes flashing behind his sunglasses.

As we rounded out our tour of village pathways our pace slowed. The sun hung over us with the weight of a wool blanket. Our time in Alliet that day was almost over, and we turned toward the village center to interview its remaining inhabitants once again.

"Why don't you let my men provide you with security from the rebels?" the commander suggested.

"That won't be necessary," Major Joseph said firmly. Pausing to look us up and down, the commander gestured his men to follow, then spun and marched toward his vehicle as aggressively as he did when he arrived.

When the dust settled after the GOS vehicles drove away, the old men emerged from the village with small watermelons to help quench our thirst. Spreading out a plastic woven mat, we took a moment to rest in the shade. I volunteered my hunting knife to help cut the melons, but realizing it was the Muslim holiday of Ramadan, when Muslims fast from daybreak to dusk, I declined to share in the treat, despite my mouth watering. This wasn't expected, but it was respectful. Two of our non-Muslim team members turned away to enjoy the juicy pulp, as the rest of our team and hosts rose for their afternoon prayers. I discretely sucked some warm water from my Camelbak.

After our break, we attempted to reconvene our interview. The old man began with the same story. Tired and impatient, Major Joseph asked, "Do you have anything else *new* to add?"

"Most of our families have fled," he said without emotion.

"Well, where did they go?"

"One hour to the west," the man pointed, "to Wash al Tool."

Anour responded automatically, "How—foot or car?"

"One hour by foot." I could now estimate this distance to be about 5 to 7 kilometers.

We thanked them and returned to our helicopter. We had just enough time to head to Wash al Tool for a few brief interviews before dusk. It was in this village that we came upon Mihad Hamid, the one-year-old baby girl whose tiny wounded body still haunts my mind.

.   .   .

When we returned that evening, Major Joseph and I met to discuss notes for a report. It was clear to me that the GOS had carried out an offensive strike on Alliet. Joseph offered another option, "Perhaps the SLA really was there and provoked them?"

"Joseph, there is no reason for the GOS to dismount with their weapons that far from the village unless they were planning an attack. Even if they somehow saw or heard vehicles in the town, it's a sizable village where a few people probably own trucks. That does not automatically mean there are rebels or 'bandits' present. There were no rounds where the commander claimed they had defended themselves against an ambush. I mean, I saw no evidence of an attack by anyone but the GOS," I insisted, slapping my notebook on the table.

"You're right," Joseph said slowly. "That does make sense." We began a draft of our report, knowing we would need to return to Wash al Tool for further follow-up.

Fighting resumed the next day with a counterattack by rebels. It took three days for the fighting to subside in Alliet. We returned on October 23 to witness the aftermath. I thought about little Mihad and wondered whether the aid groups had found her. No one had reported any news about the girl, though I had asked the Red Cross workers repeatedly. I could not forget the blank stare in the woman's eyes as she held up the infant to be examined. I remembered Mihad's silent fear. Who would she have been if she had been allowed to live? Why the hell hadn't I just brought her back on the helicopter with us? I had been given a chance to save at least one life and I didn't take it.

.   .   .

Now, back in her village, it appeared the GOS had all but obliterated everything in sight.

We met again with the same GOS lieutenant colonel, this time settling under a large nim tree a short distance from the village. Protocol required that we listen objectively to the GOS version of what had transpired, taking notes before investigating further. The commander nonchalantly gave his account of what happened: "We were continuing our route-clearing mission to open up this road for commercial traffic so that villagers could receive their goods. It was a routine mission. But the road had been blocked by bandits." It was obvious that these GOS military operations had nothing to do with bandit activity along the roadway. They rarely did. Instead, the GOS was using the excuse of clearing the roads for commerce as an opportunity to launch a strategic military campaign of destruction, integrating the Janjaweed militias when possible, as part of their operations to intensify their impact.

While he spoke, we watched as GOS soldiers passed by with empty jerry cans to collect water. As they neared the well, a row of grass huts burst into flame. In about thirty seconds, each hut was completely incinerated. The soldiers returned with empty soda bottles, which clearly had been filled with gasoline. Now, rather than claiming the fires were caused by bullets, they were burning the town right in front of us.

As the GOS commander continued his story, I was distracted by a buzzing sound. I could not place it. It reminded me of the subtle humming of high voltage power lines. I looked about, trying to find its source—perhaps a bee hive? When he finished, we demanded to see the town for ourselves.

"Let my men escort you. There may still be rebels." Like hell you will, I thought.

"As the African Union, we will go alone," Major Joseph insisted. We moved forward alone to assess the damage.

About two hundred meters into the village, I staggered as I finally identified the sound. Flies. Thousands, probably tens of thousands of flies diligently at work. They had come there to feast on the dead—donkeys, horses, camels, goats, sheep, dogs, and humans. They didn't discriminate. The dead were everywhere.

Suddenly, I took in the stench. It was so putrid it almost knocked me over—a mix of rotten meat, burned hair, and death. Only a few meters away was a bloated man who was rapidly decomposing. It had been at least a day since he'd died. I breathed through my mouth and forced myself to keep looking. His eyes were nearly popping out of his head and the whites were a sickly green color. His tongue was swollen, protruding outward, overwhelming his mouth. His body had distended to twice its normal size, and his crisply burned skin was covered with potato-sized blisters from exposure to the sun. He had been stripped of his shoes—the only useable possessions that remained on him when he died. From the gaping hole in his rib cage, it looked as if he had been shot in the side. Flies crawled over and through him.

Just to his left was another man who apparently had been locked in his grass hut as it was burned by the GOS. All that was left was a charred mass of bone and flesh. I could see him lying on his left side along the center support pole of his former hut with his arms outstretched above him, as if reaching out for help. His right arm had been broken above the wrist, and it now hung awkwardly, like a broken twig. His innards had exploded out of him toward the ground.

"What the . . . ?!!" a guy next to me exclaimed before rushing away to throw up. Half the team would not venture further. I looked away. But I was now the team photographer. I had to bear witness to this carnage. I felt ashamed as I looked at these two bodies; they were so vulnerable. At the same time, I felt cowardly for not looking. I focused the lens and began shooting, muttering a short prayer for the two victims. Ahmed shook his head and said nothing.

Just 10 meters away from this scene of death sat six or seven GOS soldiers. They greeted us casually and we returned their gesture. They were sitting under a tree, drinking water, and cooking their breakfast in a pot over an open fire.

I put my camera down. I did not need photos to remember this. I joined the team gathering outside the village. After a few minutes of discussion, Joseph suggested that we probably did not need to explore further to complete our investigation. For once, I welcomed his reluctance to proceed. We had seen more than we would ever need to see in a lifetime that morning.

.   .   .

In the evening, I lay awake in my bunk. I had only been out on patrol in Darfur for two weeks and had already seen hundreds of thousands of internally displaced people, evidence of chemical weapons, torture, rape of the elderly, murder of civilians, children who had been shot, the torching and looting of homes, attacks on IDP camps, well-trained and vicious Arab militias, GOS obstinacy, police intimidation, AU incompetence, and, worst of all, apathy. The things I had witnessed in Darfur were not meant to be seen. Still the image of little Mihad loomed above all other horrors. For me, she was the most potent symbol of this senseless war. Part of me wanted to make it disappear, and part of me wanted the whole world to see it.

I was tired. It was amazing how tired you could get. We'd been doing patrols six, sometimes seven days a week. Up in the morning at 0700 and in bed by 2200, and yet I would lie in bed forever staring at the top of my tent. I could no longer sleep, at least not in the way I used to know sleep. We Catholics on the Darfur teams joked that that we would not have to go to Purgatory when we died because we had already served our time. Under deep stress, any and all coping mechanisms were welcome.

I called Gretchen on my cell phone, telling her all the good and all the bad. I felt like I was seeing the extremes of both worlds here. There were people in Darfur who simply did not value human life. They cut ears off, plucked eyes out, and burned people alive. They shot children. The government leaders would sit there, smile, and shake our hands, but I knew that when we left, they would go out and do it again. What was amazing was that the humanitarian aid workers willingly served their victims day after day. Most of them were only working for a stipend. Some even paid their way to get to Darfur. I couldn't do what they did.

I was going on break in November for a few weeks. I knew I would be coming back, and that thought put a knot in my stomach. I wanted to fast-forward to the end of my tour. Yet, I knew that even accounting for its flaws the AU had the potential to help. We were there, on the ground, when no one else was. We so often felt unbearably powerless. But someone had to witness this. And that was why I would finish my one-year contract. For another three months, I expected to end each night the same way, lying down for eight to nine hours before doing it all over again the next day.

Chapter 14

"The Janjaweed came in two trucks. They took everything, and then they came back and raped eight of our women." The omda, a wiry, fierce man of medium height, shook his finger at Joseph. He was dressed in a white jelabia through which poked a small round belly, marking his prestige as the village leader. A small amount of spittle formed on his lips as he recounted each violation.

Our team sat on plastic mats under the shade of woven grass coverings in the village of Duma. These roofs atop wooden stilts normally served as the stalls for the town's weekly market. I listened with resignation as we interviewed the chief.

One of the other two elders sitting by the omda jumped in: "They stole our things, they looted the entire town!" The leader raised his hand sharply, and the elder grew silent.

"When did this happen?" Joseph asked, and then yawned.

"All the time—for six weeks they have been attacking us. They stole 150 goats! Then, five days ago, they ambushed a bus. My people were on that bus," his voice quickened.

"Okay, okay, just tell me how it happened," Joseph attempted to calm the angry man.

"They fired on the bus, shooting two people. The bus driver stopped and the Janjaweed forced all the passengers to get off the bus. They separated the men from the women. And then," he clenched his fist, "these Arab attackers threatened to rape all our women." He lowered his voice and spoke slowly and carefully with both hatred and humiliation, "They asked the men what they thought about that."

"Go on."

"One woman—she has a medical condition—she pleaded with the Jan-jaweed to spare her. She would die if they raped her. She was afraid and started to run. They chased her down and many men raped her in front of the entire village."

I took a deep breath and let out a long sigh.

Duma was extremely vulnerable. The north–south road from Nyala to El Fashir was the only paved road in the region. It cut straight through the town, serving as a channel for violent ambushes. It was well known that the Janjaweed had hijacked a stretch of road less than 50 kilometers to the north. The village was now completely surrounded by Janjaweed-held territory, and attacks or abductions in the surrounding areas occurred every few days. The GOS police station, located only 5 kilometers up the road, was useless, its so-called policemen unwilling to take any action to protect civilians. I found myself wondering why the SLA did not set up its own convoy to ambush the soldiers or track down the Janjaweed perpetrators.

The omda was nearly shouting, rocking back and forth as he alternated between shaking his finger and pounding his fist on his crossed legs. "I have filed complaints with the African Union over and over again. And still these attacks continue!"

This was the first time I realized that not all of the public supported our mission. We were not allowed to protect civilians or seek justice against perpetrators, but the local villagers still expected us to stop the attacks. On the one hand, I wished they knew that all we could do was observe and report. On the other hand, how can you tell a woman who has been raped or a man who has just lost his brother that there is nothing you're going to do except interview them? Aside from joining the fight as rebels, we were helpless to intervene.

Toward the end of October, a man showed up at our gate exhausted and desperate. One of our guards called our team to meet him. His jelabia was torn and muddy. His lips were cracked, and he spoke in a whisper when he asked to meet with us. We invited him into a small tent and brought him a glass of water. After gulping his drink, he collapsed onto a wooden chair with gratitude. Quietly, he rested his head in his hands, his elbows balancing on thin knees. After a moment, the man sat back, wiped his forehead, and began to speak.

"I have been walking for two days to find you," he started. "They ambushed my truck and one other truck headed to Nyala to deliver goods."

"Who ambushed you?" Joseph asked.

"The SLA."

"How do you know they were SLA?" Anour jumped in quickly.

"Because they said so," he replied. The SLA representative turned away and said nothing. The man continued. "The SLA took us hostage and then drove our trucks to a place they called the 'Hamada forest.' They tied me to a tree!" his voice cracked.

"What did the area look like where you were taken?" Joseph inquired.

"It was a wadi in a clearing at the edge of the forest. The land was full of hills. We camped there for a night. They emptied our trucks and took all of our goods."

"What kind of cargo were you carrying?"

"Orange juice packets, toothbrushes, other supplies for NGOs and for the market."

"Was anyone injured or killed?"

"No, no one was hurt. They finally untied us and let us go, but we had to walk many kilometers."

I glanced over at Anour, who was feigning disinterest as he fiddled with his pen. I knew that the moment we were finished, he would be on the phone with his SLA guys, letting them know that we would be looking for these same trucks in the morning.

The next day, we headed out to find the site of the ambush, driving up and down the road near the estimated kilometer mark of the attack. We studied the road for skid marks, oil that would have spilled if the engine had been shot, shell casings, or smashed-down brush, but found nothing. We returned each of the next two days to resume our search.

From my truck, I got the attention of the team members in the other truck with my radio. "Okay, guys, let's conduct a military analysis of this road. We'll start 10 kilometers south of the estimated mark and drive slowly another 10 kilometers north. What we're looking for are sites that might serve as a good ambush point. You've got to put yourself in the minds of your attacker. Consider areas that offer cover and concealment, a higher elevation for a surprise attack and a good route for retreat. Then we'll stop and take a look at the best sites for more ground evidence."

For a few hours we drove along the road, talking back and forth via radio.

After we picked out each site, we got out to see whether it was feasible to pull large commercial trucks off the road into the forest. Where there was a wadi or loose sand, we knew it would be impossible. Elsewhere, trees prevented a truck's passage from the road. When we selected the most advantageous position, sure enough, we found tracks leading into the high grasses toward the tree line 5 kilometers away.

"Well, I'll be damned!" Joseph declared as he came around the vehicle from the passenger side. We jumped back in our trucks and headed through the dense grasses, following the tracks toward the forest of nim trees. It was not far before we came upon a clearing near a wadi, which was plainly the site of the looting. Orange juice boxes, medical supplies, and toothbrushes were everywhere. The stock of a Kalashnikov rifle had been left behind. There were old fire pits and goat droppings, which meant the hijackers had definitely camped here. We saw the direction the tracks headed and we proceeded on foot for about five more minutes.

A hill rose above us in the distance. Suddenly, we heard a gunshot. We froze. Two more shots rang out in our direction. Whoever was out there seemed to be trying to deter us from continuing, rather than attacking us deliberately.

"Let's keep going," I called to my colleagues, turning toward the shots. Ahmed agreed, continuing alongside me.

"I don't know," Anour hesitated stubbornly. "I think it's too dangerous to continue."

"Look, we're the African Union," I argued. "They won't go beyond warning shots." I suspected that he knew it was his colleagues who conducted the attack and was thus more reluctant to expose them than he was concerned about the risk of personal harm. The SLA had been known to steal goods to sustain operations.

Without discussion, Joseph said, "Okay, let's go," and took off toward our trucks. I looked around to see if anyone would protest.

"Let's go, they're shooting at us. We're leaving," he repeated. I would not have expected him to walk into gunfire. I was willing to bet they were warning shots, but I knew arguing with Joseph would get me nowhere.

We returned to our base, wrote a report, and closed yet another AU investigation.

.   .   .

I feared for this mission and this country if the AU was supposed to stop the violence. I was reminded of that early 1980s TV show, "The Greatest American Hero," where the hero couldn't fly right and kept hitting walls. He ended up discovering the clues in each mission by accident. Or maybe it was more like the animated Inspector Gadget—he had all the tools, he had all the capabilities, but he was an idiot and could never get the job done. It always had to be his little daughter, Penny, or the dog that saved a life or saved the mission. This was not a TV show, and yet it felt just as absurd. Who would help us here?

To make matters worse, we were developing enemies on all sides. There were the local villages like Duma that were increasingly frustrated by our inability to prevent ongoing harassment and attacks. Also, one of my embassy contacts told me of a new movement called the National Movement for Reform and Development, or NMRD. The initial rumors characterized the NMRD as a break-off faction of the JEM, started by a former GOS officer from Khartoum. It wasn't clear why they had formed it—possibly trying to make a name for themselves. But the faction had already allegedly attacked the JEM in the Jebel Marra, stolen two vehicles, and then headed across into Chad. The embassy had documented that the Chadian government was supplying the NMRD with weapons and vehicles. Though their whereabouts were unknown, my contact estimated that the NMRD had about 50 members at that time. What was known, and which gave me chills, was their reported mission: to fight against all NGOs, the UN, and the AU. We had no confirmation, but the hearsay was hardly encouraging.

.   .   .

On October 29, a dead body showed up in Nyala with a sign that read "AU come and find us," signed by the Janjaweed. Intelligence suggested that the Janjaweed were going to call a jihad against the AU. I learned about the incident during one of my daily briefings with a local UN contact. "Oh yeah," he had added casually at the end of our discussion. "There was a message for you the other day from the Janjaweed."

While this might have seemed frightening in any other setting, here in Darfur it was no longer a big deal for someone to use a corpse as a piece of stationery. Every day hundreds and hundred of people were dying. This small threat could just as easily have been the SLA trying to instigate a conflict between the AU and the Janjaweed as it could have been the Janjaweed actually taunting us. The AU took all threats of violence into consideration, but we continued on with our work, unarmed.

LEFT: Child in El Fashir, North Darfur

MIDDLE: Women often have to walk miles, risking rape by the Janjaweed, to find firewood to cook their daily meals. Here several women collect firewood outside of El Fashir.

BOTTOM: Darfurian refugee children

Unless otherwise noted, all photos taken by Brian Steidle

Sitting with Darfurian refugees in Kounoungo Refugee Camp, Eastern Chad.
Photo credit: Gretchen Steidle Wallace

With Anour and other members of the Sudanese Liberation Army (SLA), Muhajeriya

TOP: SLA soldiers in Haskanita.

MIDDLE: Government of Sudan (GOS) soldier reinforcements.

LEFT: Major Ahmed (center) confronting Janjaweed members who were prepared to fire on us when we approached them. The Janjaweed member on the right has a small bottle of petrol in his pocket, which is usually used by the militias for setting fire to huts.

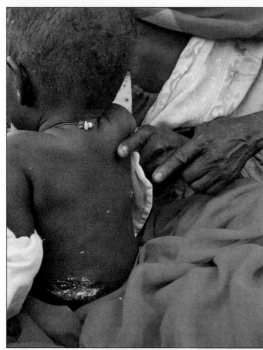

Mihad Hamid, a one-year-old Darfurian girl from Alliet, held by her aunt in Wash al Tool.

This was the scene when we arrived at Al Gheer Internally Displaced Persons Camp. Each dome is constructed of sticks and covered with garbage. A truck had driven over these shelters in the middle of the night, driving the displaced out of their homes.

GOS military and police preparing to bulldoze Al Gheer IDP camp. After we left we were told the GOS pushed it into a pile and burned it.

OPPOSITE PAGE, MIDDLE: We came across Fatima Adouma Akhmed Ibrahim (left) and Salha Adouma Akhmed Ibrahim (right) in Wash al Tool. They had fled Alliet as the town was being attacked. Both had been shot in their legs.

OPPOSITE PAGE, BOTTOM: It was three days before we could return to Alliet where we found this man burned alive in his hut. GOS soldiers had set up a camp site only meters from this corpse.

Looted shops in Amaka Sara after an attack by the GOS.

The remains of a burned hut in Um Zaifa.

GOS soldier burning food stores in Marla. These food stores contain the grain necessary for a village to get through the year until the next harvest.

We found this bound skeleton in the bone fields of Adwah.

Another victim in Adwah

A wounded villager from Jayjay

One of fifteen villages burned by the Janjaweed in one day, as seen from our helicopter one week before I left Darfur.

Chapter 15

One evening I walked into our camp kitchen and, through a haze of hundreds of flies, I saw our cook hacking up a goat leg on the floor. I flinched. With an abrupt about face, I left the room determined to find an alternative. Our meals at the AU camp usually consisted of rice, the occasional fresh tomato or dry cucumber, and a meat sauce of chopped goat including bone. I had already chipped three teeth and had no desire to return to my Khartoum dentist.

That night John and Dave from Operations invited me to join them and grab some dinner in town. I enjoyed hanging out with these two guys. Dave's calm, easy-going nature balanced well against John's frantic intensity. They took me to a Nyala restaurant where they knew the cook, an Egyptian, was very good.

"You've gotta meet this guy," John exclaimed as we pulled up to the small cement building. A low mud wall delineated an outdoor eating area, which was illuminated by a string of colored bulbs. A mix of aid workers, foreign contractors, and local Sudanese laughed and conversed around plastic tables. Dave and I found some seats, and John dashed inside to let the cook know we were there. From where we sat, I could see an open kitchen in the back corner of an otherwise empty room. I sat down in a small plastic chair that immediately sunk into the soft sand floor.

The cook came out smiling and wiping his hands on a towel. Shaking my hand, he introduced himself as Rashid and exclaimed that he was very happy to meet another American. He handed us a set of simple one-page menus. Proudly, he announced the daily special: grilled chicken, freshly baked flat bread, chips, salad, and a side of his famous green herb sauce.

"I'll have that," I said with a hunch that I might finally get something decent to eat. John and Dave ordered the same, with a round of sodas. We leaned back—carefully, of course—and took in the light mood. It felt good to be in a place where people were enjoying themselves. I had almost forgotten what normal life was like. When our drinks arrived, we offered each other a toast and let the memories of what we saw each day slip away.

While we waited for our meal, a few aid workers we knew stopped in and we invited them to join us. As others arrived, our string of tables grew into a long, rickety banquet, and our small talk, peppered with laughter, grew more jovial. We were prohibited from discussing the details of our investigations, but we tried to learn as much as we could from the NGOs about the movement of troops, attacks, or even rumors and threats of imminent attacks by the GOS or rebels that had not yet been reported.

Nobody talked much about life back home. Here, we were sharing the most intense experience, perhaps of a lifetime and yet, as I looked at John and Dave across the table, I realized I hardly knew a thing about them. I might know their home town, possibly whether or not they were married or what they would do when they finished their assignment. Otherwise, we kept to ourselves. Part of it was about remaining professional. But we also seemed to share a certain reluctance to make friends in a place where life was so fragile. We never discussed how we felt about what we saw each day. It was an understood taboo. We were military professionals trained to accept the worst in human nature. We were not supposed to feel.

In a place like Darfur, this professional ethic was an important coping mechanism. There was just too much to get angry about, from the scale and degree of the violence to the inaction of the international community to the blatant lies of the government to the inefficiencies of the monitoring mission. We would all go insane if we let ourselves really think about it, so we didn't. We didn't talk about it either.

Our meal was delicious, and Rashid was delighted when he saw that we'd cleaned our plates. I smiled when I got the bill: about $4 each for the best food I'd eaten since arriving in Darfur. We began to frequent the restaurant as often as we could. Sometimes we ordered take-out. We would always make sure Rashid knew we were visiting, and he always made sure we had a table. The daily special, specifically designed for us, was always fantastic. This small but important ritual gave us a taste of normal life.

Back at our camp, the AU cooks attempted to support local commerce by buying all of their supplies in Nyala. The sad and unintended consequence was a sharp rise in the prices of food, gasoline and the other goods we consumed. Merchants began to rely upon our business, knowing we would pay the higher prices, and the local population suffered. We felt increasingly unwelcome in town.

One night, as we were dining at Rashid's, a few young kids started tossing sand at some of the NGO patrons. The restaurant staff told them to get lost, but something about the incident felt wrong. Dave and John also picked up on it, and the three of us began to survey the scene. Suddenly, a firecracker came flying over the wall. The sound was so loud we nearly all hit the deck, expecting a drive by shooting. We quickly checked that everyone was okay—everyone was, though many people were shaken. A few moments later, it happened again. This time we watched the children run up to the driver's window of a car that sat idling in the distance. It seemed like the supplier of the fireworks was probing us to analyze our reactions and responses. The three of us stood up and began walking in its direction, and the car immediately sped away. We began to watch our backs more closely even when we were off duty and in what we had considered a safe environment. I shared this information with the embassy, and my contacts there urged me to keep sending in reports. Foreigners were becoming possible targets.

Shortly after making this restaurant our home, we were devastated to discover that Rashid had only two more weeks of working at the establishment before he had to return home to Egypt. He had come to Sudan because there were more lucrative work opportunities, and he was sending money home to his family. But this job was ending due to a change in management.

Rashid's dream was to cater to the tastes of the international NGO community. There was no one in Nyala who offered anything remotely close to what he envisioned. We asked him what it would take to keep him in town. He said the only way he could stay is if he could open his own restaurant. I asked him what he thought that would cost, and he considered it a moment, then proposed that he do a little research and get back to us.

A few days later, Rashid walked us through a thorough business plan, ending his presentation with a modest suggestion that it would take $1,000 to open his new restaurant. John, Dave, and I said we thought we could come up with that money easily, and quickly found 10 other hungry expats, each of whom was willing to invest $100 to keep Rashid in Nyala. When his new restaurant finally opened, it was a night of major celebration. After that, his business was packed to the brim every single night. We called our new investment "The Egyptian." Though he offered to pay us back within a month, we refused. We were happy to support him; he made a serious contribution to our quality of life.

In Darfur, the small diversions became very important. Whenever I had the time, I would try to go for a run or work out. Sometimes I borrowed a bicycle from the UN so I could ride up the huge hill that spanned the distance between the airport and our camp. Ahmed gave me a homemade dumbbell constructed of two paint cans filled with cement and connected with a small pipe. Working out kept me sane and helped me release some of the tension we did not speak out loud about.

We had Fridays off except in cases where complaints were urgent or an attack was underway. In the mornings, I would catch up on writing reports or logging notes into my MP3 player, while most of our Muslim team members would visit the mosque. By mid-afternoon, it was time for our weekly barbeques.

UNICEF distributed volleyball nets and volleyballs to the IDP schools. One Friday, John, Dave, and I convinced them to donate an extra set to the AU, and we went about building a volleyball court in the center of our camp. Our camp commander was thrilled and arranged to have a truck bring in fifteen loads of sand from the riverbed to create a smooth playing surface over the rocky pebbles that covered our central courtyard. When the court was ready, we spread the word to all the NGOs to join us for what would become a celebrated, weekly escape.

A few of us would go down to the meat market each Friday and buy several half-cooked goat legs and chickens. We would stock up on locally-made natural charcoal to fire up our homemade barbeque grill, which was fashioned from a metal barrel sawed in half. Dave, John, our Australian medic, and I each kept our own stash of liquor and cases of beer, which we would donate to the party. We would move a huge top-loading fridge out into a shade tent, plug it in with an extension cord, and set up the bar. We joked that our volleyball tournaments were played on the largest beach in the world—a claim we defended by calculating that sand actually stretched 1,300 miles from where we stood to the Mediterranean Ocean. It was the only real social part of my week. For brief periods most Fridays, we forgot where we were.

While it was not illegal for AU personnel to consume alcohol, we were operating in an Islamic country where alcohol was strictly forbidden. As a result, we had to "import" our alcoholic beverages. Whenever an AU or humanitarian aid flight was headed toward Abeche, Chad, where another AU base was located, we would call our contacts on the ground. They would buy the cases and we would make sure the plane dropped off its cargo in Nyala first on its return to base. We never made any profit on beer, but would sell it at cost to the NGOs as a favor because we valued their information. We also could buy gin, vodka, whisky, and the occasional rum. Later, we made a valuable contact at a European diplomatic mission in Khartoum; he would place orders for his mission and order extra for us, too.

In particular, I made sure our Australian medic was well supplied. He had a remarkable ability to obtain information. Wandering into the market, he would stop to talk to locals about someone's injury or sickness, and before they knew it they were filling him in on all levels of valuable intelligence. If we wanted to know something, he was the man to ask.

Though the AU was not required to adhere to Nyala's 10:00 p.m. curfew, we tried to honor it when not on official business. Returning to our camp would require passing multiple checkpoints. Most of these checkpoints involved a GOS soldier or policeman sleeping in a chair in the middle of a road or against a small guard house. Any time we drove an official vehicle, we had to make a cursory stop. A disinterested GOS soldier would shine his flashlight in our window before absentmindedly waving us on. We found that when returning back to camp alone, it was better to travel by bicycle at high speeds. The guards wouldn't see us coming until we were right up next to them. They would jump to their feet, scream something in Arabic, fumble with their weapons, and maybe fire a few warning shots into the air.

Our limited diversions helped to make Darfur and what surrounded us bearable in some small way. I called home every few days and came to rely on telling my family what I was seeing. I had a local cell phone for calling home or communicating with our team within Nyala, and a back-up satellite phone for when we were outside the city limits with no cell phone service. I did not speak to my parents as frequently as I spoke with Gretchen and her husband, Andrew. I did not want to worry my mom, and I knew my dad respected the work I was doing. I loved hearing what Andrew, who built wooden boats, was doing in the wood shop or about the hunting trips he was taking in the New Hampshire woods. I couldn't wait to join him. We made plans for Thanksgiving. The leaves had already changed, and the snow would soon be falling. Andrew was a great, unbiased sounding board for my stories—fascinated about every little detail. Gretchen gave me pep talks when I called her on the worst days. These calls brought life on the other side of the earth a little bit closer and helped me process what I was witnessing day after day.

Chapter 16

"Captain Brian," Dave called out to me from the operations room. "Save the Children just called to say a large GOS military convoy is on its way down the main road in Nyala. See if you can get some shots from up there on the water tower."

I grabbed my camera and hustled up the 30-foot ladder to the top of the square tank. Lying down on my stomach, I pointed my camera toward the road and waited. After a few minutes of nothing, I got out my cell phone and called Dave to ask him if he was sure they were headed in this direction. I flipped open my phone and saw the cell phone system was down. Another reign of terror was about to begin.

The GOS controlled the cell phone system in the country and could easily order it turned off at its convenience. While there was only cell phone service in the larger towns, the SLA had satellite phones in the field, and its contacts in the cities would call to warn others when attack helicopters were taking off. It did not take long for the GOS to undermine this critical communication link.

Not fifteen minutes later, two GOS attack helicopters took off. The first helicopter flew low along the road and then turned off into the distance. I snapped a few pictures to capture the Sudanese flag on its tail and rockets attached beneath. As soon as I lowered my camera, I saw another flying straight for our camp. I held my arms over my head to protect my ears as the attack helicopter buzzed our camp only 50 feet above me in a show of force. The wind surged over me only seconds before the roar of the engines.

I sat there knowing there was nothing I could do. The GOS helicopters flew low and fast, and our team would never be able to mobilize fast enough to follow them, especially when we had no idea where they were going.

Furthermore, our helicopters were usually in need of refueling—despite my efforts to insist that we refuel at the end of each day. The pilots preferred to refuel for each trip, taking only a little more fuel than we needed so that we would not be too heavy for short journeys. As a result, when we tried to respond to an attack in progress, we were vulnerable to the whims of the government-owned fuel company. Their workers might explain that the fuel truck had a flat tire or that the pumps were broken and we would have to wait a few hours for more fuel. It was infuriating.

.   .   .

On November 1, we set out toward the village of Amaka Sara. We had two incidents to investigate. The first was a reported ambush that took place near the village three days earlier on the Nyala–Kas road. The SLA and JEM reportedly carried out the attack on two commercial trucks, one of which was carrying medical supplies for Médecins Sans Frontières, the medical services NGO, known in the US as Doctors without Borders. Policemen from the neighboring village of Bulbul had responded. We wanted to locate the ambush site first and then proceed to Bulbul and Amaka Sara to speak with all parties involved.

On this particular stretch of road, which runs northwest between Nyala and Kas, there were more ambushes each year than on any other road in Sudan—or, I was told, in Iraq. The car jumped like a jackhammer over the perilous tracks. The thoroughfare had been paved nearly 10 years earlier, but it had never been maintained. Huge potholes had pitted the pavement like concave mines waiting to disable passing vehicles. Most drivers chose to drive next to the road on the loose sand, where they could travel above 10 miles per hour.

We easily identified the site of the ambush from the vultures circling above. A thick, foul stench found our nostrils as we opened our car doors. We had to check that all windows were rolled up to avert the thousands of flies from seeking refuge in our Land Cruisers.

One tractor trailer had been overturned, and discarded trash from the looting was everywhere. Beside the road, vultures devoured two slain donkeys and two dead horses. As we wandered around the scene, we discovered a number of spent rounds from an RPK machine gun and Kalashnikovs. One monitor called to us from the other side of the road, saying he thought he saw clothing in the bushes. "Affirmative, we've got a casualty over here," he said a moment later.

We headed in his direction. I nearly ran into the guy in front of me as he suddenly froze.

"What?" I asked, peering around him.

He ran to the bushes to vomit, leaving me to face one of the most gruesome sites I had ever seen. The entire team was getting sick around me. Before us, on his back with arms stretched out like a crucifix, was a man who had been lying in the sun for four days. His body was completely distended, his abdomen huge, and a pile of hair lay in a clump beneath his head. His entire left leg had been stripped down to the ankle, and vultures picked at the muscle around his exposed bones. Maggots were pouring out of his mouth, nose, and eyes. On closer inspection, it appeared that the skin under his palm, arm, and face was moving. The skin itself was hard and crusty from its exposure to the sun, but within the moist flesh beneath, larvae were consuming any life that had once existed. The body smelled worse than anything I had ever experienced.

And still, despite the ghastly site before me, I found myself curious. Perhaps it was a survival tactic that enabled me to cope with how much death I had already witnessed, but now even small details were fascinating. For example, I learned that after two or three days in the sun, a corpse's hair would fall out. I wondered how many other people besides doctors, cops, and coroners knew about these bizarre and gruesome facts. Most people would not want to know and probably would never have to. I raised my lens and took a few photos.

The cadaver was clothed in a GOS police uniform top that would obviously have been too small for him even without his swollen belly. It looked as if it had been hastily wrapped around him after he died. As with all Muslims in Sudan, the GOS would have buried their man immediately. Yet this man had been left here for four days. Clearly, this was not a member of the GOS, and the uniform had been planted so that the GOS could claim one of its men had been killed. We could not determine how he died, so we took our notes quickly and headed toward the police station at Bulbul.

.   .   .

Bulbul was a stopover point for people passing through the area. Off to one side of the road, a one-room mud-brick structure sat as a poor substitute for a police station. Outside, there were cots for police supposedly on watch, and inside, there was a single desk. Eight of us tried unsuccessfully to jam into the room to hear their story. The police commander, a corporal, three other police officers, and one security man in civilian attire met with us. They politely produced several bottles of soda before offering their explanation of the incident.

The corporal spoke rapidly. "We received a complaint at around 2200 hours from a truck driver. He told us that two trucks, escorted by GOS forces, had been attacked by bandits or rebels. The drivers and the GOS troops had fought back as best they could. One of our men was killed." He took a sip of his Fanta and continued.

"Naturally, we called upon a Mujahadeen battalion to help us." I knew the Mujahadeen, which basically means "holy warriors," were also part of the People's Defense Force. We considered all of them Janjaweed, though there was a slight distinction between the PDF, a more formal force, and other Arab nomad militias, which were less formally organized.

"The Mujahadeen and a few of my men were able to organize a force of 30 militia and headed out to the ambush site. Rebels immediately fired upon us. We returned fire from the other side of the road. Suddenly, 100 men showed up in vehicles. They had heavy weapons and a firefight ensued until 3:00."

Joseph paused to clarify that this was 3:00 a.m., not 3:00 p.m. the following afternoon. Ibrahim nodded. He was having a hard time keeping up with the corporal's overview. Though he tried, he was not always perfect in his translation. When someone said 1600, he would often translate it to us as 4:00, without specifying a.m. or p.m.

"One bandit was shot in the head after he tried to escape from a disabled truck." I assumed this was the man we had discovered, despite the fact that the GOS also claimed one policeman had been killed. "We were able to seize five weapons in the battle, including one rocket-propelled grenade, three Kalashnikovs, and one G3 rifle."

"Where are the weapons now?" Joseph inquired.

"Ah, that is an interesting question," the corporal responded. After a moment he added, "After the attack, we attempted to take the weapons back from our militias, who refused." I found this fascinating. Clearly, the GOS had almost no control over the Janjaweed when they were not paying them or allowing the militias to enjoy the spoils of war.

"What happened next?" Joseph prompted.

"The attackers withdrew about 400 meters north beyond a tree line near the road leading to Amaka Sara. The next morning, I traveled to Nyala to find our commander so that we could survey the scene. By the time we returned to the site, Mujahadeen from five villages had arrived, prepared for battle. We dissuaded them from counterattacking because we knew the bandits had withdrawn to a location near a village. You see," he paused to look Joseph in the eye, "if we had ordered them to attack, the Mujahadeen would have burned the village and killed everyone and their families." He sat back, satisfied. Though he seemed to be happy to pin such destruction on the Janjaweed, to me his story was another frightening indication of the minimal control the GOS had over the militias.

.   .   .

Our next stop was the village of Amaka Sara. We had just heard that only two days after the ambush, the GOS had moved on the village, apparently in retaliation, attacking with helicopter gunships. The unbelievable thing was that the AU had also received a letter from the commander of the 16th Division of GOS forces, a brigadier general, announcing he was going to move his troops to Amaka Sara to retake the village and reestablish his GOS post. Basically, he had notified us in advance that he planned to break the Ceasefire Agreement. All parties to the Ceasefire Agreement were required to notify the African Union of the movement of their troops. Though it was part of our mandate to monitor these movements, we were very rarely informed of such movements and thus filed no reports on these incidents.

When we arrived at Amaka Sara, a village with a population of about 5,000 people, we found the town looted and mostly deserted except for the GOS presence. A few buildings had been torched, but most were still standing. We saw a few dead animals but no human bodies. We cut loose several donkeys that had been tied to trees and had already eaten all the vegetation around them. They would likely starve to death if left that way much longer without water. As we came into the central market area, we found a long stretch of shops standing with every single door ajar, locks shot off, contents looted, and spent rounds lying on the ground. A few GOS soldiers were still there rummaging through the merchandise when we arrived, and they left quickly when they saw us. I was able to snap a few shots of the looting.

Wandering farther into the village, we came upon two older gentlemen walking with a donkey. Both looked frail, and one leaned awkwardly to the side. Boney ankles stuck out from below their yellowed jelabias. The men probably hadn't been able to escape into the bush and yet had avoided harm somehow. We pulled up beside them and rolled down our window. Joseph, who always rode shotgun in my Land Cruiser, leaned out to speak with them. Ibrahim translated from the back seat.

"What can you tell us about this attack?"

One man looked at us sideways, sizing us up. "Well," he started with an air of resentment, "about a month and a half ago, the Janjaweed came and stole our cows. To get back at them, the SLA attacked the police camp. Then a few days ago, at about 1:00 P.M., government troops came into our village firing at us with big rifles. Gunships flew over shooting missiles. All of our families left for Tama, but there were three men taken prisoner by the government."

"Were there Janjaweed who came with the government?"

"Oh yes," he said, and they nodded. "There were many Janjaweed on horseback and on foot. They broke into our shops and stole all of our food and our belongings." This was yet another example of Janjaweed backed by and fighting alongside GOS troops in an attack on a village.

Just then, gunshots rang out from the south. I counted 10 bursts. There was no way to tell who was shooting. The men looked toward the noise and then started walking again with their donkey, unfazed. We immediately turned back and headed toward a GOS encampment on the edge of the village.

The GOS offensive position, located in a peanut field about 200 meters away from the village, was our last stop. November was the time of year when peanut harvesting began, and the field was lush with small bushes. Farmers had just begun gathering the peanuts into large piles to dry in the sun before the attack.

With stiff formality, the soldiers brought us chairs and we sat down. There were peanuts strewn everywhere. A few officers had handfuls of them, others reached into their pockets, pulling them out one by one to peel. "Groundnut?" one soldier offered, from a bag he was holding in his lap.

"No," we refused. These were looted crops.

The GOS commanding officer on the ground in Amaka Sara was a lieutenant colonel. A GOS police captain and several other military lieutenants surrounded him. I made some quick notes: two military trucks, one dump truck, two Land Cruisers—one of which had a B10 recoilless rifle or giant cannon affixed to the rear—three 60 millimeter mortars, a couple of RPKs, some small arms, and loot clearly acquired from the town. Scattered about the field were mattresses, clothing, oil lamps, and chairs. The two trucks were completely filled with household goods; bicycles and beds, which did not fit inside, were tied to the sides.

The military officers waited for us to begin. Joseph asked them for their side of the story.

The lieutenant colonel did not have much to say. "Look, my unit came to reestablish our camp. When we arrived, all the villagers left."

"Did you attack with helicopter gunships?" Joseph asked.

"Well, a helicopter did accompany us here," he admitted, "but it did not fire. We fought briefly with rebels who were using the town as cover." He shrugged. "Maybe some civilians were hurt, but I cannot know for certain."

"Were any of your men wounded?"

"Yes. We have already taken four soldiers to the hospital in Nyala."

When Joseph was finished questioning the lieutenant colonel, he turned and asked me directly—with none of the annoyance he sometimes displayed—if I had any questions to add. I took the lead.

"We saw GOS soldiers in the village looting. Were these your men? Can you explain what they were doing?" I asked.

"My soldiers don't loot," he said flatly.

"Look," I said, "we know you looted. Just return the loot. These villagers didn't do anything to you."

"The villagers must have been the ones looting," he insisted. "That's why my soldiers are in the village—to protect the civilians' goods from anyone who would steal from them."

"I saw with my own eyes six or seven GOS soldiers coming out of some huts washing the dishes they had just used to eat with. They had been sitting around having a party," I continued.

Despite his stubbornness, for some reason, this man seemed decent, someone with whom we could reason.

"Look, I know you sometimes take your beds to battle, but you don't bring your bicycles to war," I said, pointing toward the trucks with the bikes lashed to the sides.

He looked at me for a moment. "Ok," he said. "We will return some things."

Was it possible, in an army committed to genocide, to come across a decent man? Maybe. But only by comparison. I was under no illusions about this GOS lieutenant colonel and what he might be capable of.

Climbing back into our vehicles, we drove back through the part of the village that the SLA alleged gunships had attacked. Since the GOS had denied that the helicopters had fired, we wanted to find some evidence of the SLA claim, if possible. Sure enough, a few pieces of shrapnel from attack helicopters remained, though it appeared as if someone had gone over the ground and picked up most of the evidence. To us, this was final and undeniable proof that gunships were being used to attack villages—and that the GOS was engineering coordinated attacks with support from the Janjaweed.

Chapter 17

Awakening the next morning with the call to morning prayers, I splashed some water on my face and headed over to the meal tent to grab some breakfast. I made my usual cappuccino—powdered milk, instant coffee, sugar, and boiling water, all stirred quickly with a spoon. I rarely had much more than a hard boiled egg and some fresh mango or orange juice. Most of my AU colleagues would pile their plates high with baked beans, soggy pancakes, and little sausages, but the stuff turned my stomach.

Our plan for the day was to interview the four injured GOS soldiers from Amaka Sara at the military hospital in Nyala, but that would have to wait, it turned out. As we drove into town, Dave at Operations radioed us about an attack on the Al Gheer IDP camp. We turned to head in that direction.

By the time we arrived at Al Gheer, the GOS military and police had cordoned off the entire area. The camp looked like so many—domes constructed with sticks and twine, then covered with plastic bags, cardboard, and other garbage. It was evident that trucks had driven over and crushed a portion of the camp. We brought our Land Cruisers to a halt near a group of GOS police. Stepping from our trucks, Ahmed and Mohammed approached the group and located the police commander. He walked toward us.

Joseph stepped forward, "What's going on here?"

"We are carrying out our orders. HAC (The High Committee on Coordination of Humanitarian Aid in Darfur) has requested that we relocate this camp to a more secure location away from the town." HAC had estimated that the camp held 500 occupants. Upon GOS instructions, NGOs had built another camp for the residents elsewhere.

"When we came to ask the IDPs to move, they refused and threw rocks. We had no choice but to defend ourselves. Only two people were shot."

I looked at the scene before us. Based on visits to other camps in the area, I reckoned that this camp was home to more like 5,000 people. This forced relocation would displace the other 4,500 or so people once again. The camp's original location near town was safer from Janajweed assaults than its new GOS-chosen remote location. The government was strategically and intentionally endangering people who had already fled their homes. I began to take a few photos of the destruction. Out of the corner of my eye, I noticed someone else taking pictures as well.

Just then, a large contingent of armed police, GOS soldiers, and security men with CS grenade launchers and Kalashnikovs showed up in pickup trucks. They had noticed that people were sneaking back into the rear of the camp to try to retrieve some of their belongings. I watched with disbelief as the police rounded them up, preventing them from returning to the camp. A few civilians tried to rush past the officers, who pushed them back. One man fell down. As he attempted to get up, a policeman began beating him with a stick. The officer swung at the other villagers, moving them toward a waiting truck. After dragging the man on the ground by the arm, two officers picked him up and shoved him into the rear of the truck. Then they herded the other stunned villagers in behind him and took them away.

My ears buzzed as about 50 shots were fired on the west side of the camp. I turned to Joseph as another burst rang out in the air. "Kalashnikov fire," I said. The next blast I could identify as rounds from an M14 rifle and a 40 millimeter grenade launcher. What were they doing?

At that moment, the police commander excused himself. I noticed that the police officers were shouting at each other, gesturing to get their men's attention, and then moving away from the area. Suddenly, one of the soldiers tossed a CS grenade right in front of us, flooding the air with tear gas. I saw the grenade a split second before the gas was on us.

"Dammit!" I cursed. I had been gassed many times in Marine Corps training. The purpose was to teach us how it would feel so that we would know we could survive and wouldn't freak out in a battlefield situation. But it was far from pleasant. Your eyes burn, your skin feels as if it is on fire, your eyes water uncontrollably, while phlegm builds up in your throat and runs out of your nose. Enough gas in your throat can cause a gag reflex and make you want to vomit. I fought the pain as calmly as I could. Most of the AU officers started screaming, throwing water on their faces, and rubbing their eyes, which only made it worse. Tear gas contains small pieces of fiberglass that create tiny cuts into which the chemical can seep, and rubbing it causes more cuts.

Joseph roared, "What the hell is going on?" Ahmed was fuming; a huge vein bulged out from his forehead. I wasn't sure whether he would tear his clothes to shreds or rip someone's head off. We had to calm him down, just to keep him from hurting anyone.

"Enough, Ahmed!" Joseph ordered. "This isn't going to help."

Anour and Ali were both shouting at the top of their lungs in Arabic. They wiped tears from their eyes, screamed at the sky, and pulled at their hair. The GOS monitor had been gassed along with the rest of us. He paced around erratically with his arms stiffly by his sides, fists clenched, trying to control his rage. I did not have to understand Arabic to know what my team members were yelling. Through my tears, I could see the policemen watching us from a distance.

Joseph marched up to the police commander. "I demand an explanation!"

The commander turned and narrowed his eyes at our team leader. A long minute passed. "Oops," the official said.

Noticing a group of UN and USAID workers about 50 meters away, I decided to warn them. My blood-shot eyes and running nose were enough to alarm them, and they stopped talking to look at me. "Hey guys, the GOS just tear gassed us. You better get out of here."

As soon as they departed, I heard a roar from behind me. I turned to see a large orange bulldozer moving in. Slowly, the bulldozer began destroying the miniature homes, consolidating the entire camp into one pile. Wiping my eyes, I kept taking pictures. Because of my diplomatic immunity, they couldn't arrest me or physically prevent me from taking pictures. The GOS apparently thought tear gas, their only alternative, would get us to leave. But there was no way in hell they could keep me from capturing this.

The team waited another fifteen minutes or so for the pain to subside, leaning on our vehicles in the open breeze. When the burning from the gas diminished enough for us to resume our investigations, we left. We were done here for now. Driving out of the area, we saw the lieutenant colonel turn from his men toward us and offer us a wave.

. . .

Later that day, we learned that the GOS had finished piling the entire camp into one mound and then burned it. The UN later told me that the other photographer was from *The Washington Post*, and had been arrested by the GOS. Though the officials later released him, they confiscated the memory card from his camera. I was the only person to get photographic evidence of the incident. A separate story on the Voice of America reported that there had been a GOS forced relocation and destruction of another IDP camp to the north of Nyala. As they had in Al Gheer, the GOS apparently denied access to all UN and NGO personnel, cordoned off the area and bulldozed the settlement. I had no idea where the IDPs would go.

. . .

We passed through Amaka Sara on our way to Tama village to speak with the residents who had been displaced and to discuss the attack with the SLA. As we drove through the town, I noticed that, true to his word, the GOS lieutenant colonel from yesterday had returned some of his loot by dumping one of his trucks in the middle of a courtyard outside a children's school. Colorful mattresses, chairs, pots, bicycles, utensils, and other precious items had been carelessly tossed from the truck bed. As we neared the GOS outpost, we saw the lieutenant colonel. We slowed our trucks and rolled down our windows.

"The GOS will not harm civilians if they want to return," he offered. We thanked him for his gesture and continued on to the village of Tama.

. . .

Tama was located deep inside rebel territory between Amaka Sara and Duma. The AU had likely flown over the village but had never before landed. It felt good to show we were following up on complaints. Most of the time we didn't visit the sites of attacks until days or even weeks after they took place.

We met with the chief of Tama, the SLA commander, and his deputy.

When we had assembled in a circle, the chief began. "Around 1330 hours, I heard firing and saw gunships and an Antonov fly over our heads. Later, several villagers rushed to me to tell me they saw the same thing."

Joseph turned to the SLA commander, "Were there SLA that fought back?"

"No, none of our forces were able to defend Amaka Sara. We cannot always get to a village in time," he replied quietly.

Joseph continued, "But the GOS said there were people firing back at them. Who were they?"

The chief responded, "Some of the men have their own weapons and try to defend themselves as best they can. Our villagers tried to help too. But four of my people were killed. Many are hurt, and 44 are still missing. Those who know they cannot fight will instead flee. At least 3,000 villagers from Amaka Sara have already come here to Tama."

The SLA commander handed us a list of names of those killed in Amaka Sara and an accounting of the damage: 31 shops looted, and 2,600 cattle as well as 4,200 sheep and goats stolen—a huge blow for a village of 5,000. This was their livelihood. I was impressed by how detailed his accounting was.

The chief directed a comment toward me in Arabic, prompting laughs all around.

"What? What?" I asked.

"You are the first white person ever to come to Tama," Ibrahim explained. "The chief wants you to autograph his house." I was a little embarrassed by his request—and, of course, honored as well. I was a white man from the West, and that simple fact seemed to elicit respect. I was again very conscious of the responsibility this involved. Most of the time, I wasn't treated any differently by my team because of my race and, frankly, I preferred it that way. Awkwardly, I scratched my name in the rough mud wall. The chief smiled proudly and pumped my hand.

The chief and the SLA commander gathered hundreds of the displaced families from Amaka Sara, and we delivered the message that the GOS would not harm anyone returning to their home. They looked at us with tired and uncertain eyes. A few men and women whispered to each other while keeping their gaze fixed on us. One man shouted toward us.

"He asks how they can know it is safe to return to Amaka Sara," Ibrahim translated. It would have been ridiculous to suggest to these displaced villagers that the GOS commander had given us his word.

"The African Union can escort you," Joseph offered instead. A few men nodded and began speaking to their wives. Most villagers remained standing with crossed arms. A small group of about 50 people volunteered to return, and the women and children began gathering their belongings. We helped to load them onto the back of a large commercial truck that had gotten delayed in Tama due to the fighting. We moved out ahead of them, agreeing to meet them shortly in the village center.

We had reports that helicopters had shot down a number of people in a field on the outskirts of Amaka Sara. As we neared the village, we found the remains of four people in a meadow. The bodies lay where they had fallen. We took our pictures and did the best we could to determine the causes of death. One body beneath a stack of peanuts was missing its head. A direct hit by a missile or gunshot had decapitated him. These were the family members of the villagers to whom we had just spoken. Nobody said a word as we searched the grasses for more shrapnel. When we found what we needed as evidence, we continued into the village somberly. Joseph had to explain where the bodies were located so that the families could bury their dead. I did not envy him at that moment.

When we arrived in the village center, the truckload from Tama had already arrived. The GOS lieutenant colonel was there again, telling them they could go home safely. Given the horror that normally surrounded us, I was not sure whether the returned loot and this gesture of reassurance from the GOS was a miracle or a trick. In actuality, all hell was breaking loose.

Some of the intelligence we received suggested that 2,000 Janjaweed were planning to move on Muhajeriya, an SLA stronghold, within three days. If they did, the SLA could be crushed. If SLA fighters succeeded in repelling the attack, they would give new meaning to their cause, strengthening their resolve. But the SLA could only succeed if it had some advance notice to mobilize. I truly hoped they too had this information.

Other intelligence stated that the Janjaweed had just been supplied with 20 vehicles by the GOS. They were expected to take Duma on the way to Muhajeriya. I thought of the angry omda of Duma. After taking Muhajeriya, they would move on the Jebel Marra, where the SLA and JEM headquarters were located.

There was clearly no stopping the GOS. Ceasefire? There was no ceasefire. How could there be in these circumstances? The AU, as a monitoring force, was understaffed and overwhelmed. The UN made noises about an intervention force, the Western powers chanted their disapproval of the killing in Darfur, and the occasional news story briefly captured public attention. But the Sudanese government rebuffed efforts to impose a robust intervention force. And the rest of the world was too far removed in physical distance and in spirit from what was happening here. Now it was about to get even uglier.

Though I had planned my leave to begin in 17 days, I did not know if I could take it, if I would even be able to get out. I packed my bags so that all I had to do was throw on my clothes and boots. There was nothing I could do for now but my job. And wait.

Chapter 18

I was surprised by the shiny tiled floors and bright clean rooms. The Nyala military hospital was a stark contrast to the civilians' clinic. We ducked into a few of the large motel-style rooms, searching for the GOS soldiers injured at Amaka Sara. To our amazement, the hospital was packed. The GOS rarely shared its casualty figures, so we never had a sense of the injuries. Despite the crowded facility, no ailing people waited in lines or sat on the ground against the walls. Each room was fully occupied but held a comfortable number of patients who looked well-attended.

Three of the four GOS soldiers injured at Amaka Sara had already been discharged. But we did locate one man who claimed to have been shot in the pointer finger while firing his weapon. The GOS record said he had also been shot in the leg, but when we found him, his hand wound was the only injury he had sustained.

He greeted us. "My name is Mohammed Ali Akhmed. I am part of the Mujahadeen Battalion."

"Tell us how you were injured," Joseph began.

"My commander brought me in to fight on November 1."

"When was the actual start of the battle you fought in," Joseph pressed.

"I don't know."

"Who is your commander?"

"Uh, I don't recall."

"Okay, then what unit are you with and where is it based?"

Mohammed raised his eyebrows and blinked, shaking his head. "I think my unit is from somewhere near Amaka Sara." He seemed to be looking to us to confirm. But he did not realize that the unit involved in the attack was based in Bulbul. The ambush occurred on October 28, and the GOS had attacked on October 30.

"Where was the ambush site?" Joseph asked, testing him further. I had already stopped taking notes.

"I think it was somewhere along a road with a signboard that read '40 km from Nyala.' The police had been attacked by people from the hills, and then I was asked to go help them."

"Who was it who actually attacked the police?"

"The Toro Boro," he proclaimed. *Toro Boro* is a term adapted from the Tora Bora mountains in Afghanistan, where Osama bin Laden was said to reside. It was what the Janjaweed typically called the rebels, which we were told was meant to signify "people from the hills," since the rebels' stronghold was also in the mountains.

"Tell me a bit more about the Toro Boro. What do they look like?" Joseph asked.

"They are a mix of people who are brown, red, and white."

"White like me?" I jumped in with disbelief.

"Yes, white like you." Each successive response was increasingly vague. He could not provide any more detailed information, nor did he have an ID card on him to prove his identity.

We turned to his wound. Mohammed held up his left hand ceremoniously so that all of us could see it. The bandage was spotless.

"I use my left hand to fire my weapon." Showing us his pointer finger, he explained, "A bullet hit the tip of my finger and went through my hand into my thumb." *Right*, I said to myself. If he had been shot through his pointer finger by a round from a Kalashnikov rifle, he would no longer have a hand to bandage. It was also virtually impossible for the bullet to travel as he claimed if his finger was on the trigger. This injury was staged for us. It was looking more and more like there had been no exchange of fire with rebels at all.

As we headed out the front gate, a man approached us.

"Did you say Amaka Sara?" he asked, looking at us to see who spoke Arabic. Ali stepped forward to greet him.

"I overheard someone say Amaka Sara. That's where I'm from," the man said.

"What are you doing here?" Anour asked. "This is a GOS military hospital."

"They took me here." The man spoke guardedly, looking around. "I was returning to my village a few days ago after spending some time in my field. I had no idea that there had been an attack or that the military was in my village. As I came around a turn, I surprised a few soldiers. I turned to run. They screamed at me to stop and then shot me. The bullet hit me here, in the back of the right arm." I took a picture of his bandaged arm; given the blood stains, the wound seemed authentic. I wondered how long he would stay in this GOS military hospital after what he had told us. We checked the logs. He was not even on the rosters. We hadn't found any civilians that had been injured at Amaka Sara in the civilian hospital either. Strangely, the GOS had taken him to get medical care but hid him here so we would not find him.

Most of the reports initiated by the GOS involved a similar wild goose chase. The perception of fairness in our investigations was a critical commodity and seemingly in short supply, given that most complaints we received involved GOS and Janjaweed attacks against SLA-supported villages. That imbalance simply meant that we had to follow up each and every GOS complaint. Many GOS complaints could not be confirmed. Still, we did what we had to do to live up to our mandate. We did not want the Sudanese government to have any reason to think we were biased because we knew such suspicions could compromise our mission. However, I was increasingly convinced that the reports were meant to confuse and distract us from ongoing attacks elsewhere. I wasn't sure whether they thought we were stupid enough to believe their complaints, but they obviously wanted to waste our resources. It was working. After all, we only had two monitoring teams operating in all of South Darfur.

· · ·

The following day we headed out on a ground patrol to the villages of Tiesha, Mirrel, and Nitega to talk to all tribal leaders, including those believed to be Janjaweed. We were following up on something that threatened to escalate into a major crisis. Reportedly, rebels had stolen 350 camels from the Janjaweed, and this is what caused the Janjaweed, willing to die for their camels, to plan an attack on the SLA stronghold of Muhajeriya. Over a few days, they had already burned 14 or 15 villages. While we went in search of their leadership, Team D was going to the villages to survey what had happened.

As we neared Tiesha, we came across eight men. These were Janjaweed, armed with Kalashnikovs, magazine pouches, and bottles of gasoline—the fuel of choice for burning villages. As our vehicles approached, the militia spread out in a military formation within the brush, ready to fire on us. They fired a few warning shots in our direction, then immediately dispersed, finding concealment behind trees. They moved carefully—the way a highly trained professional force moves, more skillfully even than the GOS. I pulled my Land Cruiser to a stop about 100 meters from the men. Without warning, Ahmed jumped out and ran straight toward them. The Janjaweed aimed in his direction, poised to shoot.

"What the hell are you doing?" I screamed. "They'll kill you!"

He had to be crazy. Unarmed, he approached the militiamen, yelling in Arabic and shaking his fist. They remained absolutely still, with weapons drawn. I was in awe of his fearlessness. Maybe it was insanity. Adrenalin rushing, I realized that this might become the first official attack on the African Union. I remained in my Land Cruiser, with my camera discreetly poking out the window. If the Janjaweed were going to attack the AU, I was going to capture it. I kept my body behind the engine of my car to protect myself from bullets. From a distance, I saw Ahmed continue to shout at them, his arms flying. Amazingly, within a few minutes they slowly lowered their weapons and raised their hands, attempting to calm him down. From this distance, I could not determine what he might have said. It was unbelievable.

At that point, we all got out and walked up behind Ahmed to speak with them. Two of the men continued to aim their weapons at us.

One Janjaweed spit his words angrily, "Rebels stole 350 of our camels and 600 cattle. My men went to take them back when rebels in 20 vehicles ambushed us near Labado. They shot the camels we were riding on and killed 15 people!" The men were now walking back to their settlement on foot, clearly furious and probably paranoid. I knew how seriously they took this theft. There were only a few banks in rural Sudan, and obviously no opportunities to invest in the stock market. Instead, you bought a cow, and when that cow reproduced, you doubled your money. Camels were even more valuable. The only thing was that these cattle and camels were most likely stolen by the Janjaweed in the first place. The African tribes had lost so many animals to theft, time and again in this conflict; I had no doubt many of these men were guilty of stealing from the Darfurian people.

"Where are you going? What are you planning to do now?" Ahmed led the discussion this time. But that was all the Arab would tell us. He glared at us. I guessed that someone had tipped off the SLA that the Janjaweed were planning an attack on Muhajeriya, so the SLA had launched a preemptive strike instead.

We left the Janjaweed in the bush and continued toward Taisha. I did not ask Ahmed what he had said to get the Janjaweed to lower their weapons, but I was really glad to have him on our team.

As we entered Taisha, we saw two people lying injured in a makeshift hut. Next to an adult militia member, I was surprised to see a boy. He was around fourteen years old, dressed like a miniature Janjaweed fighter, and stretched out on a cot. We stopped our trucks and got out to speak with them.

The older of the two was dressed in camouflaged fatigues, and his head was wrapped in a very long yellow scarf. He looked up at us and nodded his acknowledgement. We introduced ourselves and asked him what had happened.

"Rebels stole 350 camels and several cattle from us. The omda himself lost 58 cattle. About a hundred of us gathered to follow the rebels' tracks. We were ambushed!" He pounded the side of his cot. We thanked them and jumped in our vehicles to follow a Land Rover pickup truck full of Janjaweed that rushed by us toward Mirrel.

·   ·   ·

As we entered Mirrel, a few kilometers away, we came upon a meeting of nearly 300 Janjaweed armed with Kalashnikovs and G3s. Seven to ten men rushed out from the surrounding buildings, aiming their weapons at us, yelling for us to stop. We skidded to a halt.

"Mohammed, get out there and straighten this out," Joseph commanded. Ahmed was already getting out of his truck. "Tell them we are looking for the sheikh of Nitega." A sheikh was a tribal leader, higher ranking than an omda. The sheikh of Nitega was the tribal and military leader of the Janjaweed in all of South Darfur.

The conversation was quick. Mohammed returned to our vehicle to explain, "The sheikh just arrived in a Land Rover pickup truck. We can find him on the other side of the wadi." He pointed to the west.

Mirrel was situated in the middle of Janjaweed territory, divided in two by a dry riverbed. Populated with Arab tribes on one side and African tribes on the other, Mirrel was one of the villages where the original conflict had started. The African portion of the town had long been destroyed and abandoned. We crossed the wadi to meet the sheikh.

He glowered at us with a Kalashnikov in his hands, showing no interest in our presence. Ahmed introduced us as the African Union.

Before we could ask a question, he stated with annoyance, "I just got back from Khartoum." He paced around complaining, "We're Sudanese too. The government offers no recognition. They are coming down hard on us. They refuse to give us any further support."

It was interesting that he, the Janjaweed leader for all of South Darfur, had been in Khartoum meeting with the GOS, and I was surprised that he would share this much discontent in our presence. We had observed that the Janjaweed were increasingly upset that the Sudanese government was not providing the level of support they wanted. They claimed the GOS would not give them money to buy ammunition, but this I did not believe. We had also received a recent report on a Janjaweed battle with GOS police, though it had not yet been confirmed. If the Janjaweed were to get really angry with the government, then we would have serious trouble; the Janjaweed—like the rebel forces—actually outnumbered the GOS forces.

"Can you tell us anything about the recent incidents involving stolen livestock?" Joseph inquired.

"They stole from us," he roared. "And then they had the nerve to attack us when we were searching for what belonged to us!" He expelled each syllable with rhythmic force. We later learned that this group of angry militiamen had been burning villages as they tracked their stolen camels.

We had started to leave when the sheikh called to us. "Oh, one more thing," he said. When we stopped and turned around, he looked me in the eye and said something in Arabic.

"What?" I looked to Ibrahim.

"Uh, he congratulates you on Bush's reelection," he said. The hair on my neck stood on end. It was one day after the US elections. I had heard this information right before I went out on this patrol, and yet this Janjaweed leader in the middle of nowhere knew just as much. These forces were not only well trained, they were also extremely well informed.

The more I learned about the Janjaweed, the more I saw them as the government's loyal attack dog. The master loves his dog because of its devotion, even if it has the capacity to kill. Part of that love is also rooted in the master's ability to control the dog's power. At some point, the dog starts getting a funny look in its eye, and the master has to let him loose to attack someone, to taste blood, to feed. Otherwise it could turn on its master. After tasting blood, the dog is satisfied for a short while. Yet before long, the master has to let it loose again.

If the GOS did not let the Janjaweed attack a village, and rape and burn and pillage, the Janjaweed might turn on them. So the GOS would unleash them on a village, the Janjaweed would do their thing, and then they would be loyal again—the loyal Mujahadeen, the loyal Janjaweed, the loyal PDF, they were all the same. What no one understood was that the more they tasted blood, the more they needed it and wanted it. It was an addiction. It was an endless cycle of power and violence. The only way to end the cycle with an attack dog is to kill it.

Chapter 19

"AMIS? What's that? You're not getting through here," the young GOS soldier said with a smirk. We sat in our Land Cruiser, and I fought back the urge to get out and kick him in the teeth. Our old vehicles had been painted with the large letters "AU/CFC," denoting African Union/Ceasefire Commission. The new trucks we had just taken delivery of were painted with the acronym AMIS, for African Mission in Sudan. The change in notation seemed to confuse all of the GOS personnel who regularly manned the many checkpoints we had to pass through every time we left Nyala. Though they knew who we were, they played games, refusing our entry.

"Mohammed, get out there and tell them to let us pass!" Joseph demanded. One of the reasons that we had a GOS representative on our team was to assist in such petty matters. But Lieutenant Colonel Mohammed seemed to delight in being uncooperative.

He stepped out of the car, walked over to them nonchalantly, and began to converse with the officials in Arabic. We watched as they smiled, shook hands, and seemed to be getting to know each other. Mohammed lit a cigarette for the guard and continued to chat with him for another five minutes or so. He returned to the car window and explained through Ibrahim that unfortunately these men could not help us.

"Then ask for their superior!" Joseph was losing his patience.

Mohammed returned to the checkpoint officials. One ducked into the guard house and shortly thereafter another soldier emerged. They shook hands and a second round of greetings kept us waiting another five or ten minutes. This time Mohammed came back shaking his head.

"The officers have their orders," he shrugged.

"Look, unless you want to sleep here tonight, order them to let us by. You outrank every one of these GOS soldiers here," Joseph fumed.

"Okay, I will try again," Mohammed sighed. Ahmed, driving our other truck, was not as tolerant. He jumped out of the vehicle and stormed up to Mohammed and the other guards. I could see him shaking his finger in the commanding officer's face. The man's smile diminished. He was not amused. I wondered how long this standoff was going to last.

Finally, the GOS officials relented. Mohammed got back into our truck looking somewhat smug. These little inconveniences were wearing on me.

.　　.　　.

On November 7, we investigated a Janjaweed attack on the village of Halouf. According to the complaint, several people were killed and wounded. When we arrived, we found the village almost deserted—except for a large number of camels grazing throughout town. We knew to be wary of the Janjaweed, the Arab nomads tending these animals. As we approached, one armed man on horseback galloped away toward other armed men in the distance.

We looked out past the fields surrounding the village and saw two cattle herders standing in the wadi. As we walked down to interview them, a shot was fired in our direction. I immediately fell into a watch position, climbing up the far bank with binoculars to make sure the Janjaweed were not moving toward us. As the team interviewed the cattle herders for a few minutes, I remained behind a tree keeping a lookout for Janjaweed returning to the village. I saw the militiamen moving back into the village about 100 meters away. They fired a few more shots in our direction. Jumping back down into the wadi to return to my team, I relayed the situation.

"I can see four or five armed men in the village. I think they are moving this way. It doesn't look good. I recommend we leave," I stated.

Joseph accepted my assessment. "Okay men, let's go." As we evacuated the area, we were shot at again.

Back at our base we contacted the villagers who originally lodged the complaint and who were staying with friends in Nyala for a few more days, inviting them to speak with us further. Two sheikhs, one teacher, and a medic showed up for a more detailed interview. We convened in our interview tent and offered them a glass of water.

"A year ago this past October," one of the sheikhs said, "the Janjaweed led a massive attack on our village. Five of the Janjaweed were actually arrested by the GOS. Two were sentenced to death, but the other three were detained for a few hours, then released. The Janjaweed promised to avenge the deaths of their two brothers. This resulted in several attacks on our village over the year." He wiped his forehead. "It has been very bad the last month and a half."

The other sheikh picked up where he had left off. "On the one-year anniversary of the big attack, we formed a delegation to seek protection. We came to Nyala to speak with five different GOS agencies. We got nothing."

"Over the last week, there have been many incidents," the first sheikh jumped in again. "One day several young girls were attacked and all their goods stolen. A few days ago, many of our women were beaten and raped when they went to collect firewood. The Janjaweed kidnapped one woman and kept her for three days . . ." the leader's voice trailed off. He did not elaborate about whether she had been physically or sexually abused.

"Where are your villagers now?" Joseph asked with concern.

"The remaining families fled Halouf about fifteen days ago, when the Janjaweed kidnapped another person in a separate attack. Most villagers are either seeking refuge in IDP camps or staying with family members in Nyala. Our village is destroyed!" he cried.

. . .

It was still Ramadan, and most of our team had been fasting during daylight hours for weeks. The team was pretty tired, and our Sudanese representatives were constantly getting into arguments. They got into it again the day of the Halouf-related interviews. The sheikhs jerked their heads toward the back of the room as we noticed Anour and Mohammed arguing in Arabic. Instead of leaving it to Joseph to sort out, I stepped in immediately to keep them from embarrassing our team any further.

"Knock it off! We are professionals here. Act like it," I shouted, thrusting them apart with my arms. I knew Mohammed would not necessarily know what I had said, but he got my drift. I had never jumped in before, and because I had taken the initiative to do so, then they must have known it was looking pretty bad.

Anour threw his pen down. Mohammed sunk into a chair, his arms folded across his chest.

The men we were interviewing seemed surprised at our disarray. What was happening to us, I thought? How the hell were we going to get anything done?

Chapter 20

"The GOS and Janjaweed came from every direction—on foot, on horse-back, and in trucks. Soon gunships were overhead, firing on the middle of the village," the chief was saying. It had started like every other investigation.

We were sitting down with members of the Um Louta people's protection force, a group of local civilians who had come together to protect their village, but were not aligned with either of the primary rebel groups. Joseph handed me the list of those killed, which had just been provided to him by the defense force. Um Louta had been home to 400 to 500 residents from four different tribes. I looked at the quarter page of a dirty piece of notebook paper. The note had been folded several times and spent time in someone's pocket. The paper was filled with names, separated by tribes. I strained to count them. In all, thirty-four people had been killed, five had been wounded, and the entire village had been torched to ashes. The injured had fled to Muhajeriya.

Muslims almost always bury their dead immediately, so we rarely found bodies in an investigation and often would only have the count provided by witnesses for our reports. This could result in obvious discrepancies. Sometimes when we were investigating a backlogged incident, witnesses were hard or impossible to find, leading to what we figured to be an under-estimated count of the dead. In other cases, the estimated death toll was too low because many people—the precise number was unknown—had fled into the bush and probably died from their injuries.

There were also incidents where the number of people killed or injured was exaggerated. If the number was given by a chief, it would usually be accurate because he most likely had a list of names of those villagers who had perished. When the town provided a list of families missing, we would estimate around seven people per family. But local villagers often provided inaccurate—and inflated—numbers. Sometimes this was simply ignorance; on other occasions, it was because they wanted to make the attack look more serious than it actually was. Who could blame them? Many towns had been attacked over and over again.

"What time did the attack begin?" Joseph asked. I looked around at the villagers standing behind their leaders. The men shifted from one foot to the other, peering at Ibrahim, listening intently to what Joseph was saying. I still could not get used to the distress in their eyes and the eagerness with which they observed our investigations. They wanted us to know every detail, even though we had already heard this kind of story hundreds and hundreds of times.

The leader of Um Louta's protection force was more subdued, "The attack began in the early afternoon, November 2. That was six days ago. We mobilized a response force and arrived here four hours later. We were able to chase away one Land Cruiser filled with Janjaweed. But that didn't end it. After we returned to our base, the Janjaweed burned one empty village to the south, then torched another village to the north just 2 kilometers away. Then the next day, the Janjaweed and GOS attacked again, this time together. They used helicopter gunships to force people back into their huts or to flee into the open land."

"Which direction did they come from?" Joseph asked without looking up from his notebook.

"They came from the northeast, from Ghazawal Jawzet. There is an animal research center there."

"Tell me about your casualties," he asked in a monotone. Joseph was on automatic response today.

The man took a second to reply. "Most of them were burned to death." His words, barely a whisper, pierced the silence. Joseph was startled out of his trance.

"What did you say?" he stammered.

"Thirty-four people were locked in their huts and burned alive."

I took off my canvas hat and ran my hands over my close-cropped hair. When would this be over?

Our team wandered through the village unaccompanied. We discovered the fresh graves of the attack victims covered with damp soil and thorny branches. A villager approached, pointing at the dirt. He leaned toward Ali, who was standing nearest to him, and muttered something. Ali translated, "He said this one contains at least six bodies." Despite the glaring sun and intense heat, I felt a chill deep in my bones.

I continued, photographing the destruction. Crumbling and charred, mud-brick huts partially enclosed the ash skeletons of bed frames and clay pots. As far as the eye could see, compound after compound had been leveled. The smell I once associated with expired fire pits after a night of camping took on a new significance. I touched the side of a building, and clumps of mud broke off from the curved wall. Everything was so fragile.

.   .   .

We headed next to Ghazawal Jawzet to meet with Sheikh Wida Mohammed Al Daorok. He was chief of the area's Rezigat Tribe and head of the Government Workers Union for the village. As we flew over the animal research center in our helicopter, we could observe no animals and no animal pens. At first glance, it looked abandoned. Yet, to one side we could see what appeared to be an obstacle course, suggesting that the GOS was now using the center as a training facility.

As our helicopter touched down, a crowd of nearly 200 people came out from the bush. They were clearly not Sudanese. Even my untrained eyes told me that they looked foreign. They seemed to wrap their heads differently, and many looked of a different ethnicity: lighter skin, lighter eyes, higher cheek bones, and more facial hair. The men wore a mixture of jelabias, military uniforms, and civilian clothes.

I whispered to Ahmed, "Where do you think they come from?"

"Yemen or Syria, probably for export," he said.

"What do you mean, 'for export'?"

"They are trained here to go to Iraq to kill people like you."

Osama bin Laden had been in Sudan a decade earlier, using it as an Al Qaeda training ground. Under pressure from the United States, the government in Khartoum had booted him out. Now, according to Ahmed, this place in South Darfur was being used to train foreign fighters to join the insurgency in Iraq and kill American Army soldiers, Marines, and civilians. What the hell was happening here?

My stomach sank. "Don't introduce me as an American," I said slowly. "Alright. No problem."

Unfortunately, Ahmed did not conduct the introductions that day. At that moment, I saw Ibrahim pointing at me. I closed my eyes and heard him say "*Amerki.*" I opened my eyes and saw every one of the men staring at me with hatred in their eyes.

I swallowed hard, reached down to feel for the small hunting knife at my side and unsnapped it from its sheath. Here I was, an American, dropped right into the middle of their terrorist training practice. What were the chances I would make it out alive? I fully expected that I could die on this day. I looked around me. There were about 25 men near me, a mixture of Al Qaeda and local Janjaweed, holding Kalashnikovs. Who would I go for first on my way down?

"We have got to go. *Now.*" I said to Ahmed. My hands were sweating.

But, the team was already walking away with the sheikh and his deputy toward the animal research facility for a chat, presumably inside one of its buildings. I figured it was better to stick with the group. I wasn't going to be left alone with these terrorists. These men had been trained to kill people exactly like me, and here I was in their territory—unarmed. I don't think my team really understood how hated I felt in that moment. My heart was pounding, and the adrenalin rush was almost making me dizzy. I might as well be on a death march. I took a slow, deep breath. This was my job. I had to continue. I followed my team as they walked toward the closest compound. What I really wanted to do was head straight for the helicopter and offer to pick up the guys later when they finished. I continued to look in all directions, watching the men slip back into the bush. We were only giving the snipers more time to set up outside.

The long cement building was a mess, with broken screens covering open windows that revealed empty rooms within. We passed between the high walls and turned the corner to speak underneath a tree in the courtyard.

I tried to focus on the investigation.

The sheikh was explaining, "This region has always been fairly secure and peaceful until October 29." Um Louta was the last such town to be burned and looted. Apparently, the town had had good relations with the sheikh.

"When the militias began to harass the villagers from Um Louta and kidnapped a man, they came to me to ask for my help. Unfortunately, I am not responsible for these militias. I told the villagers that this was Khartoum's problem. Then, two days later, some of my cattle were stolen. I believe the villagers caused the rebels to steal my animals."

"What happened next?"

"My men and I tracked down my animals. When we finally found the cattle, we were shot at from the bushes. We chased the shooters to a water hole outside Um Louta. There the thieves fired on us again. This was early afternoon. By 1700 hours, we were surrounded. The attackers were using mortars and heavy machine guns. They even killed and injured some of my men! There is no excuse for this!" the sheikh shouted furiously. "We could not even rescue our wounded until the next day. And then the rebels attacked us again at the water hole. We fought back, and many people escaped into the bush. We chased them down. And then," he said, shrugging his shoulders, "what happened . . . happened."

"What do you mean, 'What happened, happened'? The entire village of Um Louta has been destroyed!" Anour interrupted in a harsh voice.

"Our men first approached the village on foot, raising a white flag attached to a stick. I tried to go talk to them about the situation, but no one was there. Look, these are thieves. And no one would help us. We had to take matters into our own hands."

"The villagers report that there were Janjaweed militia involved in the attack. Is that so?" Joseph asked.

"As I said, the Janjaweed are not my responsibility. I do not know them and do not want to be associated with them." I was not sure whether he truly meant this, as he was living side by side with them. But as far as I could tell, when the Janjaweed were sitting around too long during a time of peace, they seemed to get hungry for more violence. If what he said was true, the chief could not even control members of his own tribe.

At last, it was time for us to leave. The team stood up, shook the sheikh's hand, thanked him for his time, and headed towards the exit. Anour and Ali were chatting loudly with each other. Joseph and Ibrahim were making small talk with the sheikh. Ahmed was following behind silently with Mohammed. My team members seemed completely unaware of what I felt to be an imminent threat. No one was on guard for what could await us on the other side of the compound.

As we emerged from the buildings, I positioned myself directly next to the sheikh, figuring that snipers wouldn't fire on me because of my proximity to their leader. Each step toward the helicopter seemed to take forever. The men were still sitting with their weapons under nearby trees. Others smoked, leaning against the walls. I felt every eye pressing into me. I continued to glance around and behind me as we walked until we reached our helicopter. I almost sprinted the final steps up into the fuselage. My heart was pounding in my ears as I collapsed into my seat. I pulled at my drenched T-shirt and wiped the back of my neck. I tried to make myself as thin as possible, pressing back against the jump seat, still feeling myself a target inside the gaping, open door. When we finally lifted off, I fully expected a missile to blast us out of the sky. As we safely turned toward Nyala, I realized how long I had been holding my breath.

Chapter 21

Two days later I was in the operations room listening to Dave explain the details of a reported GOS attack on the village of Abu Sofia involving helicopter gunships and Antonov twin-engine prop planes. His hand passed over our British colonial map, now peppered with notes from the villages we had visited.

"We have no idea where Abu Sofia is except that it is in the northernmost reaches of our sector. I recommend you take the helo to Haskanita first." Haskanita was an SLA stronghold in the southern area of North Darfur, outside our area of operations.

When they saw our helicopter land in Haskanita, over 100 SLA members walked out to greet us. We jumped out from the chopper and gathered with the SLA in a tight circle. Ahmed conducted our introductions, pointing me out last. One of the men looked at me closely and then remarked in English, "Hey, you were in the Nuba, right?"

He looked vaguely familiar. "Yeah, I worked for the Joint Military Commission," I replied. I gazed at him for a moment, searching my memory. I suddenly realized he was an SPLA member from the south. I was surprised he had recognized me from my previous mission. He had caught me off guard in this context, and I wondered what he was doing here. "The SPLA is not supposed to be here," I said questioningly.

"I know," he said.

It was curious that Africans from the south were assisting the groups fighting the Government of Sudan in Darfur. The Sudan People's Liberation Army is made up mostly of Christian and animist tribes that had fought for an independent south. In Darfur, the Sudanese Liberation Army and Justice and Equality Movement were African Muslims fighting for freedom throughout Sudan. They had different ideologies, they had different religions. Though the GOS had used similar tactics to suppress and crush opposition in both regions, many of the soldiers conscripted by the GOS to fight in the south were from tribes in Darfur. Most importantly, in light of the fragile peace treaty, this kind of collaboration could destabilize the situation and renew GOS violence in the south. There were too many possible explanations, and I wished I had more time to spend with the guy, but we had to continue on our investigation. It was also remarkable that you could run into someone who knew you from a previous post because Sudan is just plain huge—the largest country in Africa, roughly a third the size of the United States.

But, I suppose I was unusual. In the Joint Military Commission, there were only around five Americans in the entire mission; here, there were only three. The encounter with the SPLA guy was another reminder that I needed to be aware of the impression I made on others.

The Yemenis, Syrians, and other trainees we had encountered in Ghazawal Jawzet already regarded me as an enemy. As an American in Sudan, wherever I went I represented my country—and whatever those I encountered *thought* about my country. At this point, most Sudanese seemed to respect Americans, but that could quickly change. Neither the Sudanese nor the African Union wanted Westerners to interfere. I was fully aware that my presence on this team came at the insistence of the US, which was funding the majority of the mission at the time. Depending on how effective or ineffective our presence was, the locals could easily come to see me as part of a Western plot to control Africa and its resources.

The SLA leader explained that we were misinformed about the bombing in Abu Sofia. "It never happened," he insisted. "However, there were a series of bombings here in Haskanita and the nearby village of Isban. This was back in late October, over four or five days. If you like, we can take you over there to show you the bombed out area of the village."

We piled into two SLA Land Rovers and headed for the village. The SLA parked near three large holes. I got out to take a closer look. Sure enough, these resembled impact zones created by bombs. Metal scraps were scattered about. I grabbed a piece of shrapnel and joined my team under a tree to learn more.

An omda and a sheikh joined the conversation, along with four SLA field commanders. The SLA leader introduced them in turn and then began his explanation.

"The conflict began on October 18 when the Janjaweed attacked civilians in Isban. The Janjaweed looted and burned several of their homes. Over the next two days, the GOS came and bombarded the north side of Haskanita. Within a week, the helicopter gunships and Antonovs were back, bombing both villages. Fortunately, no one was injured here."

I realized we were talking about the same time period as the attack on Alliet. Alliet was approximately half an hour east of Haskanita by air. On their way back, the GOS had probably just dropped their extra bombs on these other small villages. I whispered this possibility to Joseph who, in turn, asked the SLA leader about Alliet.

"Yes, we know that the same day the government was bombing us, they sent a reinforcement of 30 to 50 troops to Alliet. Troop strength in Alliet is still increasing. A separate force of 3,000 PDF and Janjaweed are now massing there, and the GOS has been running reconnaissance missions into our territory."

I was alarmed at this reported build up of troops. What would they do next?

"What about your injured and those who have fled?" Joseph asked.

"Haskanita now has approximately 10,000 people living here, including IDPs from Alliet. There are probably still 40,000 displaced from the Alliet area, 22,000 of whom are still missing by our count. With so many people displaced, without homes and vulnerable to attack, we absolutely cannot risk giving up our position here or this whole region could be attacked again."

We decided to reroute our investigation to head to Isban. When our helicopter touched down, the entire village came out to meet us. That saved us the trouble: we always tried to gather the entire village at the start of an investigation so we could tell everyone directly what we were there to do. It was important that they see who we were and what we were doing, rather than wondering who might be in trouble. Further, it showed them that the African Union actually investigated their complaints. That acknowledgement was important—to them and to us.

Ahmed first introduced the three team members who were parties to the conflict. Anour and Ali were cheered with chants of "SLA, SLA!" and

"JEM, JEM!" When the audience quieted down, Ahmed introduced Mohammed. The crowd began to boo and scream at the man. Someone threw a rock.

"Okay, okay!" Ahmed called to them in Arabic. He needed to calm them down before a riot started. Next he introduced our team leader from Kenya, the deputy team leader from the Congo, and himself.

"Last," he explained, "every African Union monitoring team has an EU or US representative. They are here to offer us additional advice and support. Our representative is Captain Brian Steidle from America." The entire town of several hundred people got to their feet and applauded me. I raised my hand and nodded.

Our quick investigation with the village leaders confirmed that the GOS had bombed and set fire to several huts on one side of the village. Three individuals had been killed, some abducted, and four burned, and many huts had been torched. When we finished our meeting, a few villagers came up to me.

"We are so happy that America is here to save us like you have done for the people of Afghanistan and Iraq," Ibrahim repeated in English on their behalf. I shook their hands. As always, I was there just to take pictures and write reports, and I was not sure that any of those reports would help them anyway. I felt helpless. But I was thrilled and humbled that they thought so highly of my country—and reminded again of the heavy responsibility that attended such admiration.

.   .   .

Things were heating up. A Janjaweed attack we investigated a few days later on the village of Sanam Al Nanger yielded another horrifying picture. The majority of the 37 dead had been locked in their huts and burned alive when the Janjaweed snuck into their village before dawn. This was the first time in our experience that the Janjaweed had attacked at night. The militias almost always attacked during daylight hours because they often were reinforced by GOS troops using helicopter gunships and Antonov prop planes.

The violence apparently began on November 2 with a dispute over a water hole. A week later, the Janjaweed attacked, stealing 300 cattle. The villagers mobilized and attempted to take back their livestock. The next day they were ambushed. On November 12 around 4:00 a.m., heavily armed Janjaweed in formal military uniforms arrived on 24 camels, two men per camel, to attack and loot the village. Some of the villagers followed them, and six more people were killed in action; three people were still missing, and many were wounded.

"We lodged a complaint with the police, but we have heard nothing," another tribal leader was saying. "If we do not receive a response in the next two days, we intend to retaliate, even if it means dying for our animals." We asked them to give us a little more time to investigate before taking further action. We needed to diffuse their anger even though we could not tell them that our investigation would bring any level of justice.

Chapter 22

The last day of Ramadan was a Friday and a well-deserved day off for Team C. The conflict was intensifying, and I was looking forward to going on vacation in a few days for Thanksgiving. That morning I spent a little time going over my finances and thinking about my options for the future. I also practiced the art of doing nothing, looking forward to our afternoon barbeque and volleyball tournament. Tomorrow was the first day of Eid, the festival marking the end of Ramadan. Our Muslim colleagues would spend about half a day at the mosque, then take a few days to celebrate. The AU gave our teams one or two days off from our field investigations in honor of the holiday. We could catch up with our reports and maybe watch a few rugby games on satellite TV. I could feel the tension in my shoulders beginning to ease.

Joseph stopped by my tent. He saw my packed bags. "You cannot go on leave," he announced. He knew I didn't need his permission, so his tone surprised me.

"Look," I said. "I just need a short visit home with my family. I'll be more useful to the team once I've had some time off," I replied as diplomatically as possible.

"Yes, I understand," he said, "but the team really needs you here."

It was a rare show of support. I was flattered and grateful that he finally saw me as an essential part of the team.

"I appreciate your confidence in me, Joseph. But I've been in Sudan since January and have not been home since last May. I really need this break." Joseph had arrived in Darfur shortly before I had been transferred to Nyala.

"You've been here for ten months?" He paused for a moment. "I didn't realize that."

"Can I bring you or the team something back from America?" I added.

Joseph thought for a second, then asked me if I could bring back a laptop and a book on how to use it.

"Of course," I said.

Joseph had always been a stickler for protocol at every level, demanding complete respect for his authority, but he wasn't very tech savvy. This was where I came in. Though he'd never admit that it was because he did not have the skills, he often turned to me to manage technological tasks, such as logging GPS coordinates for each attack. I was more than willing to take on these extra duties so as to have control over operationally significant data. Over time we had developed a certain level of respect for each other's ways of operating. It wasn't exactly a friendship. I knew almost nothing about his background, and he always maintained a certain formality in our interactions. But he had come to value my military experience, and I appreciated his professionalism.

. . .

It was great to finally make it home. My parents lived in rural Virginia. I took some time to take a hike in the woods near their house before Thanksgiving. The smell of dried leaves was so comforting, and it was great to wander alone without the threat of attack. As much as I enjoyed the peace and safety of Virginia, I also realized how sheltered Americans were from how the rest of the world lived and suffered. I was shocked at the skimpy news coverage about the genocide in Sudan. Even worse, it seemed to me that people just didn't want to know.

One night I was out with some friends in a bar.

"Where'd you get so tan?" the bartender asked as he handed me my pint.

"Sudan. Just home from working in Darfur."

"What's Darfur?" he asked. I looked at him. I wasn't sure if he was really interested, but I continued.

"You haven't heard of it?" I asked.

"No, is that a nonprofit or something like Doctors without Borders?"

"Darfur is a region in Sudan. There's a genocide going on there—the government has already killed a few hundred thousand of its own citizens."

"Whoa. That's intense. So, like, isn't everyone in Africa killing each other, if they're not starving already?" he asked. Annoyed, I tried to give him a quick summary of the conflict.

After a few minutes he broke in. "So, why do we have Americans like you there? What do we get out of it?"

"What? Nothing," I told him. "You get nothing."

"So, why should I care?"

I almost knocked my beer over. "Shouldn't we care about massive killing?"

"So what? Africa is a mess. I don't really care if they keep killing each other," he said.

"Are you serious?" I stood there a second stunned. The guy turned to take someone else's order. I dug in my pocket, threw a few bills on the bar and grabbed my friends to leave before I got myself into trouble.

Even some of my best friends showed a similar level of callous disregard. But my family and the majority of my close friends understood the moral dimension of what was happening in Sudan and wanted to know what I thought should be done to stop the violence. As I sat around the dinner table one night with my parents, we talked about the situation.

"I'm really proud of you, Brian. You're doing a good job," my dad told me.

"Thanks, Dad," I smiled. In the military, there is only room for excellence. There's just no room to screw up. That's what my Marine Corps training had been about, and in a sense, my childhood had been shaped by that philosophy too. A career Naval officer, Dad had always had tough standards for us growing up, and it felt great to have his support.

"Are you ok? Are you safe there?" my mom asked.

Dad reassured her. "Marcia, Brian is a neutral noncombatant with diplomatic immunity. That means he has special protection and is not considered part of the conflict. But he's also a trained Marine. He'll be just fine." Turning back to me, he asked, "Don't you also have protection forces?"

"Yeah, we've got Nigerian and Rwandan soldiers. Sometimes we take them with us on a patrol to guard our trucks or helicopter. Each of them has extensive combat experience, and they were all hand-picked by their government for this mission.

"They're also really fun. They play soccer together every afternoon. In fact, I was told, when Rwandan soldiers deploy, they always go to battle with their soccer ball, cleats, and jerseys as well as their combat gear. The best thing, though, is that they really understand our mission, and I think they actually want to do some good. I get the sense that some of the other people on my team just think of it as a job. They don't really care what happens one way or another as long as they get their paycheck. There are exceptions, of course. I know Anour and Ali are invested in helping Darfurians. The same thing goes for Ahmed and Ibrahim—and even Joseph, despite his even-handedness."

Later that evening, I spoke to my younger brother, Eric, on the phone. He was stationed in San Diego with the US Navy. Eric was completely fascinated and genuinely surprised that no one was doing anything about the genocide.

"What are people doing about it? What can I do?" he asked me.

"You know, Eric, I really don't know. I've been so in the middle of it, I haven't thought a lot about what people need to do. I guess just tell everyone what's happening. I've watched the news every single night and read the paper every day since I've been back and haven't found one mention of Darfur yet."

The most shocking thing about coming back to America was the waste. I saw everything through the new prism of nearly a year in a country where the vast majority of the people have little or nothing. There was just too much of everything here—too many frills, too many toys and gadgets, too much food, and too much wasted water. Still, I loved the fact that I could say, "I want curried chicken for lunch" or "I think I'll have a slice of pizza" and just go and get it. Some days I would open the refrigerator and just look inside, marveling.

I had volunteered to collect all kinds of things from the US for my fellow AU monitors. Joseph wanted a laptop and a book on computers. Ibrahim wanted some English textbooks. A few of the Rwandans asked me to get some US clothes—blue jeans or anything American. Many of the guys wanted US desert camouflage, which I had to order online. In Africa, the military officers wore whatever uniforms they could find. To be able to wear American camouflage would be a sign of prestige. James and another monitor from Team D asked for digital cameras and a color printer. I also planned to bring back plenty of batteries, chewing gum, suntan lotion, and American snacks—all rarities in Darfur. I was happy to have this task. It was something concrete I could do to help make our lives easier in Darfur. I decided to make a trip out to Wal-Mart where I could get everything in one place. I was not prepared for how severe the disparity would feel that afternoon.

When I walked into the store, I lost my mind. I had been away less than a year, but I felt as if I had just entered Oz. I kept getting lost in the store and forgot half of the things that I was supposed to get, even though I had the list in my hand. I kept looking up at all the row signs, searching for what I needed. It was bright, loud, and too damn colorful in there. And there was so much for sale that people didn't even need.

Everything was a distraction. I would be in the food section looking at the different kinds of cheese puffs when I'd suddenly remember I needed electronics. Then I would walk past sporting goods and forget about the digital cameras, thinking the Rwandans might like a new soccer ball. Out of the blue I'd find myself staring at Wiffle ball bats and remember to pull out my list again. In the pharmacy aisle, I got stuck counting the varieties of soap and lotion. People seemed to be looking at me. I felt confused. I saw the reams of fabric and thought that if I could bring just one of these reams back to the women, I could clothe an entire village.

It took me over thirty minutes to pick out a digital camera. When I finally determined what to buy, the sales clerk brought out two four-foot-long boxes.

"That box is huge. How many cameras are in there?" I remarked.

"Just one. Oh, and it also comes with two AA batteries," she said. It was all about the packaging.

"I gotta get out of here," I said out loud to no one in particular. I paid in cash, forgetting half of what I came to buy.

The men had given me a ton of cash. I had walked into the US with $25,000 of my teammate's salaries in dollars. They could not send funds out of Sudan. But they trusted me to take it all the way to America, deposit it in my own account, and then wire it back to their home countries in Africa. I knew what this money meant to them. And here I was, surrounded by all kinds of unnecessary stuff Americans wasted their paychecks on daily. I always knew there was a wide gap between the poor and the developed world, but for the first time I could really feel that divide. It was staggering. The people in Darfur just wanted to plant their fields and live to harvest their crops. They wanted the choices that we took for granted: to go to school and get an education, to vote for their government, and to live reasonably free of fear that they might be killed, that women would be raped, that children would become orphans or slaves.

.   .   .

My brother-in-law, Andrew, and I decided to take a few days to go deer hunting on his father's land in Connecticut. Mom, Dad, and Gretchen joined us to celebrate my birthday with a lobster dinner at his home. A thoughtful and generous man, Gretchen's father-in-law, Emmett Wallace, had spent a career in foreign affairs and international development. He was intrigued by all that I could tell him about the politics and culture of Sudan, the crisis in Darfur, and the complexities working against international intervention.

One afternoon he invited two of his friends, authors Karl Meyer and Shareen Brysac, to take a look at my photographs and hear my stories. They were absolutely riveted. Karl was a former editor at the *New York Times* and editor of the *World Policy Journal*. He was very engaged in the events in Darfur but had not heard of the extent of the violence or the systematic nature of the destruction engineered by the Sudanese government.

"So the government is supporting the Janjaweed?" he asked.

"Absolutely. They're like another arm of the military." Most people I spoke with thought that it was simply a tribal conflict between the Arab militias and African farmers. Many were even more surprised to find Muslims were killing Muslims.

"I know someone who would be very interested to hear your stories and see these photographs," Karl suggested. "Have you heard of Nicholas Kristof? He is a columnist at the *Times* who has been writing pretty consistently about Darfur lately. I'd be happy to make an introduction."

"I appreciate your offer, but I'm not sure I'm ready to speak with the media. I'm going back over there soon, and I have to be careful about what I say publicly."

I hadn't spoken with any journalist since I began my contract with the

African Union. I was not certain I wanted to risk my career and possibly my life by doing so now. I felt that the best channel for sharing information was the US State Department, through my contacts at the embassy in Khartoum. However, it was reassuring to know people like Emmett, Karl, and Shareen who were eager to learn more about the crisis. They also helped me think about the situation from an international policy perspective and what the range of reasonable options might be for intervention.

In September, Colin Powell had officially called the crisis in Darfur a genocide. But since then, the US government had not taken definitive steps to intervene. Article 2 of the Geneva Convention on the Prevention and Punishment of the Crime of Genocide defines genocide this way: "In the present Convention, genocide means any . . . acts committed with intent to destroy, in whole or in part, a national, ethnical, racial or religious group. . . ." Article 1 states: "The Contracting Parties confirm that genocide, whether committed in time of peace or in time of war, is a crime under international law which they undertake to prevent and to punish."

As far as I was concerned, once we called the human rights abuses in Darfur *genocide*, we had the obligation to do whatever was in our power to stop it. Most people interpreted this as military action. The US government seemed to believe that by engaging in diplomatic talks, we were "undertaking to prevent" genocide and meeting our obligations under the Geneva Convention.

That wasn't enough. The United Nations needed to deploy peacekeeping troops immediately to disarm the Janjaweed and help the displaced people return to their villages safely. If the UN was unwilling to do it, NATO should shoulder the responsibility. Every nation had an obligation to prevent such atrocities. To me, whether or not to use the word *genocide* wasn't what was important. People were dying in large numbers and we had the means to stop the violence. Unfortunately, we did not have the will. They are "just Africans," someone said to me once. It made me sick.

While I was home, the UN passed Security Council Resolution 1574 on November 19, "expressing its serious concern at the growing insecurity and violence in Darfur, the dire humanitarian situation, continued violations of human rights, and repeated breaches of the ceasefire." The Resolution also said:

[The United Nations] *reiterates* its readiness, upon the signature of a Comprehensive Peace Agreement, to consider establishing a United Nations peace support operation to support the implementation of that agreement, and *reiterates* its request to the Secretary-General to submit to the Council, as soon as possible after the signing of a Comprehensive Peace Agreement, recommendations for the size, structure, mandate of such an operation, including also a timetable for its deployment, . . . [and] *demands* that Government and rebel forces and all other armed groups immediately cease all violence and attacks, including abduction, refrain from forcible relocation of civilians, cooperate with international humanitarian relief and monitoring efforts, ensure that their members comply with international humanitarian law, facilitate the safety and security of humanitarian staff, and reinforce throughout their ranks their agreements to allow unhindered access and passage by humanitarian agencies and those in their employ. . . .

The acknowledgement of what was happening on the ground was gratifying, but actual UN intervention still seemed a pretty remote possibility.

I was frustrated by having no mandate to protect the Darfurians, whom I saw attacked every day. But I still felt that our presence in Darfur gave the people some sense of security and hope, even if it was a fragile promise. As my three-week break came to an end, I pulled myself away from my family and my comforts and prepared to return. I had given the contracting company my word that I would serve one year in Sudan, and I intended to live up to that obligation. I also needed to gather more information. I did not know why, but something was urging me to keep going. I still had no plans to speak out; doing so would have jeopardized my position and prohibited me from gathering any more information. I said my goodbyes and headed back to Darfur just two weeks before Christmas.

PART THREE

Genocide

Chapter 23

By this time, I had a decent sense of the various factions within the parties to the conflict. It was more confusing than the American media reports led one to believe. The Government of Sudan military was supporting both the People's Defense Force and informal Janjaweed militias. The GOS police, security, and intelligence officers also were involved in the conflict. Among the rebel forces, the Justice and Equality Movement and Sudanese Liberation Army responded to government and Janjaweed attacks when possible, but local civilian defense forces also operated out of the villages to try to protect their populations. The groups had varying experience, command structures, weaponry, areas of responsibility, styles of operation, and interaction with one another. Just when we thought we knew how to expect them to operate, something would change, break down, escalate, deteriorate, or otherwise shift. There was no broad understanding of the international rules of war among any of the parties, especially with respect to some of the specific prohibitions of the Geneva Convention, such as deliberately attacking civilians, using inhumane weapons—such as flechettes, the hundreds of tiny twisted darts contained in GOS rocket pods—taking hostages, using rape as a tool of war, and other crimes against humanity.

By the time I first arrived in Sudan, I had already worked with several foreign military forces while I was in the US Marine Corps. My impression of the Sudanese military was that it was not a well-structured or disciplined entity. Compared with Western standards, its capabilities were poor. One reason was short training periods; another was that soldiers were conscripts, not a volunteer force. They were usually conscripted from areas of the country at some distance from the conflicts in South Sudan and Darfur to avoid anyone having to fight members of his own tribe. Conscripts had no dedication to any underlying values and often had no understanding of what was at stake in the conflict.

The officers, on the other hand, were professional soldiers. Using strict punishment, including the threat of death, these officers enforced their orders to subordinates.

At one point, our sector's two teams of monitors and the operations team started to create structural diagrams of the Sudanese military by printing out several photographs of leaders and matching faces with names. But our information was limited principally to those in lower-level military units we met during our investigations.

We knew that the permanent posts in our region were subordinate to the GOS command in Nyala and that they would communicate via satellite phones and high-frequency radios. In contrast, according to our observations in the field, mobile advancing units had often been brought in from other areas for a specific purpose and received their orders directly from Khartoum. Higher-level officials made regular visits to Nyala; we figured the row of black cars passing our compound every couple of weeks was bound to be carrying people from various Sudanese ministries.

The regular GOS military used mostly small arms, which we came across in the course of our investigations. Heavy weapons included the B10 recoilless rifle, the Howitzer 105 millimeter artillery, and the 120 millimeter and 82 millimeter mortars. At the Nyala airport, the military maintained five helicopters (three Mi–24s and two Mi–8s) and two Antonov 26 propeller planes, although they were not always there at the same time. I monitored their movements and noted the tail numbers of all helicopters and aircraft that landed. I never saw tanks being used in any operations in South Darfur, even though two tanks that looked like Russian T–55s were positioned at the airport. I was told by other observers, however, that tanks were used in several operations in North Darfur. The GOS would sometimes "drop" bombs by kicking them out the back end of the Antonovs. Other reports claimed the GOS would target civilians by throwing mortar rounds out the back as they flew over villages or packing 55-gallon drums with explosives and shrapnel and just rolling them out. It was not a very high-tech operation, but it could be pretty lethal.

. . .

The permanent military positions were established when the military was advancing. When I first arrived, the area in South Darfur was approximately 75 percent rebel controlled. There were two main rebel areas, one around Adwa, another around Muhajeriya. There was also a smaller concentration of more mobile groups around Ketil, south of Nyala. During the months I served in South Darfur, I watched the government-held areas increase dramatically as the rebel strongholds began to wither away. The Adwah pocket was eventually pushed east into Khor Abeche and then farther east to the Shariya area about 50 kilometers north of Muhajeriya. Muhajeriya still had some rebel presence. I was not aware of where the Ketil group went when the GOS military advanced into the area, but my speculation was that they moved to Muhajeriya.

Most crimes committed by the regular GOS troops usually occurred because commanders just let things happen, such as the looting of smaller items that could be easily carried by a soldier. But larger items that required transportation—beds, oil barrels, and motors, for example—were looted on express orders from a commander. We heard that GOS soldiers were sometimes paid in food or loot instead of money. I had no knowledge that looting incidents were ever reported up the chain of command. Similarly, I was not aware of any GOS-conducted prosecutions or trials relating to the crimes we investigated and reported.

What we typically referred to as Janjaweed in Darfur consisted of both the formal PDF force and informal Arab militias. They were most easily distinguished by the difference in their uniforms. The militias would have either no uniforms, partial uniforms, or a mix of uniforms; the regular PDF had matching formal uniforms, its own bases, and proper equipment. The weapons used by all Arab militias were usually in very good shape. When we asked the informal Arab militias where they got their weapons, they often told us that they came from the PDF. The militias also told us that they got weapons from the government or the Wali, the GOS-appointed governor or mayor for a region, but they would not give us further details on how the process worked. My general impression was that the informal Arab militias in the area and the local PDF units knew each other, and when more manpower was needed, members of the PDF would gather other nomads they knew and give them weapons.

The informal Janjaweed militias were also trained by the government. I heard from my US and local contacts that there had been a graduation of a militia in mid-November 2004 from El Gardut, which is on the southeastern slopes of the Jebel Marra. My contacts had been monitoring the training of this particular group; according to their reports, some of the trainees had even been sent to a special operations school north of Khartoum to receive training. I shot a picture in Taisha on November 4 that showed Arab militias clearly trained by the government. The militias were well equipped with ammunition belts and paratrooper-version Kalashnikovs with retractable stocks and aiming sticks.

We knew that the Arab militias had villages or gatherings in certain areas of South Darfur. These nomadic villages, where the fighters lived with their families, were not located in military compounds; they were situated on the annual migratory routes that followed the railroad east and then northward on both sides of the Jebel Marra or the Marra mountain range.

When the Janjaweed and the GOS fought together, we learned, the militias were directed by the plainclothes intelligence officers from the military posts. We referred to the intelligence officers as "national intelligence," and our impression was that they were from a separate service. These officers clearly had power over the militias. The leaders of the informal Janjaweed militia units were paid a salary, but it was common knowledge in Darfur that the rank-and-file fighters were essentially paid in loot.

We didn't know much about how the Janjaweed were given their orders to move. We were told by some of the attack survivors that when the GOS and militias arrived at a village, the men on horses and camels would go in first because the animals were fairly mobile. But, we also knew that camels are not very agile and do not maneuver well between huts. More often than not, we found instead that the Janjaweed would dismount at the outskirts of a village and go in on foot or on horseback. We also knew that the Janjaweed groups sometimes staged attacks on their own, without the involvement of the regular military. The police also took part in attacks on villages, and when they did, they were under the command of the military based in Nyala.

As for the rebel side, the AU mission never analyzed its command and control structures. At the time I arrived, the rebels numbered somewhere between 2,000 and 4,000 in all, although even that broad estimate may be off because of the difficulty of counting heads. The SLA and the JEM were not distinguishable in Sector 2 apart from the different names on the sides of their vehicles and the fact that SLA fighters were more numerous than the JEM fighters. On average, fighters in both groups had little or no military training, formal or informal. The commanders on the ground were not tribal leaders; most had received some formal military training in the south or from the government before they left the service to join the rebels. For example, an SLA commander may have been a corporal in the Sudanese armed forces. Many had a relatively high level of education or were previously professionals. The rest of the rebel fighters were there because they had lost family or property or both and wanted their freedom.

To the best of my knowledge, rebel fighters did not stay in a village to stage attacks against the government. Their bases were usually outside the village, and they would go into the village only to get food or talk to the people. Local commanders were well organized and knew their district superiors' satellite telephone numbers by heart. If I needed to get in touch with a rebel leader in Khor Abeche, I could ask Anour whether the relevant contact was SLA or JEM, and he would immediately dial the leader's number on his telephone. The rebels were equipped mainly with small arms such as AK–47s and Dushka machine guns. When asked, the SLA would tell us that the weapons came from South Sudan or were stolen from the GOS.

Chapter 24

I was surprised by how good it felt to be back in Darfur. I got bored easily when I wasn't active and, after three weeks in the US, I was ready to return to the field.

As team members stopped to welcome me back, I distributed the items they had requested from America. I walked over to Joseph's tent, poking my head in, smiling widely.

"You are going to be so psyched," I declared. "I got a great deal for you on an HP laptop." I handed him his brand new computer. His mouth dropped open. He held it in his hands as if it were a Ming vase. Fumbling for the lever, he opened it extremely slowly. He didn't turn it on; he just looked at the keyboard.

"Do you want me to show you how it works?"

"No, not now. Come back later."

"Oh, and I got you this." I presented him with a book. Unfortunately, the most comprehensive guide I could find on learning how to use a computer was the *Idiot's Guide to Computers*. Joseph frowned at the book as he read the title.

"Thank you, Captain Brian, for thinking of me," he replied with a hint of uncertainty in his voice. Did he think I was making a joke at his expense?

"I hope you don't think I'm trying to offend you," I said. "This book is actually part of a series that are known all over the US as the very best if you need to learn how to do anything."

"Okay," Joseph said. "Please come back by my tent later to show me what you know," he said. I ducked out through the flaps of his tent.

The following morning, December 11, I was back on duty, energized by my conversations with family and friends. I was eager to document the crisis more closely and take more photographs. During my leave, several new

AU officers had arrived from Egypt, Nigeria, Malawi, Mali, and Mauritania. Joseph introduced me to the new monitors who would join our team. The Egyptians spoke English well and greeted me warmly. Now that we had so many AU monitors on the ground, they would be rotated onto the teams depending upon the investigation. Since each team still required an EU or US representative, I would remain as part of the core make-up of Team C, along with Joseph, Ahmed, Mohammed, Ibrahim, Anour, and Ali.

.   .   .

Back in our operations office, our sector commander informed us that the village of Um Zaifa had been attacked by GOS and Janjaweed forces the previous day. We boarded our helicopter and headed out. The wind swirling around us felt relatively cool as we soared over the familiar landscape. Having returned to the US during winter, I had forgotten how bright it got here. I cleaned the lenses of my favorite pair of sunglasses and gazed out the open door beside my jump seat. As we sped across the sparse land, scrub brush and sand stretched as far as we could see. Any grass or green that had existed in June had long since withered away.

Orange dust billowed out from the force of our rotor blades as we descended in Um Zaifa. Once the pilot silenced the engine, the stillness of the deserted town was alarming. We could hear no braying donkeys or laughing children, no constant drone of a grinding machine or the sound of a well pump. And yet the energy of what once was a bustling community was still evident in the jerry cans and clay pots hastily abandoned at the local watering hole.

What we saw was what appeared to be a small IDP settlement on the outskirts of Um Zaifa. Most structures were made of grass walls thatched together almost like a fence and then propped against a stick frame or dome. Some huts were wrapped with white tarps, plastic sheeting, or ragged clothes. I came upon a worn blanket tied to an opening, noting the gaping holes between the reeds assembled as a roof. A red gas lantern sat beside the doorway, cap off and fuel emptied. I moved farther through the camp in a small circle, listening to the wind inflating and then flapping through the plastic walls.

Within a few minutes, SLA members, who had seen our helicopter touch down, emerged from the bush to speak with us. The SLA welcomed us with sober nods as we introduced ourselves. Standing in a circle, the SLA commander began an explanation.

"Government officials dressed in military uniforms approached the village two days ago. They announced that residents could flee or die. As quickly as they could, about 1,750 families from the village and 500 families from the IDP camp left."

"Where did they go?" Joseph asked.

"I wish I knew," the SLA leader responded, "but we have no idea."

We walked into the village as he spoke, where the SLA showed us the looted tent of a medical clinic established by a German NGO. The khaki canvas had collapsed at one corner. Entering the tent, we found overturned wooden chairs and desks. The drawers had been smashed or thrown to the ground, spilling medical supplies. Examining tables lay on their sides, benches sat upturned, and torn cardboard boxes had been emptied. I took a photograph of the destruction, focusing on empty machine gun shells dotting the sand around the exterior.

Elsewhere, we found several shops that had been looted, the twisted metal of padlocks still hanging from corrugated metal doors that were bent and pockmarked with bullet holes. Canisters, boxes, and tin cans swept from their shelves now lay crushed on floors. Tracks from dragging sacks of grain outlined a path from each storage area to where they had been loaded on animals or trucks.

"Thirty people were killed here," the SLA member said, as we stood before a series of graves. I snapped a shot of several fresh dirt mounds covered with the limbs of spiky trees meant to discourage scavengers.

Joseph asked, "Where did the attackers head when they left?"

"Toward the villages of Kokono and Taisha," he answered, pointing. We thanked them for their report, hurried back to our helicopter, and flew to Kokono.

.　　.　　.

It was nearing late morning and I was starting to feel a little hungry. We did not have any French rations in the helicopter that day. Usually, I did not bother with food during our investigations, unless we had some MREs (Meals Ready to Eat) on hand or stopped off to grab something in a village market. I often had little appetite anyway, but in this case, I was still adjusting from the gluttony of Thanksgiving back home.

I sucked on my Camelbak and positioned myself in the rear-facing jump seat directly behind the pilot's cockpit so that I could take some aerial shots as we flew over the village. As soon as we were off the ground, I asked the crew to open the door beside me, gesturing to them that I was strapped in to my chair by pulling on my shoulder harness.

We flew to the northeast over Kokono, then back to the south over the village of Labado in a big clockwise circle. Within minutes, we were hovering above displaced people everywhere we looked. Every 100 to 300 meters there was a family or group sitting under a stubby tree as far as we could see. Each tree was fully occupied: as many as 40 people huddled together underneath, using every millimeter of shade. Others were walking in large groups, herding their animals. It was not immediately clear whether the cattle moving beneath us had been looted by their captors or were fleeing along with their rightful owners.

Just south of Um Zaifa, we discovered a large nomad population. The Arab nomad settlers were easy to distinguish from the Darfurian farmers because they built distinct, semipermanent structures. We could see low quonset huts made of branches and cloth clustered within a grove of trees. Next to these settlements, nomads were dividing loot and animals. Men on camels herded white goats and skinny brown cows around trees. I leaned out of our helicopter snapping pictures.

We headed west from Um Zaifa to the village of Ishma, where we understood the GOS forces had established a defensive position after evacuating the town's 400 residents. We needed to get the GOS version of the attack in Um Zaifa and wanted to hear it from the commander.

As we came upon the GOS encampment, we were stunned by the size of the military position. Starting from the edge of town to the west, soldiers were entrenched along a corridor following the main road that measured 100 meters wide and 1,000 meters long. There were likely 1,500 troops dug into temporary defensive positions. They had burned down all the brush in front of their trenches to provide a clear line of sight; their mortars were dug in, and new trucks were arriving with reinforcements. About 5 percent of the troops appeared to be officers, who were congregated in the middle of the camp around a central hill. A communication station had been established atop the mound. Their cots were set outside where they could relax and oversee operations. Men in civilian dress, likely from the security service, mingled with the officers, all of whom seemed to be of Arab descent. The men occupying the trenches around them appeared to be African by origin. Other soldiers dug holes, hauled ammunition, fetched water, and moved supplies.

I leaned over to Ahmed. "Am I seeing this correctly? Are there Arab officers commanding African soldiers down there?"

"More conscripts," he confirmed.

We brought our helicopter down so close to their position that it could have been regarded as a hostile act. I could see the soldiers looking up at us from their holes. Ahmed and Mohammed jumped down first to go find the commander. Before they could walk very far, we saw the commander and his deputy racing over to us in a Land Cruiser. The commander got out of his vehicle, lowered his sunglasses, glared at us, and walked briskly over to the shade beneath a nearby nim tree. There would be no soda or chai on this visit. The rest of us disembarked and followed him.

"What are you doing here?" he asked us with annoyance.

Joseph replied through Ibrahim that we were investigating the occurrences in Ishma and Um Zaifa.

As he spoke, I again leaned over to Ahmed and whispered: "Now, I understand the Arab GOS leadership commanding African conscripts, but this commander looks African. Can you explain that?"

"He must have proved himself in some way in the south," Ahmed said. "He looks to be from the Juba region, which is in the equatorial province. Very unusual."

The commander introduced himself as Brigadier General Ahmed El Hajer Mohammed. "My brigade, of the 16th Division, is under direct orders from Khartoum to clear the roads and railway of all bandits harassing commercial traffic between Nyala and Khartoum."

"Where are the local villagers, and have you encountered any SLA or JEM forces yet?" Joseph asked.

He shrugged as he commented, "I don't know where the rebel forces are located, and I don't know why the villagers from Ishma left, especially since we are available to protect them. In any case, I have my orders, and unless I hear otherwise, I have no plans to stop. My troops will fight anyone who gets in our way." He spoke quickly and stared at us with cold eyes before walking away.

Our team remained under the nim tree watching his operations for another fifteen to twenty minutes. The rest of the team was talking amongst themselves, mostly in Arabic, paying little attention to the GOS troops. I took time to make note of the general's weapons, capabilities, and movements before we took off to return to our base.

Mohammed went off to have dinner with his GOS colleagues in Nyala, while the rest of us ate dinner at camp that night with little discussion of the day's events. Shortly after Joseph retired, I could see the glow of his laptop screen within his zippered tent.

It was common practice for the GOS, SLA, and JEM representatives to share information with their counterparts in the field. In fact, when Mohammed "went on leave," he usually just traveled to the GOS compound in town. Some mornings we even had to pick him up there before we left for our daily mission. In turn, Anour and Ali would make a point of having private conversations with SLA and JEM commanders when we interviewed them in the field. I also knew that the Sudanese monitors would carefully save their $120-per-day salary, which was quite substantial in this poor country, to help finance their ongoing operations. In short, this so-called neutral monitoring team, designed to uphold peace by ensuring equitable representation for all parties to the conflict, was instead providing ample opportunity for each side to learn valuable information about the other's operations and anticipated moves. In practical terms, the AU monitoring mission was almost helping to sustain the ongoing war. Still, we were the only eyes on the ground and the only way word was getting out to international parties. It would be worse without us.

The following day, we returned to Ishma to see if there had been any change in the GOS position. Overnight, it had doubled in size and the troops' position now stretched for nearly 2 kilometers. Now, roughly 3,000 men were entrenched as if they expected an imminent attack. They appeared to have been resupplied with ammunition, and new mortars were dug in.

Again the brigadier general approached.

"What are you doing here again?" he asked bitterly.

"The AU is monitoring the situation on the ground here," Joseph responded to his challenge. We had his attention for only five minutes this time.

"Now, can you please explain the increase in your forces?"

"I am not at liberty to discuss that with *you*," he said with a sneer.

"Where are your troops originally based?" Joseph asked, ignoring his attitude.

"My men are from the Blue Nile region in the east of Sudan. I have been in the Juba area for the last eight years. We have only just been reassigned here."

"Unless you end your operations, we will be forced to report your actions to GOS headquarters in Nyala as a violation of the Ceasefire Agreement," Joseph said in an unusually bold voice.

The brigadier general looked at us, perplexed for a moment, then said with complete confidence, "I do not report to Nyala. I receive my orders directly from Khartoum." Strangely, he left us the impression that he and his men were not really aware of the overall situation in Darfur, but that the GOS had assigned his brigade to the area just for this specific operation. He might even have thought this conflict was an extension of the war in the south. What his remarks did reveal is that the government had explicit control over this large military operation. These were not rogue units cooperating with the Janjaweed. Genocide was a matter of policy from the highest reaches of the Government of Sudan.

We remained on the ground another fifteen to twenty minutes, simply watching. Many troops were walking outside the perimeter of the encampment in front of their line of fire to collect firewood or to relieve themselves. Most were sitting on top of their fighting holes and were not even manning their weapons. We could see smoke from their fires, and many of the soldiers were chatting loudly. In the Marine Corps, when we would "dig in," we would even dig holes to accommodate our vehicles. We were completely silent, leaving no trace of our existence. In contrast, these troops seemed to be a beehive of activity. Either they were extremely undisciplined or they were preparing to advance.

Over the next week, we would return to Ishma on several occasions to monitor their actions. I wanted to know exactly when to expect an advance on another village, and I wanted the brigadier general to know we were watching him.

We took off toward Labado to make our clockwise air patrol again, passing over Um Zaifa and its neighboring village of Hashaba. As we neared the villages, we saw smoke funneling upward. The cylindrical mud-brick foundations of a number of huts smoldered while other homes continued to burn. We could see the fire snaking furiously around the walls of several compounds. Fragile fences assembled with sticks or live bushes surrounded each individual compound of two to five huts. Each complex stood as distinct as a single city block. Given the limited undergrowth, there would be virtually no way for a fire to spread from compound to compound over dirt paths. These compounds had been torched. Attackers had returned to Um Zaifa and Hashaba to set fire deliberately to each family homestead.

Suddenly, one of the monitors pointed to a Land Rover pickup truck and a Toyota Land Cruiser speeding away from the village, loaded up with contents from local homes. Each contained around ten men crammed into the truck bed with their loot.

"Fly in closer," I shouted to our helicopter pilot. I knew it: the Land Rover was the same truck the Janjaweed and their leader from Mirrel had used to race by us once before. Slightly rusted and dented, the tan Land Rover was painted with an orange and yellow insignia on its dirty white doors. Men in camouflage, armed with Kalashnikovs, hung on as the vehicles sped along a vague path between fields of sorghum stocks.

From the air, we followed the Arab militia in their vehicles as they drove in the direction of Kokono. The trucks pulled under some trees as they arrived. The ground surrounding the village, perhaps twenty or thirty acres, was littered with loot and animals the Janjaweed had likely stolen from Um Zaifa and Hashaba. Kokono itself looked to have been abandoned some time ago. Stiff grass huts stood crumbling and vacant among the Arab nomads' domed structures. Men walked out from under the trees to greet others returning on camels with more loot. We circled in the helicopter four or five times as I snapped photos of the families distributing household goods, beds, food, and livestock. Children bounced on cots, around which were strewn grass mats, metal tubs, jerry cans, and sacks of grain. Donkeys grazed, oblivious to the chaos.

We continued our air patrol over Labado, a town of 20,000 people. Labado supported the second largest concentration of SLA in South Darfur and, in addition to Muhajeriya, was one of the only rebel strongholds left by this time. Looking down on these Darfurian villages, I thought of the labyrinth game I played as a child, maneuvering a metallic marble through a grid of passageways and obstacles. The compounds were beautiful in their precise organization and balance of sharp angled fences and conical roofs.

Like many large towns, Labado was also host to an IDP camp that sat on its outskirts and accommodated populations forcibly removed from another village or those who had fled during a GOS or Janjaweed attack. Hundreds of white canvas covers fluttered below, loosely holding together their grass walls. Huddled closely, the shacks flowed around the permanent compounds at the edge of the town like sea foam pushing at the beach. We could see no women, children, or animals walking between the tents. In fact, the camp appeared completely empty from the sky, indicating to us that the people were anticipating an attack.

Soaring over Um Zaifa a second time that day, there were now five complete compounds burned to the ground. The white ash formed an outline delineating where each compound once stood. We noticed smoke starting up in another region and dropped down to document the action. We caught approximately 50 armed militia and military men in GOS uniforms looting and burning. This time, there was no attempt to hide from our helicopter. A man stood next to his camel, gazing up at us just a few meters from the grass fence he had just set on fire. I shook my head in disgust.

Unarmed, we would not have been able to intervene safely even if we had the mandate to do so. We were low on fuel because we had flown a loop larger than we had anticipated. I hung out the door as far as possible to capture unobstructed shots of the burning and looting. The pilot circled one burning hut a few times for me. Every few minutes I had to retreat into the helicopter for relief from the searing heat of the flames. We made a final pass and turned toward home in Nyala, tracking the smoke for nearly 15 miles along the way.

As soon as we refueled and resupplied, we headed back for another air patrol over the region. By this time, the entire villages of Hashaba and Kokono and 90 percent of Um Zaifa had been destroyed by fire. Every single nomad hut and every item of loot distributed by the Janjaweed three hours earlier had been moved. All we could observe in any direction was white or gray or charcoal outlines of what had recently been places where people lived. I had never seen systematic destruction on this scale.

Chapter 25

That evening, at about 10:00 p.m., Dave and I were hanging out in one of the tents when a guard from the front gate came in.

"There is someone out here who needs you right away," the guard said. Dave and I looked at each other, wondering who would visit us here at this hour.

"I'll go," Dave said.

Moments later, he returned. "Get your camera."

I grabbed my little digital camera and caught up to Dave, who was gesturing to a Save the Children UK truck that had pulled up in front of the compound. The driver got out and, visibly shaken, pointed to the rear of the vehicle. Dave explained to me that the SLA had just attacked a Save the Children convoy north of Nyala, hijacking its vehicles and shooting and killing two of its local personnel when they tried to run. The SLA then sped off in four of the organization's new Land Rovers, leaving this driver to return with his dead colleagues.

We pulled open the rear door of the truck to find two dead men, one face down, the other face up. They had become twisted in the tarp from the drive, and blood was everywhere. I took a few pictures of the man facing up; then Dave helped me roll the other man over so I could get his photograph as well. He wore a white Save the Children T-shirt with red lettering. We were unable to assemble a complete monitoring team that evening, so we advised the staffer who had driven the truck to return to the Save the Children compound, clean up, get some sleep, and come back the next day to provide a formal statement.

Team D investigated and recovered the vehicles the next day. I knew that various forces in this conflict sometimes ambushed vehicles to obtain supplies. In fact, the World Food Program had recently reported the theft of eleven of its trucks, which we also suspected the SLA of hijacking. However, no NGO workers had ever died in such raids.

We eventually learned that the commander of the SLA unit who attacked the Save the Children convoy had been drunk. It was a tragedy that shook up the entire NGO community, and news of it spread throughout Darfur, blotting the SLA's reputation. The SLA took this seriously. Anour informed us that soon after the SLA executed the commander.

.   .   .

Team C headed the next day toward Labado. As our helicopter flew over the town, we noticed several large trucks parked outside its central commercial district. Dozens of one-room, mud-brick sheds with light blue doors lined the main dirt road. Adjacent to the main street, a group of thatched-roof pavilions in a grove of shade trees defined the open market. Beyond the commercial district, compounds of grass huts spread in all directions. As we finished our pass over town, I noticed a patch of darkened, moist soil, where women tugged on the pulley and rope of the village well. Young girls teetered beneath jugs and followed donkeys heavy with canvas bladders into the town's network of paths.

As our helicopter set down, we were immediately surrounded by women and children. The women wore brilliantly colored dresses, one piece of twisted fabric wrapping them from head to toe as if the wind had spun them around. Taking a brief break from their work, they stood in groups whispering to each other. A few children knocked on the fuselage and cupped their hands to peek through the glass. Others skipped around the helicopter, waiting for us to disembark. We jumped to the ground, shaking tiny hands and playing a game of copy cat with the children's cries: "I am fine, how are you? I am fine, how are you?"

Beyond the welcoming villagers, we spotted a large contingent of SLA and JEM fighters heading our way. The men were wearing either camouflage fatigues that didn't match or dark full-length robes with heavy jackets and mustard-colored head scarves. I was always surprised by how comfortable they appeared in the intense heat despite so much clothing.

Following brief introductions, we gathered with seven of their leaders under a tree, sitting cross-legged in a circle to seek more information about their intended response to the GOS build-up of forces in Ishma.

"The SLA is prepared to attack within the next few days if the government does not withdraw," the SLA leader threatened. I could certainly understand their desire to strike back, but I had to remain neutral.

"What can you tell us about the government-backed forces in the region?" Joseph asked.

"We know that Hassan Azeer Abdullah Haliik controls the Janjaweed groups. We saw him yesterday with his men," he responded. I jotted this name into my notebook.

"There are eleven missing World Food Program trucks that some allege the SLA has taken. Can you provide us with more information about that?" Joseph asked directly.

"We've never heard of any such ambush taking place and certainly would have no information about the trucks," the SLA leader answered with a straight face. We figured we would probably never find evidence of them again.

With that, we were done. Anour and Ali went for a walk with their colleagues while other members of our team took the opportunity to rest or pray. I snapped a few more photographs of girls carrying tubs of dishes on their heads and the crowd of men and camels wandering beneath the trees.

As we took off in the helicopter, sure enough we saw World Food Program trucks hidden under the trees. I captured the evidence as we departed.

From Labado, we flew over Um Zaifa and could see many people dashing between huts and looking for the remains of their property. We landed briefly to investigate and learned that these people were Um Zaifa villagers who had come back to see if they could salvage anything from the wreckage of their torched community. It had taken them two days on foot to return. We were there just long enough to find out that five other small villages in the region had been burned over the last few days. I tried mentally to calculate the number of civilians displaced just in the past three days. It was simply too difficult to calculate the precise number because we did not even know the sizes of all the villages. Where would they relocate for food, water, and most of all, safety?

Upon our return to Nyala, I only had a few moments to set down my gear and splash water on my face before someone noticed the cell phones had gone down again. I grabbed my camera and climbed up our water tower to photograph the GOS helicopters I expected would soon take off. What I saw first was a terribly sad sight—a long convoy of Save the Children SUVs evacuating the organization's operations in Darfur. Ten Land Cruisers, top-heavy with luggage, with Save the Children UK flags streaming from their antennas filed by in a somber procession.

A few minutes later, a GOS military convoy arrived via the main road from El Fashir. Ten orange and army-green trucks—looking more like large livestock trailers than armored personnel carriers—were packed with troops. Zooming in with my camera, I counted fifteen to twenty troops sitting atop the cab and along the sides of each tractor trailer. Dozens more were inside the trucks. A few Land Cruisers and fuel trucks accompanied the convoy. All in all, these were significant and alarming reinforcements. Within moments, as expected, attack helicopters were airborne at Nyala airport. I took photos of the helicopters, rockets clearly displayed and Sudanese flags painted on their tails.

The next morning was December 14. I was curious to see whether we had received a complaint that coincided with the troop movement and attack helicopters we saw the previous evening. I hated having to wait to learn where an attack had occurred, knowing there were wounded and displaced people wandering vulnerable out there. But we heard nothing. Our sector commander instead instructed us to head to Adwah to investigate a Janjaweed complaint of stolen cattle.

In Adwah, an armed Janjaweed militia member stopped us on the outskirts of the village. He held out an arm. The other held a Kalashnikov. We rolled down our window so Joseph could address him.

"We are the African Union here to investigate your complaint of stolen livestock."

"Very good. Let me summon the others." Walking several feet away, he fired a few shots in the air.

"That," he said, "was to let my men know that you are not SLA or JEM and that it is okay for them to come out to meet you."

It didn't take long. Almost before the words were out of his mouth, Janjaweed started coming out of the bush from all directions. The straw reeds stood nearly shoulder high, providing cover for the men as they approached on foot, weapons strapped to their backs. Others followed on horses and camels—about 35 in all. We quickly introduced our team. The Janjaweed seemed particularly taken with the new Egyptian monitors, who got big smiles and friendly handshakes from the Arab militiamen. I was surprised because they had never greeted Mohammed with such enthusiasm. On this occasion, he stood to the side without expression.

"Okay," the militia leader stated. "Let us begin." He waited to make sure we were prepared to take notes. "Last week the SLA kidnapped and killed several of our family members. During this attack, a few cattle were also killed. Then, the SLA stole our camels and remaining livestock. We demand that our property be returned." I found it odd that he did not make a similar demand of his kidnapped family members.

"We can show you evidence of the livestock they killed as well as the site where the SLA executed our brothers," he offered. Joseph nodded.

Gesturing, the Janjaweed leader called a rider on horseback over to our gathering. The militia member dismounted, untied a series of cattle carcasses from the back of the horse, and spread them out on the ground before us. Were they joking? One of our monitors lifted the side of a stiff, nearly petrified skin with the tip of his boot. These were not skeletons or even the remains of whole bodies, just five large patches of leather lying together in the dust, all of which could have come from two or three cows. I did not have to be a specialist to see that these remains were significantly older than a week. But we nodded professionally, took some photos, and made a few notes.

"Finished? Now, we shall go to the site of the attack." The Janjaweed leader and a few other militiamen jumped in our vehicles, and the rest guided us by camel and horse to a dry, grassy area perhaps a kilometer or two away. "Here is where we must leave your cars and travel on foot."

As we walked, the Janjaweed pointed out bodies. "Here is one of our brothers who was killed. Here is another. And here is another." The bodies were as much as 300 meters apart. One skeleton was missing its head, its arms bound and pants pulled below the knees. Apparently, the perpetrators had sexually assaulted the individual before executing him. In a nearby ditch, we found a naked skeleton missing one of its legs. Another body lay in a torturous position with broken or dislocated limbs; its skin looked mummified, like tightly stretched parchment. Elsewhere, a dark stain in the soil and two casings from a Kalashnikov marked the site of an execution, but nothing but a few bones remained. We walked for about an hour, identifying several more bodies and becoming increasingly nervous about the situation.

One of the Janjaweed said something in Arabic and pointed at me angrily. I looked up questioningly.

"What did he say?" I asked Anour next to me.

"They don't want you to take pictures." I lowered my camera to see where this was going. Though I needed to document the scene, I wasn't going to defy an armed and fuming Janjaweed member.

Soon enough, the Janjaweed leader and one of his men were in a heated argument with Joseph, Ahmed, and Mohammed. A few militiamen sat on their camels and horses watching the exchange from a distance, weapons at the ready. Terrified, Ibrahim barely said a thing and kept making mistakes in his interpretation. He cowered near Joseph, looking fearfully at the Janjaweed screaming at him. Ahmed quickly relieved him of his duties.

After another ten minutes, Ahmed was finally able to convince the Janjaweed that we needed the photographs to document their complaint in our report.

"Go ahead," their leader disdainfully conceded in my direction. Once the militiamen understood that the photos would validate their claims, they watched my actions with a careful eye. I guess I was a little more tentative than before. Before long, the same leader began pacing around, yelling in Arabic and pointing at me, agitated.

"Okay, what did I do now?" I asked Ahmed.

"They don't seem to believe you are actually taking photos," he replied. The leader came near and made a specific demand. "Take a shot of this corpse here and then show him the photo," Ahmed instructed while trying to calm the leader in Arabic.

I complied as ordered, and turned my digital camera around so that he could see the image I had just captured. Then I quickly reversed through my catalog of shots, proving to him that we were indeed documenting the scene. Satisfied, he walked back to his men. I wiped the sweat from my forehead and rubbed my camera display with a rag.

"Why don't we go get our trucks so we can have them close by—just in case we need to make a fast exit," Ahmed whispered.

"I'm all over that," I breathed.

We returned with the vehicles, meeting the team in another field. I pulled over when I saw the first few bones. Jumping to the ground, I waved for Ahmed to slow down, but he swerved around me and continued on toward our colleagues. He did not realize where he was driving until he stepped from his truck.

"Oh . . . I didn't see," he muttered.

Thousands of human bones were scattered in all directions over an area about 50 meters in diameter. Single rib bones were strewn around an outcropping of rocks. In front of me, a lower jaw bone had fallen beside a foot connected to a single leg. I could see the upper jaw a few meters away, but the remainder of the skull was nowhere to be found. Darkened soil or deflated clothing marked the location of each death.

I could not be certain how long these human remains had been here, but I recalled an attack that reportedly took place at Adwah two weeks earlier involving mass rape and the abduction of 35 people who were never heard from again.

"These are remains of our men. We buried some and left the others for you as evidence," the Janjaweed leader declared. I found it hard to imagine that they would selectively bury their own, leaving others for the vultures until we could get there.

The militia man pointed at what he described as fresh graves. I bent down to stick my hunting knife in the soil, finding it hard as rock and unsuitable for digging. Someone had sprinkled fresh dirt around one site next to a collection of rib bones.

"These are the shoes that belonged to the man buried here." The militia leader produced three flip-flops of different sizes, which he dropped by the purported grave.

We regrouped to ask if the Janjaweed had any further details to report. The commander brought up an incident that reportedly took place either in 2003 or 2004, he couldn't be sure; rebels purportedly stole 1,050 camels and abducted 75 people in an ambush while the nomads were traveling to Libya. The militia leader was furious that the AU had not yet done anything about the situation.

He then leaned in toward us: "We have tracked our camels from Adwah to Jurof, Hamada, and Khor Abeche," he spit out. "Until we retrieve our camels, we will go to these villages, we will rape the women, we will steal their property, we will burn their houses down, and we will kill everyone. No one can stop us. You can't stop us." The Janjaweed commander then looked directly at me, "You bring George Bush here and I . . ." He drew a finger sharply across his throat and gave me a grisly smile. I took a deep breath.

Chapter 26

Later that evening I was delighted when the Egyptians brought out a *shisha*, a large water pipe used socially to smoke fruit-flavored tobacco, and we sat outside one of the tents to talk and smoke from the towering glass. I sat back in a metal folding chair to relax, listening to the mellow chant of the Egyptian album they had playing in their CD player. After some small talk, the Egyptian monitors remarked casually that they had noticed I always knew what was being said in Arabic. By this time I had spent nearly a year in Sudan and was beginning to pick up some of the language. I nodded.

Our conversation eventually turned to a discussion of Islam. I'd spent some time reading about Mohammed and admired him as a spiritual leader. I shared my thoughts openly and asked more questions, to which they enthusiastically responded. The Egyptians claimed radical Islamic fundamentalists had misinterpreted the Koran and what Mohammed had preached. Mohammed, they said, promoted peace. This would be only one of many conversations we had about the beauty of their religion.

Another evening, my Egyptian colleagues concluded definitively that I was Muslim. They also would joke sometimes that I was CIA, noting that my never-ending supply of beer, liquor, and MREs always appeared after my regular meetings with guys from our embassy. I denied their claims, but they weren't buying it. Eventually, we would return to our shisha with a smile.

·   ·   ·

Tensions were soaring, the conflict was escalating, and our team was going to high alert. I was a Marine: I was accustomed to a constant state of readiness. Among my AU teammates, however, I felt an awkward sense of foreboding because we all knew our mission proscribed intervention.

Over numerous visits to Ishma, we had observed a steady flow of GOS reinforcements, including troops, weapons, and vehicles. By now the GOS had brought in nearly 15 huge civilian trucks and another 15 pick-up trucks filled with supplies. We anticipated that government troops might try to bait the SLA and JEM into an attack so they could counterattack in force. We also heard reports that a GOS Mi–8 helicopter had ferried the GOS 16th Division commander to Ishma so he could meet with the GOS brigadier general in charge of the area. I sought any intelligence I could find on their plans, without much success.

The following evening, SLA rebels attacked the GOS position in Ishma. The massive GOS defensive force counterattacked, driving thousands of SLA soldiers 10 kilometers to the east, where the GOS then established a new position outside of Labado. We knew Labado would be the next to fall and tried on several occasions to get to the region to monitor the situation and make our presence known. More than once, when we tried to leave our compound, the state-run fuel company said the fuel pumps were broken.

"What do you mean they're broken?" Ahmed questioned.

"I'm sorry, they're not working right now," the fuel worker insisted.

We were stranded on the tarmac. At that moment, we watched as a GOS Mi–8 transport helicopter touched down to offload its wounded and load new ammunition. The fuel truck headed for the GOS helicopter and began its refueling right in front of us. A few minutes later, an attack helicopter landed to refuel.

"What is this, what is going on here?" Ahmed said to the security man who had joined us.

"The GOS is refueling. We demand that you bring us fuel immediately," Joseph shouted.

The airport worker shrugged and looked at us blankly. "The pumps are not working. We cannot refuel your aircraft."

Joseph was outraged and turned to Mohammed to insist that he straighten out the situation. Mohammed wandered over to the refueling area to talk with the officials. A half hour later, they agreed to let us refuel. The GOS helicopters had long since departed. When we finally got off the ground, heavy fighting was underway, prohibiting us from landing or even flying over the combat zone.

On December 16, I traveled up to El Fashir to escort a fuel convoy and to pick up new vehicles for our sector. I also arranged to pick up my usual shipment of 25 cases of beer, which had come in on a flight the previous evening. Frustrated and reminded of the three-day attack on Alliet in October, I sought out Dan and Oscar, my US contacts from the embassy.

We sat down in my contracting company's compound. They had their own room in which we would regularly meet. Paperwork covered a small table, and a series of charts and maps plastered the cement walls. We walked through the most recent attacks, looking over the maps.

"There's a new class of Janjaweed trainees that has just graduated from the training facility in El Gardut," Oscar informed me. "Intelligence suggests that many of these graduates have trained to be specialists such as snipers or reconnaissance experts. Some militia will move on to special forces schools north of Khartoum, in the desert just south of the Egyptian border. Have you seen any special weapons in the field?

"Yeah, I caught a glimpse of a Janjaweed with a Dragunov in the village of Adwah," I told them.

"Are you sure?" They were amazed.

"Absolutely. One hundred percent sure."

A Dragunov is a Russian-made sniper rifle. It is a highly specialized piece of equipment with a range of about 1,000 meters. They were not often seen in this part of the world. Seeing a Janjaweed militia member with a Dragunov was as significant as discovering an active Al Qaeda training camp. Someone was seriously investing in these Arab nomads—and the destruction of Darfur's black population.

"This is unbelievable," Oscar remarked. "These guys are obviously well trained and getting some major support."

Dan spun around in his chair and pulled his laptop closer. "Take a look at this. A team in North Darfur retrieved this during a field investigation with a Janjaweed member." I looked at the image. There was a scanned version of what looked like an official document with an English translation.

I read it with disbelief. "Damn, can I get a copy of that?" I asked, and plugged in my memory stick. The translation was poor, but its contents were shocking:

THE LIGHT AND FRIGHTFUL FORCES OF MUSTERIHA
Attention of:
Commander, Western Military Area
Commander, Training and Operations Department
Commander, Intelligence and Security Department
Director, Security and Military Intelligence and National Security
Director, Security (AMN IJABI) Organ

Peace and the blessing of God be with you.

Subject: Execution of all directives from the President of the Republic that were issued during a secret meeting in the residence of Gibril Abdallah Ali, in your presence and other officers from the Intelligence and Security Leaders from the Arab States (*in Darfur?*)

Firstly: you are informed that directives have been issued to raise maximum alert for all Arab Leaders in the whole region of Darfur, in the towns and villages, in their province to face the American and European danger (threat) and readiness to go for war and military operations on a large scale. To implement the aims of the Arab Coalition in Darfur and change the demography in Darfur and make it void of any African tribes and face the rebels and destroy them with poisonous weapons.

Secondly: Killings, burning of villages, farms and terrorize and rob properties from African tribes and force them to migrate outside Darfur, killing of intellectuals, the youth that may participate with the rebels in fighting and celebrate by raising the Arab Coalition flag after two years.

Thirdly: Ninety vehicles have been received equipped with Iranian weapons and munitions and materials for the manufacture of rockets and twenty personnel from the forces who are graduates in preparation (*or field*) of traditional poisonous (*chemical*) weapons, and anti-aircraft weapons and

الدائرة الخاصة بالقيادة القطرية التنظيمية

لعناية كل من

السيد قائد المنطقة العسكرية والسيد رئيس منظمة العمليات و التشكيلات ...

... السيد قائد القوة الجوية ... وبعد ...

والموضوع تنفيذ كل التوجيهات الصادرة ...

... في اجتماع السري في ...

...

400 pieces of guns (American Dogs*) through vehicles or El Treifi' Transport Company.

Fourthly: The arrival of vehicles loaded with guns have arrived in Chad and have been handed to the Arabs safely at (Umtiman) to strengthen the Arabs to gain authority.

Fifthly: After graduation of 45,000 men, they were added and merged into the police, military and security organs and are now in position.

Sixthly: Sums of money have been allocated to be transferred to abroad to some Arab countries to destroy the American Interest and some leaders of the Popular Defense Force and these sums of money have been received by the Arab leaders in Chad from Damagha El Jerih (*the Stamp of the Wounded*) Fund and the Amal Benevolent Organization and El Zabair Benevolent Society through Wadi Hawar Popular Agency.

Greeting to all Inspectors of Arab Coalition Work:
1. Wali Northern Darfur
2. El Taiyib El Gadal
3. Abdel Hamid Musa Khasha—Minister of External Trade
4. Husain Gibril
5. All Walis, Minister and Commissioners for the sake of Arab Coalition and brotherhood

Musa Hilal Abdallah—Secretary, Arab Coalition Movement in Darfur

and thanks are due to Abdlla Safi Nur

Lt. Colonel Abdel Wahid Saeed Ali Saeed
Commander
The Light and Frightful Forces
Mustreriah

XXXXXXXXXXXXXXXXXXXX END OF TRANSLATION XXXXXXXXXXXXXXXXXXXX

---

*A Sudanese reference to U.S. weapon systems.

I couldn't believe what I was holding in my hand. Here was clear evidence of orders to commit genocide against the black African tribes of Darfur—*from the government*—"to change the demography," as the directive so clinically put it. I didn't want to seem too amazed that the GOS had held a meeting to hand down its strategy for carrying out widespread ethnic cleansing. So I just said, "I'll keep my ears open for any mention of anything in this document."

.   .   .

After that, I ramped up my efforts to collect information, tracking both teams' investigations so that I could report back to the embassy as well as build a better intelligence picture for our operations on the ground. The only way to stop the violence, I felt now, was to provide our government with the intelligence it needed to intervene forcefully on the diplomatic level. Many of our official AU reports, which should have made it to US officials, seemed to disappear along the lengthy journey to the top. During my time in Darfur, between the two teams in my sector, we wrote more than 80 reports. I later learned that only four reached the American embassy through official channels. My interpretation was that the AU had to balance conflicting interests. On the one hand, it was operating in Sudan at the invitation and approval of the Sudanese government. The members of the AU did not want to be kicked out of the country. On the other hand, they did not want their mission to appear a failure to the international community. I decided to take this responsibility into my own hands. I was on the phone with Oscar and Dan at least thirty minutes a day.

.   .   .

The citizens of Labado and Muhajeriya had requested AU protection out of fear of an imminent attack. Our hands were tied: we were unarmed and still had no mandate to protect. By December 17, the GOS brigade had advanced on Labado, and Janjaweed militia were working side by side with GOS forces to loot and burn the village. Team D conducted a brief pass over Labado and witnessed two helicopter gunships flying over the village and an Mi–8 parked on the ground. Simultaneously, the GOS had deployed a company of 300 men to travel southwest of Labado to attack the neighboring village of Marla, with a population of 1,000 people.

The government's eastward offensive appeared designed to isolate all SLA and JEM forces in their final stronghold of Muhajeriya, a city of 40,000 people. Back in October, the GOS had moved west from the Darfur-Kordofan border. Now it was systematically destroying all villages along the railway that ran southeast out of Nyala. Marla and Suleia were on the south side of the railway, and GOS forces had already taken Suleia. On the north side stood Ishma, Um Zaifa, Hashaba, and Kokono—all virtually destroyed in previous weeks. Then came Labado and, finally, Muhajeriya. These were not small attacks carried out by small militias. This was a large-scale military operation led by battalions on the move.

.   .   .

Our sector commander assigned our team to damage assessment in Marla. I was disappointed that he had not sent us to Labado since we had already been dealing with the brigadier general for some time. I talked with John and Dave, but unfortunately they could not sway the sector commander. They explained that our team had been especially effective in our investigative documentation, which is what our commander needed now in Marla. We were assigned there, while Team D would monitor the ongoing fighting in Labado.

We assembled three vehicles, including one troop carrier to transport a protection team of 10 Nigerian soldiers to accompany our monitoring team of 13 men. With the conflict escalating, we felt it necessary to strengthen our protection force whenever we went into the field.

We knew where the GOS military position was located, so we headed there first. As we neared our destination, I saw several people in military uniform running from the village with loot under their arms. I slowed to snap a few shots. We pulled up to the GOS military position, where men were dug into a trench; four vehicles with mounted weapons were parked behind them. One soldier hurriedly pulled a colorful rolled carpet into his trench as we approached. The officers, of Arab descent, rose from their crouching positions under a central tree, and the GOS company commander and his deputy walked out to meet us.

He introduced himself as Omar Bashier Al Nur and his deputy commander as Mahmoud Mahamed Tom. Joseph asked him to explain his mission.

"My orders are to secure the area so that the police can establish a post in the town," he explained. It sounded familiar: the GOS used the same rationale in Suleia and Amaka Sara. He told us his forces were part of the brigade that was now positioned in Labado.

"Were you provoked?" Joseph asked, looking for a specific motivation for this attack, though we knew the government needed no excuse.

"There were no rebel fighters when we arrived; therefore, we had no need to fire into the village."

Joseph confronted him. "Your men are looting. We have seen them."

The commander replied with confidence, "My troops don't loot." Smoke rose in the village beyond us. We needed to see the destruction up close.

Back in town, walking up a row of shops, we found every metal door ajar, locks shot off, and loot scattered everywhere. We heard gunshots elsewhere in the village and saw widespread damage from bullets, but could not find any spent rounds. We saw holes in the sand caused by rockets, but no rockets themselves. It was as if the attackers had picked up every single piece of evidence that could connect their weapons to the attack.

Brazenly, the GOS troops continued to burn and loot the village even as we conducted our investigation. We came across one soldier setting fire to a food storage facility. He had just lit sacks of peanuts on fire and closed the door to walk away. Ahmed rushed toward him yelling for him to put it out. Startled, the man initially began shoveling sand on the blaze, then his efforts slowed, and he shrugged and said that he could not put it out. I snapped a shot of the soldier in his army-green uniform, the fire growing behind him. We walked around the back side of the structure and found another line of corrugated metal shacks with their contents spilling out into the sand. What wasn't burned resembled a landfill.

Compound after compound in the village was smoldering. A lone donkey, long abandoned, was the only remaining life. The scene here in Marla was familiar and heartbreaking. Charred foundations, burned-out vehicles, smoking trees and charcoal fence posts amid the ash that now blanketed an abandoned settlement. We returned to our vehicles.

We had noticed that Marla had its own IDP camp, which we approached from the other side of the village. Located on the edge of the town, the camp now hosted the residents who had not been able to flee the attack. As we drove into the camp, I leaned out of my window to call to a woman walking by. I always approached a woman because it was unlikely that she would be a spy for the GOS. You could never be sure with a man. Mohammed was in the other vehicle, which gave me more latitude to ask GOS-related questions without his intimidation. We still had found no bullets or evidence of rockets. I asked the woman if the children and other villagers had collected any shrapnel. She replied that they had and agreed to have the children bring it to us.

We stopped outside a medical tent, where we found a nurse's assistant treating a man who had been shot in the head. The medical personnel from the NGO had left the region a few days earlier, and this assistant had enough basic medical skill to treat the remaining wounded. The man with the head wound sat on the ground bundled in a dark green winter jacket with a hood. Five bandages held a piece of gauze to his scalp. The villager explained that he had been shot by the GOS when he tried to fetch water from the local water hole. The GOS was now barring these IDPs from using their only source of water.

We emerged from the tent to find a crowd gathering in wait. The woman I had spoken with on the side of the road gestured to the children. One by one, they stepped forward to make a pile of shrapnel on the ground before us. The majority of the air ammunition was Chinese or Russian, based on the writing on the shrapnel. They brought us shells, pieces of rockets, and dozens of flechettes. Helicopter gunships typically carried four rocket pods, each of which contained twenty rockets. Each rocket could house more than 500 of the tiny twisted nails. The helicopters would release their rockets to shred the bodies of their targets on the ground.

Mohammed grew defensive.

"We don't know where this came from," he said. "These people could have saved this from other villages. No one can prove this came from here!" He would continue to debate the evidence up to the submission of our final report, writing an addendum disputing the findings.

We made a final sweep through the village, snapping pictures of many more soldiers looting and running into the bush with arms full of goods.

Though they hurried away from us, they seemed less concerned about our witnessing their activities than they had been in previous months. We passed the village food storage facility, which by now had burned to the ground. The unfired bricks had cracked and crumbled from the intense heat, and the roof had collapsed into the flames. This store of food, which its rural farmers had so recently harvested, was expected to have lasted until the next harvest. Now, famine was a real threat, with Marla's suddenly vulnerable population dependent, at least for a year, on international humanitarian aid.

We were silent during most of the two-hour drive back to Nyala. Back in Operations, John said that our AU air officer had something to report. The AU had assigned us an air officer to coordinate travel, maintenance, and all other logistical needs from a small office at the airport. When he first arrived in Nyala, John and I had asked the officer to observe every move of the GOS; we also made a point of keeping him well supplied with beer. Today, he had witnessed the GOS offload an estimated 5 metric tons of ammunition from an Antonov 26. We also had numerous reports of C–130s with Saudi flags painted on their tails bringing in ammunition. Our AU officer got a glimpse of their flight manifest and recorded the tail numbers of each aircraft, which he turned over to us. Every bit of data we could collect was important: it would tell us how many gunships there were, help establish the government's patterns of attacks, teach us about the pilots and who directed them, and thus give us a clearer picture of the government's capabilities in carrying out its offensive strikes. I made another call to Dan and Oscar in El Fashir.

Chapter 27

The smoke rising from Labado filled the sky with haze, and from afar the city resembled the impact zone of an atomic bomb. It was still late morning. Though the relentless glare of the sun was normally at its peak by this time, today the smoke cast a thick, grim shadow that covered the land like an approaching hurricane. It was the second day of this battle; Labado was still under siege by GOS forces. Military aircraft were flying around the area, including Mi–24 and Mi–8 helicopters. I was able to capture many photos of GOS gunships attacking the city. We were just 1,000 feet above the village, and we watched first-hand the attack helicopters firing their rockets.

A wide ring of trenches and individual holes surrounded dozens of trucks. We estimated the GOS troop strength at 4,500 men, including 1,500 Janjaweed. I could easily distinguish the Janjaweed positions from the GOS military positions. The Janjaweed were dressed in mixed attire and walking in and out of their defensive positions to add to the growing pile of loot before them. While Janjaweed were often well trained for offensive strikes, this was the first time that we had seen them digging in alongside the GOS in a defensive position. Their positions were what we in the Marine Corps would describe as "undisciplined"—made up of hand-dug holes without any semblance of unity. In contrast, the GOS forces occupied square holes of equal size and spacing, every two situated side-by-side and linked by a trench for moving under cover. The entire force was positioned in a huge ring that, judging from above, measured approximately 1,000 meters by 500 meters. It was chilling how many forces the GOS had mobilized for this attack.

Returning to Nyala in the afternoon, we spotted a military convoy traveling along the road from El Fashir to Labado. The convoy contained 19 Land Cruisers, each carrying 10 troops, and four large trucks packed with up to

50 troops each. Each vehicle also carried heavy weapons, including six Dushkas, one B–10 recoilless rifle, and two Katyusha rocket pods. Meanwhile, Mi–8 helicopters continued their flights back and forth from the front lines to Nyala, offloading injured troops onto stretchers and reloading with fuel and ammunition. The injured GOS soldiers meant the SLA was fighting back. The military convoy meant the GOS was not giving up. This battle was not going to end any time soon.

The sector headquarters team flew another air patrol in the evening to Muhajeriya and Labado to observe any change in the situation. They invited me to join them to take pictures. The AU was finally recognizing the need for photographic documentation, now that all-out war had broken out in the region.

We were 1,500 feet above Labado, which was still burning and appeared to be totally destroyed. Again, we caught a helicopter gunship circling the town at about 50 feet and firing rockets into the village, and we spotted another Mi–8 on the ground. We knew the GOS helicopter gunship and Antonov pilots were Russian, just like our pilots. In fact, our pilots had previously overheard the Antonov pilots speaking in their native tongue, coordinating with the attack helicopters to fly low after a bombing run to strafe the villagers. These men were mercenaries. As we were circling above the conflict, I leaned over to our pilot and asked him, "What would you do if one of those gunships down there came up behind you?"

Without looking at me, he pulled a body armor vest from behind his seat and sat on it, offering me one word in response: "Pray."

In the morning, we returned to Muhajeriya to speak with the SLA, the JEM, and the local village defense unit. Our objective was to get an approximate death toll and a count of how many people were wounded so we could attempt to escort a medical NGO to the area to provide immediate assistance. We also wanted to determine how many people had fled Labado and where they had relocated so that we could notify the humanitarian aid groups providing food, water, and other resources to IDPs.

The mood was understandably somber in Muhajeriya. There were few villagers who initially met our helicopter. We asked a young man to get the SLA. We waited for nearly thirty minutes as a large circle of people gathered around us quietly.

Finally, a group of 20 SLA and JEM soldiers drove into the village to speak with us. We formed a tight circle with the rebel leaders, omdas, and sheikhs, sitting in the shade on the ground cross-legged. About 50 villagers moved closer, standing around us. We began to ask their leaders questions about what had happened in Labado.

They reported that 400 wounded people in need of medical attention had already arrived in Muhajeriya. An estimated 85 people wounded in the attack remained outside of Labado, unable to flee, and GOS soldiers were preventing them from receiving any medical aid. They had been rounded up by the GOS and taken to a nearby wadi. Some had been executed and the rest left to die.

Looking up behind me, I noticed the group had grown to about 150 people, now standing nearly 15 deep around us. Their mood quickly turned from sadness to anger. Villagers began chiming in, interrupting their sheikhs. First, they made their comments quietly, but soon their voices started to rise. The SLA and JEM leaders, respecting the positions of the omdas and sheikhs, let them lead the discussion. Several times the tribal leaders raised their hands, and the group calmed down briefly before rising to anger again.

Then one villager shouted, "You haven't done anything to stop the killing and destruction of our villages. This has been going on for months, and all you ever do is come and ask us how many were killed and wounded and take your pictures and leave. Then the next week another village is attacked."

"What good are you?" another screamed. "You can't protect us!"

And another: "We told you that Labado was going to be attacked. We asked you for protection and still you couldn't protect them. If you can't help them, how can you help us? They're coming here next!"

The villagers were frantic. Ibrahim was trying to focus on the core conversations between the tribal leaders and Joseph, and he skipped over much of the yelling. But I could see the panic in the villagers' eyes. Sitting next to Ahmed, I leaned over to get his insight. "Ahmed, these people are really angry. They want someone's head, and I don't want it to be ours. What can we do?"

"I don't know, Captain Brian. It's not looking good."

The crowd surged forward. I stood up and a number of other monitors did likewise to avoid people stumbling over them. "You must get our wounded from Labado!" they screamed.

Joseph spoke through our interpreter, "We are doing everything in our power to help. We need to know exactly where this wadi is. And we need to know how bad the injuries are so we can be prepared to help." He glanced at me and Ahmed. The people were turning hostile. A number of them had Kalashnikovs and pushed their way to the front of the crowd, demanding that we depart immediately to bring their people back. Joseph and Ahmed again explained that we needed more information.

"We can't carry that many people in our helicopter," Ahmed told them. If we knew exactly where they were, we could get medical personnel from the NGOs in Nyala, where our base was located, and bring another helicopter to assist. That was the best we could do. But I could see many villagers frowning and shaking their heads. Our reasoning, in their eyes, was just another excuse for inaction.

I looked at Ahmed: "We have got to change this situation now."

Ahmed grabbed Joseph by the back of his arm. "We have to go." Joseph nodded. We broke through the circle and headed toward our helicopter. Walking backward we thanked them hurriedly for their time. I could see the expression of contempt in the face of a man just a few feet from me.

"What about our wounded?" another man shouted.

Joseph responded that we would go look for them right away. Ahmed and I were nodding.

"That's not good enough," one of the villagers barked. He stepped forward with his weapon drawn.

At that moment, John called my satellite phone from the operations room. I swung around my backpack and fumbled in the pocket for it. I felt a burst of relief. I could receive calls on this particular phone, but I could not place them.

"John, we've got some angry people here. There are wounded in Labado that can't get out. We need to get Team D to go look for them. Apparently they are stranded on the outskirts of Labado, but within the GOS position. We're told the GOS captured them and are holding them in a nearby wadi."

"What do you mean we can't leave?" I heard a monitor say.

"We are taking your helicopter to find our people. You are going to stay here under guard as insurance that nothing will happen," Ibrahim tentatively translated a villager's order.

"Hold on a moment, John," I said, lowering the phone.

"Ahmed, what the hell is going on?"

"They're refusing to let us leave and want to take our helicopter to find their people themselves," he called as he walked toward me.

"John, this is bad. I think the village is trying to hold us hostage. Let me see if I can handle it. Call me back in fifteen minutes. If I don't answer, send a team in to get us."

I called over to our three Nigerian protection forces and told them to keep everyone away from the helicopter. They were young, maybe eighteen years old, and they looked extremely nervous as they watched the group of 150 enraged men with weapons.

I grabbed Anour and Ali and walked away from the rest of the group to speak privately. "I don't believe this," I said. "You need to get your commanders over here immediately." While the SLA was not responsible for the hostage threat, its leaders were doing nothing to help convince the villagers that we should be allowed to leave.

Our monitors returned quickly with the SLA commander. I turned and looked him in the eye. "Ok, what are you going to do about this? You are the SLA. If you tell them we can go, we can go." He looked uncertain.

"Let me get this straight," I continued. "You are holding an international monitoring team hostage. You are holding an American hostage. Do I have this right?"

"Well," he faltered.

"Do you know what that means?" My voice was rising. I took my satellite phone out of my pocket and held it up as if I was about to dial. "Don't make me make this call. You and the rest of the SLA and JEM will be extremely sorry." His eyes widened. "I am going to call and tell these guys that you are holding an American hostage." I looked up at the sky to an imaginary satellite. I was almost shouting now. "They already know. Don't make me make this call. You have five minutes." I walked away.

Anour and Ali turned and started debating aggressively in Arabic. I could see that they were insisting that their commander let the team go. A few minutes later the SLA commander returned to the group to instruct the villagers to release us without further confrontations. A few of the more aggressive villagers shook their heads. Some of them continued to shout that they needed to take matters into their own hands. The SLA commander appeared to be explaining the impact of interfering with American monitors, since all eyes seemed to turn toward me. Finally, they relented. The SLA commander walked toward me and said we could go.

"Thank you," I said. "Please convince these villagers that we are here to help. We will try in every way that we can, but we cannot be forced to do something that we have no mandate to do. Look, we are traveling to Labado right now, we already have a team on the ground there, and we will all begin a search immediately for the 85 missing people. Let us do this out of good will and not by force."

He nodded, and I joined the rest of my team members, who were already walking away quickly. We jumped into our helicopter. John called back as we lifted off above Muhajeriya. He laughed when I told him I had threatened to "make the call."

"What would you have done if they called your bluff?"

"Prayed like hell you would call back," I said.

.   .   .

We returned to Labado, flying a wide circle around the city searching for bodies or groups of wounded people gathered outside the village. The smoke was still thick, and fire raged throughout the town. We could see no groups of displaced or wounded people from the air. Team D had headed off to Labado earlier that morning. John had told me over the phone that the GOS commander had refused the team access to the village and prevented them from speaking with Janjaweed militia leaders. The brigadier general insisted that if team members attempted to enter the city, their safety could not be assured. It was now early afternoon, and we decided to land to provide support for Team D and to see if we could find any of the wounded still stranded in the village. John had called ahead to alert them that we were on our way.

We landed on the outskirts of the village near Team D, whose members were standing with their vehicles next to the GOS troops. Reunited, we caught them up on the situation in Muhajeriya.

We noticed that the GOS had stolen a number of Médecins Sans Frontières tents, which now formed the officers' quarters and operations tents in the center of the military encampment. We asked a GOS soldier to tell the brigadier general that we wanted to speak with him.

Before long, the general appeared, clearly not happy to see us again. We confronted him about the wounded, and he denied any knowledge of them. Joseph was livid: "This is a blatant ceasefire violation. Look at this village. It has been burning for three days. There's nothing that could have provoked this."

The general clearly felt no remorse, explaining in a matter-of-fact tone: "This is my mission. I am a military man. I'm going to follow my orders and continue this attack." I knew what he meant: Muhajeriya, the next village along the road, was already in his crosshairs. Muhajeriya had 40,000 inhabitants, IDPs who had recently fled Labado, and several thousand rebel troops, who almost certainly would fight to the death. It was going to be a very ugly battle.

"Is that all?" the general asked impatiently. I cursed under my breath as we let him go.

Labado was burning in all directions. The heavy smoke stung my eyes and clung to my clothing. I walked a few meters away to get a better view of the activity. GOS vehicles roamed around, while steady streams of militia members dumped their loot in front of the Janjaweed's dug-in positions, then wandered back to the village for more. We could hear sporadic machine gun bursts within the town. I expected they were executions. The brigadier general walked over to stand beside me.

I called Ali over to help translate. I wasn't going to pass up this opportunity to confront a GOS general. "Why are you not stopping your men from looting?"

"These are not my men," he replied in a flat voice.

"But they are in uniform," I argued.

"Anybody can get a uniform. If you had money, you could get a uniform." At that moment, a group of men from behind his defensive position exited the area in a vehicle headed toward Labado.

Pointing, I asked, "Are those your men?"

"Yes," he said, "those are my men. They are going to fetch water." I watched as they stopped 75 meters away, entered a hut to retrieve some property, and drove away after setting the home on fire.

"Then why don't you stop them?" I cried in desperation.

"Oh, those are not my men," he said casually, changing his story. I raised my camera to take a photograph. He lifted his hand and shook his finger in front of me, clicking his tongue. Neither of us said a word. I lowered my camera as a crew of Janjaweed rolled by us in a vehicle filled with loot.

.   .   .

Later that evening, the headquarters team conducted another air patrol to Muhajeriya and Labado with the aim of escorting medical staff to care for the wounded. The AU normally prohibited us from escorting anyone by helicopter. However, our headquarters approved this special mission, given the severity of the situation. In Labado, the brigadier general refused them safe entry to the town. Meeting with a group of women on the outskirts, the team learned that all the men had fled or had been killed and confirmed that many casualties remained within the village. After they took off for Nyala, a shot fired from the village punctured the helicopter's tail boom. If it had hit a hydraulic line or a fuel tank, the helicopter could have crashed.

The AU finally obtained access to Labado the following day, after a threatening fly-by from a gunship and serious negotiating effort. After three days of fighting, the village was almost entirely destroyed. Shooting, burning, and looting continued, and the few villagers the AU patrol spotted ran away at the sight of the group in military uniform. At the same time, another team escorted MSF's medical staff to Muhajeriya to care for the wounded. The villagers and rebel groups angrily informed the AU that it was no longer welcome since it had failed to stop the GOS attacks. They even went so far as to suggest a cause and effect: the AU left an area and the village was promptly attacked. They were shouting for the UN or the EU. They wanted someone with armed forces. On that point, they would get no argument from me.

Labado had fallen. The success of the GOS attack had completely undermined our authority. Furthermore, the lack of any intervention by an international community that had helped to establish the failed Ceasefire Agreement sent a loud message to the GOS: there was no meaningful opposition to its systematic genocide.

Chapter 28

When John went on leave sometime before Christmas, I agreed to take over his position in the operations room until he returned. I was glad to have a break from the field. If we were ever going to do anything, we needed a better overall understanding of the conflict. I could help with this now that I had greater access to both teams. I continued work on our diagram of the GOS command structure. I wanted to try to predict future movements. One thing I did know was that Muhajeriya was next on its list.

About this time, our sector commander informed us that his superiors had reassigned him and that we would receive a replacement within a week. Our new sector commander was also Nigerian, but higher ranking. His name was Colonel Mohammed. We liked our existing sector commander, but it was normal for staff to transition. A few days after Colonel Mohammed arrived, Dave visited me.

"I've heard the new commander doesn't like Westerners too much," he said. "He thinks that the Westerners are trying to take over the AU mission. Apparently he's been talking about prohibiting you from operating on the ground or having access to information. Just wanted to give you a heads up."

"Thanks," I said, shaking my head.

As Dave turned to leave, he added, "Oh yeah, I also heard the colonel mention something else about watching out for the white guys. That includes me, too, but I guess since I'm South African, I have a little bit more credibility. You keep your information coming my way and I'll keep my information coming your way."

Over the next few days, my interaction with the new sector commander was less than enjoyable. He would not speak to me directly. After our first meeting in the operations room, as I was leaving he turned to Dave and said, "What is he doing in here? He's a monitor. He should stay out of the operations room." I was pissed. There was no way I was going to stop doing my work. The AU wasn't doing enough as it was without this commander throwing obstacles in front of its monitors. I didn't want to provoke him though, so I would sneak into the operations room only when I could see him in his nearby trailer office.

Within days, Colonel Mohammed had ordered a mosque built within the AU camp. This decision did not bother me in itself, though some of the Christian monitors asked why we could not then build a church. There were many mosques in town, but there was no church in Nyala. What worried me was the things the commander was focusing his energy on. He refused to authorize any patrols on Fridays, even if an attack was ongoing. Friday is a holy day in the Islamic faith, and we usually had the day off. But if there was something significant happening, we had always gone out on patrol anyway. Finally, he removed our Dutch monitor from the team. He said that there were enough monitors and he did not need any Western monitors in the field. Before long the Dutch monitor resigned in frustration.

John was on vacation, Dave and I were in the operations room, and our Dutch monitor was history. Suddenly, not only were all the white personnel restricted from the field, but there were also no longer any EU or US monitors operating in our sector.

.   .   .

I called Gretchen and Andrew back in the States. I needed some advice. The racial discrimination of our sector commander was infuriating. He continued to isolate the US and EU representatives and decrease their involvement in the mission's affairs. Our impact on the ground was already doubtful. Restricting our access to the flow of information affected the trust that we had gained among the NGOs and UN organizations over the past six months. They were our eyes and ears on the ground. If our communications link were broken or relationships discarded, all of our information would dry up.

Gretchen was speechless after I told her about the attacks on Labado and recounted my brief experience as a hostage in Muhajeriya. "I can't believe it.

I hope you're taking notes about everything that is happening," she finally said. I assured her that my notebooks were filling up.

"I know the GOS forces are going to attack Muhajeriya next," I said, "and I know the Janjaweed are going to move on Jurof, Hamada, and Khor Abeche. But our leaders won't believe me and they won't do anything about it."

"Look," she said, "what's the highest purpose here? Maybe it's to honor your commitment to your contracting company for one year in Sudan and that's it. Maybe it's to do the best you can while you are part of the AU mission even though you are under the restrictions of its authority. Do you have a greater moral responsibility to these people as fellow human beings who are being slaughtered? You have to figure out what feels right. Perhaps when your time there is done or you can't do any more, you can come home and do something about this in other ways. Nobody knows about this—or not enough people anyway."

.   .   .

Our teams monitored Labado daily, ensuring that the GOS brigade was not yet advancing on Muhajeriya. The GOS forces appeared to be consolidating their encampment closer to the core of the village, while the brigadier general continued to say that he would hold his position until ordered otherwise. On one visit, the brigadier general announced that they were going to forcibly relocate approximately 3,000 IDPs to a camp near Nyala via 25 commercial trucks. Over the next week, several air patrols verified that the village was nearly deserted and that the GOS was still burning the town, compound by compound.

Marla was faring no better. As of the fourth day after the attack, the town was 50 percent burned and looted and completely abandoned. GOS forces still maintained their established position within the town, where a police unit had joined them. They were reportedly harassing and beating the IDPs on the outskirts and continuing to refuse them access to their only water source. One man was beaten to death by the GOS as he tried to get water from the town well. By the end of December, the Government of Sudan had given the remaining occupants of the Marla IDP camp seventy-two hours to leave.

The GOS apparently attacked three villages south of Marla as well. IDPs from those villages, along with those few remaining in Marla, would doubt-less join the displaced from Labado at Kalma Camp outside Nyala. In fact, the government appeared to be attempting to isolate all IDPs in South Dar-fur in that one camp.

The village of Duma also continued to fall victim to repeated attacks. De-spite the growing frustration of the residents and their leader at our lim-ited response, we sent regular patrols to Duma. Over several visits, we heard reports of Janjaweed militia stealing livestock, kidnapping villagers, and rap-ing women and girls. On one occasion, the police arrested numerous villagers when they tried to go to Nyala. Unable to travel safely to trade, the people of Duma requested urgent humanitarian aid to help them survive. No mat-ter how many complaints were lodged, there were no brakes on the attacks and other ceasefire violations; they simply continued, almost on a daily basis.

One day the GOS invited our monitors to the PDF headquarters in Nyala to witness the voluntary surrender of 80 Janjaweed. Despite the blatant at-tacks and open looting, the GOS guys seemed to feel that it was important—if only occasionally—to demonstrate that they were complying with the ceasefire's requirement that the Janjaweed disarm. I asked Ahmed how it went when he returned.

"It was completely fake," he said. "No way those guys were Janjaweed." Apparently, the GOS had paraded around men holding old, decrepit weapons. After the official surrender, the GOS stated that it would release the men once their registration was complete. This was par for the course by this time; nothing surprised me.

.   .   .

Christmas came and went. We drank and partied and listened to music—and we tried to escape. We celebrated Christmas in style on the largest beach in the world, throwing our biggest barbeque yet. People came in from all parts of the sector for the feast, creating a line of at least 30 NGO vehicles snaking through our compound. We grilled goat legs and chickens and offered our guests multiple cases of free beer. Even the Muslims celebrated Christmas with us. With the exception of John, all of my colleagues usually spent this day in the searing heat of the equator or in the southern hemisphere's summer. Only for me was it strange to be playing beach volleyball, barefoot, in the sand on Christmas day.

. . .

A few nights later, Dave and I had an intriguing hour-and-a-half-long chat with a local tradesman who gave us in-depth information on the Janjaweed leadership. The tradesman delivered supplies to our camp, and we'd developed a relationship with him over the past few months; by now we considered him a credible source of intelligence. He'd received his training in the GOS military and suggested he may have served in its Special Forces branch. He had worked mostly in the south, around Juba, but his unit had reported directly to the military command in Khartoum, not to a regional force.

"The Janjaweed are primarily made up of the Julul Tribe. The Mahamit and Regat tribes also participate. Some members of the Rezigat and Miseriya tribes are involved as well, but only in small numbers. The GOS security officers in each region recruit the Janjaweed, and the most senior security officer has full operational control and command over that militia force.

"Originally, the GOS had simply paid the Janjaweed to raid and attack. Over time, they also decided to provide further training—to improve the nomads' military effectiveness. The principal Janjaweed training center is located in El Gardut," he confirmed. He gave us the names of the main Janjaweed leaders in the Nyala area.

"As more and more Janjaweed have graduated from training," he told us, "the GOS has realized it is becoming increasingly expensive to pay the nomads to attack. Instead, they have switched to a payment-in-kind system; the militias are now allowed to take anything they want during the raids. Only high-ranking officers continue to receive salaries as well as a cut of the loot."

The tradesman added, "The weapons and ammunition used by the Janjaweed come from a number of sources, including GOS-appointed governors, the police, and the PDF commanders in the area. However, all aircraft in Darfur operate under the direct control of Khartoum, with no regional command."

I was really excited about the intelligence he was providing and passed all information to Dan and Oscar. The tradesman was the first real "asset" I had identified and developed while operating in Nyala, and I hoped that he would continue to trust us and feed us valuable information.

New Year's Eve was a night of debauchery above the city of Nyala—a rooftop party featuring locally brewed alcohol, children throwing rocks onto the roof, and Middle Eastern techno. It was amazing no one fell off the roof. I woke up under the harsh Sudanese sun, wondering where the hell I was. And then I remembered. *That's exactly where I am.*

.　　.　　.

Our new sector commander was wearing me down. When our role should have been expanding, he was tying our hands. Samaritan's Purse, an international relief organization doing good work in Darfur, had reported an ambush on the Nyala–El Fashir road directly to the sector commander. One person was killed; two wounded people were kidnapped by men reportedly dressed in GOS uniforms. But Colonel Mohammed had refused to assign a team to investigate it.

"You won't believe the nerve of this guy," I told Gretchen on the phone one night. "Even today, an escort patrol to help another NGO travel safely into the field was cancelled at the last minute because he said he didn't approve it. We'd been planning this patrol for days, and he'd already even approved it. I swear he's bipolar. We did nothing but sit around all day!" I was pacing around my tent.

"The NGO continued its convoy alone. It risked ambush—that's how badly the IDPs needed the food and supplies. I mean, if we are going to continue to have the support and trust of the NGOs and the people of Darfur, things like this just cannot happen!" I was furious.

"When information is passed to him about things happening on the ground he ignores it," I continued. "We all understand that the NGOs and even the UN sometimes exaggerate the situation, but when over the course of a few days, three NGOs and two UN organizations report the same incident, it's at least worth checking out to let these organizations know we're here to assist them. He's on some damn power trip!"

By the end of the week, John had come back to take over his position within Operations. Even so, Colonel Mohammed would not let me back into the field. Some days, I did very little other than lift weights and jog, slipping into the operations room when the colonel was not around. In the evenings, after dinner, the Egyptians and other AU monitors would join us to smoke a shisha.

"Why are we here?" The Egyptians were asking more frequently. "We've only been here a month, and we're not doing anything to protect these people." I never knew how to respond.

I spent a lot of time talking with the Egyptians, who spoke English well and wanted to go to the US someday. They saw themselves as closer to the West than most of the rest of Africa. As I got more comfortable with them, I began to ask them for more information about the GOS, what they were doing, or what they had heard. They knew that I was close to the JEM and SLA and asked me questions as well.

"Captain Brian, do you think Israel is supplying the rebel forces with weapons?" one of them asked.

"No way," I said. "Do you think if Israel was supplying them with weapons they would be walking around with rusty old Kalashnikovs? They would have surface-to-air missiles that they would be using to shoot helicopter gunships out of the sky." Good point, they agreed.

Chapter 29

On January 5, 2005, one monitoring team conducted a routine patrol to Jurof, one of the villages threatened by the Janjaweed in retaliation for their stolen camels. The villagers reiterated the story we had heard several days earlier from Samaritan's Purse about an attack in a nearby village. Apparently, GOS soldiers in a vehicle showed up and started shooting wildly. One civilian was killed and two wounded, both kidnapped. They also informed us that an Arab militia had abducted eight women two days later. When the monitors returned to operations and reported their investigation, I felt my stomach sink. I was certain the GOS and Janjaweed were trying to provoke the SLA and JEM to attack so that they could counterattack with force as they did in Labado.

A few days later, during a routine patrol to Adwah, a team met with the Janjaweed commander who had given us a tour of the bone fields to assess the militia's situation. The commander reminded the team of the militia's 2004 complaint to the AU about 1,050 camels being stolen and 75 people being kidnapped en route to Libya. They also reported the more recent theft of camels from the area. He repeated his threat: if the rebels didn't return their people and their camels, he would attack Hamada Forest, Khor Abeche, and Muhajeriya. He was prepared to move today but had heard the AU was coming, so he decided to give us one more chance. He announced again that he would attack each village, kill all inhabitants, and burn the towns to the ground.

Finally, in an unprecedented move, the AU headquarters in Khartoum announced that within the week 70 AU soldiers and a monitoring team of 10 men would deploy to Labado. In addition, 35 soldiers with a civilian contracting team would head to Muhajeriya. Headquarters assigned the civilian contracting team the officially authorized job of establishing a base in the village, which gave the AU a reason to deploy an armed protection force. Though this force still could not engage directly to stop an ongoing attack, the hope was that its presence could deter an offensive strike.

Remarkably, neither the Janjaweed nor the Sudanese government advanced. After about a week of our AU presence in the villages, the GOS forces simply consolidated their position in Labado. Within two weeks, about 3,000 people returned to Labado to rebuild, and AU headquarters was able to negotiate a complete withdrawal of government troops from the region.

Our deterrent had actually worked. As far as I was concerned, with a force of around 25,000 troops, the AU could establish peace and security throughout all Darfur. I was not sure the AU had that many trained troops, but it had demonstrated a capacity to deliver on requests for reinforcements. By this time, the AU had 2,000 protection forces assigned to the monitoring mission in Nyala. Now we needed trained AU forces to prevent Janjaweed attacks to the north in Hamada, Jurof, and Khor Abeche.

There had been multiple signals that these villages were in danger, including the explicit warnings of the Janjaweed commander and the shooting and abductions that occurred near Jurof. In the operations room, Dave and I evaluated the maps and the data. We could predict that Hamada would be first, given the size and location of the village; that would position the Janjaweed for attacks on the larger towns of Jurof and Khor Abeche. I approached Colonel Mohammed, laying out the information and insisting that we bring in a team and protection force to deter the attack. He dismissed the idea out of hand.

"Mark my words," I said. "Hamada will be attacked and destroyed within two weeks."

Colonel Mohammed looked at me with an expression of contempt and exasperation. "How is it you think you can predict what the GOS or Janjaweed will do? And you have no place telling me what to do." He walked away.

That same day, Colonel Mohammed cancelled two scheduled patrols, including one to the Kalma IDP camp to investigate a reported shooting by GOS police. I could not understand why. The IDPs had been herded into this camp, and the GOS police had established an outpost in it, claiming they would offer protection from the Arab nomads. We all knew this was a lie.

A small contingent of seven to ten policemen situated in the center of a camp housing possibly 175,000 people could do nothing to prevent attacks from Janjaweed along the perimeter. Kalma Camp was no safe haven at all.

I called Gretchen and Andrew. "My contract is up in less than three weeks. I think I'm coming home," I said. "I can't be part of this mission and let these people die. I'd rather be home watching it on the BBC."

"Brian, there is so little information in the media on what you are seeing," Gretchen said. "Maybe there is some way to get your message out once you get back. I know there are journalists interested in your story. I've spoken to one. He really gets your security and safety concerns. He could release some of your photos or stories anonymously, if you want. Just think about it."

There was a pause. "Okay, G. I'll think about it. But right now I just want to get out of here."

I went outside my tent and sat on the ground. I knew I did not want to be in Darfur any longer, but I was also pretty certain I did not want to speak with the media. The Marine in me had strong faith that if I could ensure the intelligence I was collecting could get high enough up the political or diplomatic chain of command, something would happen. I felt uncomfortable going outside this authority. I had a code of conduct to follow. What's more, going public could endanger my colleagues on the ground. I just needed to go home and clear my head. I couldn't think anymore.

A few days later, one of the top executives from my civilian contracting company arrived from the US to visit our operations on the ground. Arriving from the airport, he stepped out of his Land Cruiser accompanied by a woman who served as director of Africa for the company. I had met with her in Washington and also during her frequent visits to the region.

"This is Captain Brian Steidle, one of our American monitors," she said proudly.

The executive seemed to saunter as he walked over to shake my hand and said casually, "Oh, Brian, nice to meet you." He was wearing what looked like a safari outfit he ordered straight from a catalog: a bright white short-sleeve, button-up shirt with khaki pants. He was the cleanest man in Darfur that day. There was something about him I didn't like.

"I heard you've seen some interesting things here," he said, smiling, as if there was some private joke between us.

"Interesting?" I asked. "Interesting?" I repeated. "Hmm. That's not exactly the word I would use to describe it," I said, looking him in the eye.

I turned and walked away. This was the boss of a massive civilian contracting company who was supposed to be making a difference here in Africa, and he was acting as if the genocide was freak-show entertainment. I was disgusted.

. . .

A few days later I informed my superiors that I was leaving, giving them nearly one month's notice. I would be staying a few weeks past the completion of my contract. Without the support of my AU sector commander, I sat back and waited for the inevitable. Within one week of my prediction, Hamada was viciously attacked.

Team C invited me along to take pictures. "No, thank you," I replied. "I already know what happened there."

When the team returned to camp, I saw them getting out of their vehicles. I could see by their faces that they were aghast. I had never seen military men so emotionally shaken, and God knows what we had seen up to that point. One of the monitors walked up to me, looking at his hands.

"I buried seven people with these hands today," he said and walked away. We were not authorized to bury the dead, but something drove them to ignore the rule this time.

Ahmed walked by me. He paused and said, "Captain Brian, you are very glad you did not go today." His eyes were glazed over. He looked deeply disturbed.

"Tell me about it," I said.

He shook his head. "I have to go pray," he said quietly and headed to his tent.

Seeing the photos from the incident is something I would wish on no one. A massacre had taken place at Hamada. Of the 450 villagers, 107 had been brutally tortured and murdered. Bodies were strewn along blood-soaked village paths. Infants had been crushed. Toddlers had their faces smashed in with rifle butts, their bodies tossed into the dirt. Deep gashes in a bloody tire bore witness to its use as a chopping block; beside it was an axe. Inside a children's school that had been looted and destroyed, a message remained on the blackboard, written in Arabic:

Faggots and donkeys. We came here to fight you. You weren't here. SLA and JEM you cannot protect your people. You stole from us. Give our property back or we will kill you all.

I was shaking with rage. I stormed into the operations room and started screaming at Dave.

"We told him a week ago! We warned him! We knew! You tell that bastard that he had a moral responsibility to protect these people and he failed. It is his fault those people died. We could have stopped this, but we failed!" I turned and walked out the door before he could say anything.

I was fed up. One hundred and seven people died because the colonel did not listen to me. I was fed up with everyone—my team, our leaders, my employer, the AU, the US—everyone. What was I still doing here?

.　　.　　.

After the attack on Hamada, about 7,000 IDPs arrived in the nearby village of Menawashi. Intelligence suggested that Jurof and Khor Abeche were next on the list of GOS and Janjaweed targets. I convinced our team to conduct a special flight to Jurof and Khor Abeche to warn the towns of an impending attack and instruct the villagers to leave. The omda of Jurof met us at the edge of town. He told us his people were aware of the brutal attack on Hamada, but they wouldn't leave. This wasn't shocking. Where could they go? Nowhere was safe.

"This is our home," he said firmly. "We will stay here until we die."

I learned that Jurof was attacked around February 2005, as I was leaving Darfur, and Khor Abeche was eventually attacked in March 2005 and completely destroyed.

.　　.　　.

Team C never had the chance to get to Labado during the fighting. I joined them when we finally had a chance to visit after we heard that villagers were returning. Even remembering what we had observed from the air, the destruction was staggering. The GOS had spent over a week ensuring that the entire village of 20,000 people was destroyed. Every house, every store, every school and clinic had been looted, burned, and trashed. We walked into a three-room clinic. Half the building had been torched. Inside was a charred swamp of medicine, supplies, tools, and equipment, smashed and broken on the ground. It was eerily quiet. There was no evidence of those who had been killed, probably because they had been buried by their families by now. As we shuffled through the mess, I noticed Ahmed kicking things aggressively. His face was filled with rage. He paced about muttering in Arabic and clicking his tongue at the shame of the destruction.

Walking out from the clinic, I said to Anour, "Ahmed's pretty upset."

"He's Zagahwa," he explained. "These are his people."

The Zagahwa Tribe, like many in Darfur, had been divided by national boundaries when Chad and Sudan were formed during colonial times. But I never knew that our neutral mediator was a member of one of the tribes most persecuted in Darfur. Nearly every attack we had investigated over the last six months had probably involved members of his tribe.

Chapter 30

The impact of Labado and Hamada's destruction—right now before our eyes—was crushing. I could no longer preserve any small belief in what we were doing. But I had to go through the motions for these last two weeks.

I sat in the operations room listening to John. "The GOS reported an SLA strike on four civilian villages. We have to check it out." This was the first incident we had heard of rebel forces attacking civilian villages. In the past, their only targets had been the GOS or police.

Our team met the GOS first in the village of Malam, where the government had established a military outpost. The GOS escorted us on a tour of the village. We saw several dead animals and torched huts. Malam was only partly burned, but the GOS said the SLA had completely destroyed the other three villages. There were only two dead bodies, most likely SLA fighters because they hadn't been buried. We hurried through the investigation, and I barely spoke.

We traveled from Malam to the edge of the Jebel Marra to meet the local SLA commander. The SLA denied the accounts and seemed upset that we were even asking them about the attack. Driving back to Nyala, I spoke privately with Anour and Ali. "Why would your guys do this? You are attacking civilians just like the GOS. This is really bad for you. You're supposed to be the good guys," I said.

"No one is helping us," Anour said defensively. "What are we supposed to do? The people who lived there were Janjaweed. The GOS post there has been helping them. These are the same people who attacked Hamada and Adwah. We looked at this as a military target. We did not kill any civilians."

"But you burned their village down," I said in exasperation.

"Well," he said, "the situation is getting worse."

. . .

The next day we flew to the villages of Gireida, Joghana, and Jayjay, all part of the province of Gireida, one of the last tribal kingdoms in Sudan. The king of Gireida, Abdulrahman Bokhit, was of higher rank and importance than the GOS-appointed governor of all of South Darfur. He even had his own private GOS police detachment to provide him with security. The fact that these GOS security men were protecting him was not an indication that the GOS itself was aligned with the king. In fact, the king was of an African tribe, but he had been able to remain neutral and maintain peaceful relations with all sides in the conflict until now. There had been no fighting inside his kingdom until an attack that occurred three days earlier in Jayjay.

We landed first on the airstrip next to Gireida to meet with the king. He arrived dressed in a brilliant white jelabia and surrounded by his military police detachment.

"There has been an attack on our village of Jayjay. I also have received a letter from an omda, warning that the Janjaweed will attack Gireida next," he reported. "I have ordered my police unit to arrest the militias and have called on every man in the province to come to defend his kingdom. They are to meet in Joghana this morning. You must go there and help them."

Before we departed, the king presented me with the cane he was carrying. He shook my hand, remarking that he had never met an American before. He said that he respected our country greatly and wanted me to remember him. I thanked him as we turned to leave.

Joghana was the next stop. We touched down outside the village, where a large group of 300 people with guns, spears, and vehicles had gathered. They told us they were waiting for us on instruction from the king to take representatives of our team to meet with a group of omdas and sheikhs assembled in the village. The townspeople could only transport two monitors and our interpreter in their small pick-up truck. I volunteered to go, and Dave, with us for the day, decided to join me as well.

They drove us into the central marketplace where a group of around 300 people were yelling and cheering. I felt a bit alarmed, wondering if they were celebrating our capture. They led us to an empty cement building that was guarded by three dump trucks filled with men carrying spears, swords, and guns. Inside the building it was bare except for a metal desk and a few chairs.

Within moments, several omdas and sheikhs entered the building and sat down with us. They provided more detail about the fighting in Jayjay.

"Around 30 Janjaweed on horses and camels attacked the village," a sheikh began. I suspected this was possibly an out-of-control Janjaweed force involved in a local dispute because the GOS was not involved in this attack.

"Our village defense force fought off the militia forces and successfully captured their leader, Mohammed. When we got him, he had been driving a car that belonged to the government-appointed mayor of Buram." The mayor had evidently lent him his vehicle to use in the attack.

"Now the militias are preparing to strike back and free their leader. The king has called on all residents to defend Jayjay. These are the people gathering outside. We are preparing to take them to the village by truck." We ended our meeting quickly and returned to our helicopter so that we could fly to the site of the conflict.

We touched down into chaos. A vehicle immediately screeched to a halt alongside our helicopter. We could see a man in the rear of the pickup truck bed with a gunshot wound to the leg. Blood was streaming down his calf, and people all around us were yelling. A group of women had gathered and were waving their hands in the background. Apparently, the villagers had not had water in three days. The Janjaweed were holding their water hole. The women were demanding that their men go retrieve water.

An old man about 65 or 70 came up to us in a white jelabia and flip flops. He was holding a huge spear, nearly ten feet long with a massive head on it. Through Ibrahim, I asked him about his spear. He said he last used it in 1976. I asked where, and he replied that he had killed an elephant with it.

"Whoa," I responded. "What are you doing with it now?"

"I'm going to go kill some Janjaweed," he said and walked into the bush.

The local civilian defense force brought the Janjaweed leader to us. He was beat up. I felt no emotion when I saw him with his arms shackled behind his back. We began asking questions but were immediately interrupted by gunshots in the distance—perhaps 2 kilometers away. The fighting had resumed, and we suspected the Janjaweed were moving on the village. Villagers of all ages were emerging from their huts with axes, spears, clubs, or anything they could find that could serve as a weapon. Ahmed and I looked at each other with eyes wide.

"They are going to get their water hole back," Ahmed said.

We heard more shooting, closer now. Anour and Ibrahim jumped up immediately. No one needed to say, "Let's go." We dashed back to our helicopter and loaded up as the pilots started the engine. The engines turned over briefly but then cooled down again. Another try, another failure. The pilots screamed back to us that they could not get the second engine started. The gunshots continued in the distance.

We all got out of the helicopter and looked around us. We were in a wide field of sorghum stocks, the earth hard as a rock. At that instant, I heard the firing of a rocket propelled grenade. The Janjaweed were getting closer. Dave looked at me.

"Well, we may be the only two white people to ever witness a Janjaweed attack firsthand," he said. "Only we won't survive to tell the tale."

Dave pulled out a satellite phone and called our operations room.

"We're in Jayjay," he yelled. "It's crazy here. You've got to get us out of here. We're about to get caught in the middle of a Janjaweed slaughter, and the damn helicopter won't start. We need a maintenance crew and as many protection forces as you can fit in our other chopper."

Dave's face went white and he turned off his phone. He relayed the news, "They'll be there within an hour."

"Within an hour?" I shuddered. We looked around, wondering what we could do when all hell broke loose. As soon as the militia poured into our field from the higher grasses beyond, all they would see would be a huge white helicopter. We had no weapons and couldn't even dig a hole.

We could see women in the village loading their belongings onto donkeys and fleeing in the opposite direction. All the men and boys, even as young as eight years old, were preparing to fight. There was no apparent strategy. Some men were heading into the field, while others were positioning themselves in front of their huts. I watched the scene in horror. They had no chance.

Minutes passed. Dave and I sat there and said nothing; all the while the gunfire was getting louder. My heart beat in my throat. I looked at my watch.

It had only been ten minutes. I swore I could hear Arabic voices shouting through the grass. I looked at Ahmed. He was kneeling by the helicopter with the other Muslim monitors praying. Joseph was pacing back and forth, holding his hand to his forehead.

Finally, we heard chopper blades in the distance. Ibrahim and Ali cheered and jumped up and down. I let out a huge breath and made the sign of the cross. A helicopter roared into sight. Three pilots, a few maintenance guys, and 10 protection forces jumped out when it landed. The new crew brought a machine gun, which they positioned at the head of a semicircle the Rwandan soldiers formed in front of our two helicopters. We weren't out of trouble yet, but we were in a much better position.

Two Russian maintenance workers opened the engine compartment on top of the helicopter and climbed up into the hood. One of the guys with a 10-pound sledge hammer began bludgeoning the engine. He yelled down to the pilot, who then started up the engine as the Russian continued pounding away. I could not imagine how long this remedy would last.

"Dave, I don't know about you," I said, as a piece of machinery flew by me, "but that looks like a quick fix to me. How about we take the good helo back?" He nodded and I turned toward the mechanics.

"Listen, you guys take this one in case it needs any more work. We'll go on the chopper you came in. Let's split the protection forces between us," I instructed.

We climbed into the helicopter and slammed the door. I peered out the window and caught the eye of a tiny girl holding her mom's leg as she loaded her other children onto the back of a donkey nearby. "Jeez," I breathed to myself. "What's going to happen to them?"

As we lifted off from Jayjay we saw the three dump trucks from Joghana pulling in filled with more armed villagers. I felt only slightly reassured. They might be able to hold off the Janjaweed long enough for their kids and wives to flee to safety, but I couldn't imagine these men with spears and clubs could save their village alone.

Our most experienced pilot was at the helm. He flew toward the fighting below tree level, swerving between nim trees. We could see some people dragging the injured back toward the village and others heading out into the conflict with axes and spears. Gunshots rang out all around us. The pilot decided to fly a bit higher so we would not risk getting shot. As we neared the Janjaweed forces, we could see a number of militiamen in offensive positions, others on camels and horses.

Suddenly, our pilot laughed and said, "Watch this." He pointed to a Janjaweed on a horse just ahead. Lowering the helicopter, he headed straight for the man. The militiaman looked over his shoulder and saw the huge helicopter heading his way. In fear of his life, he kicked his horse into a flat-out gallop, trying to outrun our aircraft as we came closer and closer. We soared over the horse, nearly throwing the Janjaweed soldier to the ground with the force of our gust. The entire team cheered in the cockpit. But the high from this small victory was short-lived. It did nothing to compensate for what we knew would be inevitable.

We flew farther, toward the place where the Janjaweed forces had originated, identifying nomad settlements on the other side of the water hole. As we continued, we saw five or six more villages smoldering. The Janjaweed had been burning villages all along their way to Jayjay.

.   .   .

A few days later I prepared to leave Nyala. Ahmed gave me a bear hug.

"Captain Brian, you must come and visit me in my own country."

"I will," I replied, and meant it.

As a gift, Ahmed gave me a traditional jelabia, including a scarf and head dress. He also had a local cobbler make me some traditional Sudanese shoes from leopard skins. Anour and Ali presented me with amulets that they believed would make me bulletproof. Ibrahim gave me a note that said, "Thank you for being my friend." Everyone was there to say goodbye. Contractors and aid workers tended to rotate so often in these conflict areas that frequent departures were common. But I was considered an old hand, having been in Darfur for six months.

Joseph walked up and thanked me for my service to the team. He spoke politely and a bit formally, but there was warmth in his voice. "It is too bad that you are leaving, Captain Brian. But, I wish you well." On the day of my departure, one of the contractors in Khartoum escorted me all the way through airport security. I had packed everything I owned in my check-in bags, not willing to risk being caught by security with any information on me, despite the fact that I still had diplomatic immunity. I passed through the final passport check and settled into a chair in the waiting room.

It was about 2:00 a.m., and the airport was relatively empty. One of the florescent lights flickered inside the stained ceiling panels. The waiting room looked like a scene out of the 1970s. Each row of connected orange plastic seats shifted with every passenger who sat down, nearly all of whom were smoking and then throwing their cigarette butts directly on the floor. A single bored vendor served bottled drinks in one corner. Each flight was announced in Arabic, and the few white people in the waiting area kept checking with each other to see if their plane had been called.

Then I saw a Sudanese official in a suit walking toward me.

"Brian," he said, "we need to check your bag."

Oh God, I thought. How did he know my name? What was he going to do with me? I followed him as he walked back through the security counter toward the baggage claim. He moved toward the hole in the wall leading to the back rooms where the baggage handlers sorted the luggage. I could see the pant legs of more than one man; I could also see the barrel of a Kalashnikov.

"Come this way," he ordered. My stomach churned. How was I going to get out of here? If I ran, I might be able to get out of the airport and find my way back to the contracting company's compound, but there was no guarantee I could get out of the country after trying to escape. I had duct taped my bag completely shut, attaching a sword that I had bought in the market in Khartoum. Inside was my laptop, my camera, and my external hard drive with duplicate photos and the details of every attack I had witnessed.

"After you," he said, gesturing toward the hole. I stepped up onto the conveyor belt and through the opening. Four other Sudanese security men in suits were standing next to my bag. The man with the weapon looked at me with no emotion. I blinked, trying to adjust quickly to the darkness. Luggage, perhaps from other missing passengers, was stacked around us, collecting dust. I could disappear at this moment. As far as the contractor who checked me in was concerned, I had boarded my flight.

"Open your bag," the man said. As an AU monitor, I was not supposed to be searched, but I wasn't going to argue with a man with a Kalashnikov.

Carefully, I pulled back the tape and unzipped the zipper. The man began reaching into my bag, rifling through my clothing. He finally came to my computer. He pulled it out of my luggage and demanded that I turn it on. I had not removed any of the photos from my files on my laptop. Nearly 1,000 of my own photographs and more than 2,000 others documenting six months of genocide were right here beneath my fingertips. I pressed the power button. It seemed like an eternity before my laptop came to life. I waited for him to begin to search my files.

Through the pounding of my heartbeat, I heard him say, "Thank you. You can go now."

I scrambled to my feet, trying not to appear nervous. My legs felt like jelly. I half expected to be clubbed over the head as I emerged from the baggage claim area, so I walked toward the opening half backwards. Maybe my bag wouldn't even show up on the other end, but I no longer cared.

In the distance, I heard them calling my flight. Clutching my passport and ticket, I boarded my one-way flight from Khartoum to America.

Epilogue

I never intended to speak out when I got back to America. To the contrary, I would have been more than happy to fade into the New Hampshire woods, where my sister and brother-in-law live, put on my best camo, and wait for whatever professional opportunity came along next. But the same instinct that drove me to collect more and more information in Darfur, combined with my gathering anger at the world's averted eyes, left me feeling incomplete. Someone had to know what I'd seen. Something had to be done—soon, right now, not later when the politicians and the diplomats thought they could tuck the issue of genocide in Sudan into their schedules.

Even before my return, Gretchen had been corresponding with Nicholas Kristof, the *New York Times* columnist whose consistent and passionate coverage of Darfur had set him apart from his colleagues in mainstream journalism. At his invitation, Gretchen and I traveled to New York to meet with him. Nick was eager to expose what I had witnessed, but he also recognized and respected my concerns about going public. We finally agreed that he would release four of my photographs and I would remain anonymous. I was not yet prepared to put my career, and possibly my life, on the line.

The response was overwhelming. Nick called shortly after his column was published to say that many news organizations had contacted him, all of them eager to talk with me about my experiences. Without pushing, he suggested that my talking to other journalists might be the best way to broaden news coverage of Darfur. I still felt tugged in two directions: the opportunity to do more for the people I had just abandoned was compelling, but so was the need to preserve my career options now that I had terminated my employment. My father recommended that I think very carefully about the consequences of my actions and consider ways to work within the system to share information without jeopardizing my own safety. Gretchen,

Andrew, and I discussed various strategies to inform the public of what was happening in Darfur.

But the energy of that initial response finally pushed me to take the risk: with my approval, Nick mentioned me by name in his second column.

Suddenly, every major news agency in the country was calling, and politicians supporting the cause were eager to bring me to Washington. Republican Senator Sam Brownback of Kansas had paraded my photographs and Nick's two columns around the Senate floor, entering them into the *Congressional Record* during debate over the Darfur Accountability Act, a bipartisan bill he introduced with then Democratic Senator Jon Corzine of New Jersey. The nation's leaders actually seemed to be listening as they pushed for a no-fly zone over Darfur, weapons embargos, travel restrictions on Sudanese officials, and economic sanctions against the government in Khartoum. Policymakers were also seeking increased funding and support for the African Union to get more troops on the ground, and to expand its mandate to include stopping the fighting. I was fired up and ready to go to bat for the people of Darfur by raising awareness however and wherever I could—in America, at the United Nations, around the world.

In Lebanon, New Hampshire, Gretchen and I headed to a local coffee shop to brainstorm ways to start a movement for Darfur. We envisioned a documentary film, a book, photography exhibits, rallies, grassroots projects, and global speaking tours. We made travel arrangements to spend at least a month on Capitol Hill lobbying and doing interviews. Like idealistic college protesters, we thought we could engineer the end of genocide in Sudan. It all seemed so simple.

Both my former employer and the US State Department thought I should hold off on the interviews—and they told me so over the course of several conversations. But at that point, I'd given it a lot of thought. I certainly had a legal right to speak out, and there seemed to be political support for my continuing to share my story with as many others as we could reach.

Gretchen and I met with many members of Congress in both the Senate and the House. We took my photographs and the document containing the specific genocide directive I obtained in Darfur to two ambassadors to the UN, Stuart Holliday and Pierre-Richard Prosper. Republican Congressman Frank Wolf of Virginia arranged for me to sit down to discuss the Darfur situation with then Deputy Secretary of State Robert Zoellick and introduced me to Secretary of State Condoleezza Rice. Congressional representatives were desperate to take action, but the Bush administration only politely acknowledged my evidence. I gave countless interviews and began speaking at universities all across the country. I testified before several congressional committees, traveled to Geneva to speak before the UN Human Rights Commission, and shared my evidence with the British Parliament.

Despite the early interest in my story, there was no serious movement for international intervention. Meanwhile, we began to feel the backlash.

I had heard rumors that people with the NGOs, UN, and AU in Darfur were upset that I had shared information with the public. They accused me of making their jobs on the ground more difficult because the GOS had clamped down on their operations to prevent further leaks. During my speaking engagements, representatives of the Sudanese government occasionally attended, taking the opportunity to publicly contest the legitimacy of my photographs. The Sudanese ambassador to the United States actually claimed to one news reporter that the photograph I took of a GOS attack helicopter was taken in Arizona.

At the same time, the US State Department was concerned that the GOS would force the AU to expel all US monitors from the mission; people from the State Department told me directly that I had made it nearly impossible for US representatives to obtain visas to travel to Sudan.

I already knew that I had destroyed any chance of working with another civilian contractor. Whistle-blowers who did not follow the appropriate chain of command were not welcome. During one panel discussion at the National Press Club, Charles Snyder, then the senior guy on Sudan at the US State Department's Bureau of African Affairs, glanced in my direction and asserted that the United States was now much better at screening its contractors. Snyder went on to discredit my assessment of the situation on the ground, claiming that the crisis was easing and that the United States was doing everything it possibly could.

An anonymous source sent several threatening and degrading e-mails. Later, I was able to identify the source as someone I had worked with in

Sudan; apparently the sender thought I was trying to exploit the suffering of the people in Darfur for my own financial gain.

The criticism hurt because it was so misguided: I really was trying to do something positive—to generate public interest that might bring pressure to bear on our lawmakers and force them to stop the genocide. I was also trying to gain more support for the AU so that its people could continue their work in Darfur. Unlike most advocates, I was not employed by an NGO. I was certainly not a celebrity who could self-finance my work as a spokesperson for a cause. In fact, by the end of 2005, I had spent nearly eight months' worth of the salary that I had saved as I traveled around trying to raise awareness.

I was plagued with doubts and frequently dreamed of Darfur. Working one night at my parents' house in Virginia, I walked outside to get some fresh air. In the moonlight across the field, I saw hundreds and hundreds of Darfurians staring at me. They didn't say a word or make a sound. They were imploring me to help them and to be their voice. Despite the difficulties I was facing, I felt confirmation that what I was doing was the right thing—maybe not for me, but for them.

Within months, the news media turned their attention away from Darfur to cover the Michael Jackson trial, the ordeal of Terri Schiavo, the ailing Pope John Paul II, and other stories they considered more pressing. In the void, Gretchen and I decided to leave America and return to Africa. We both wanted to reconnect with why we were doing this work and Gretchen wanted to look for grassroots projects to support the women. We spent a month in Chad, camping near the Darfur refugee camps, seeking those who may have fled the villages I saw attacked, and starting our documentary film. When I showed the refugees photos of what I had witnessed, they were clearly surprised that anyone knew what was happening to them. I felt an instant connection. They seemed convinced they were going to be saved. Over and over again, they voiced the same simple request—to return safely to their homes.

There were no other witnesses willing to speak out. How could I not continue? I left Chad even more certain that I was doing the right thing and determined to help these people at all costs.

.   .   .

Nearly three years and hundreds of speaking events and interviews later, there still is no UN or other international intervention force on the ground in Darfur. In fact, the violence has escalated. NGOs and government agencies disagree on the exact numbers, but a fair estimate is that between 300,000 and 400,000 have perished, and over 2.5 million people have been displaced.

In the last year or so, the situation in Darfur has become increasingly complex. In May 2006, the SLA signed a peace treaty with the government of Sudan. However, internal disagreements about the terms of the treaty caused the SLA to splinter into different rebel groups. SLA proponents of the peace agreement, under the leadership of Minni Minawi, aligned themselves with the Sudanese government and began to attack rebel groups that opposed the treaty. The government opened a large new offensive across North and West Darfur, while a number of the remaining rebel groups pulled back into Chad, reorganized as the National Redemption Front (NRF), and launched counterattacks in an all-out war.

Since 2006, several new rebel groups have revealed themselves. Most are vying for positions and representation at any future peace talks or treaty. While some represent the people's interests, many are simply pursuing power and control. This prompted new fighting leading up to the peace talks that opened in Tripoli on October 27, 2007. The GOS initiated major offensives throughout Darfur in an attempt to destabilize the region even further, resulting in the two main rebel groups boycotting the talks. Analysts are not optimistic. If the rebel groups cannot agree on a single platform, they will never achieve anything. If the GOS does not stop killing its own civilians, then the resistance will always exist.

The UN has committed to deploying 26,000 "Peace Keeping" troops to Darfur by the end of 2007. My question is: If there is no peace to keep, what will be their mission? There is no dispute that the civilians, who are caught in the crossfire or targeted by the government, need protection. But how can peace be forced upon the parties who want to continue fighting? And how can it be guaranteed to those who want it?

The UN was formed to deal with issues like this one. Yet, as of this writing, the UN has passed twenty-two resolutions pertaining to Sudan since 2004. All are too weak to stop the fighting and none have been enforced.

Furthermore, the UN has allowed the GOS, of all parties, to dictate the make-up, structure, and function of this peace keeping force. It is ludicrous.

There is still hope, however. Even if we cannot rely on multinational institutions like the UN or our governments to take the lead to stop genocide, there is a large grassroots movement in the United States, Canada, and Europe, and it is slowly spreading to other places in the world. This is one of the largest movements seen since the end of Apartheid in South Africa. As a result of this movement, twenty states and many individual cities have divested pension funds and other investments from companies that are complicit in the genocide in Darfur. The United States has increased sanctions against Sudan in response to heavier pressure from citizens, though it has had little effect on the ground. In addition, activists have been using the 2008 Beijing Olympic Games as leverage for increasing the pressure on China, a leading supporter of Sudan both militarily and economically. China has been quietly talking to the Sudanese government, attempting to persuade it to stop the killing. China also abstained from vetoing the UN resolution that authorized the deployment of 26,000 troops. Movements in Europe have persuaded their governments to assist neighboring countries affected by this conflict. As a result, the EU has committed to deploying 4,000 troops to stop violence that has been spreading into, and destabilizing, the neighboring countries of Chad and the Central African Republic.

Governments around the world have a responsibility to act on behalf of their citizens. This is most often done in the name of national security or in order to secure economic resources. If we want our governments to stop atrocities from happening when they have no interest at stake, we must all stand up together and make noise. We must make this OUR issue. These things should not be happening on this earth.

. . .

Sometimes when I am talking to people about Darfur, they ask me how they or the United States will benefit from getting involved in the issue. I can feel my anger rising. I tell them: You get nothing! You get nothing from helping these people—except to know you did something good, that you did the right thing. You helped people who couldn't help themselves.

Every human being should have a chance to grow up without violence, to make independent choices in life, to drink a glass of clean water, to be free of fear—the fear of rape or a bullet in the back during the simple task of collecting firewood for daily meals.

I then point to my photo of Mihad and say: If these reasons aren't enough for you—I give you her. Shouldn't she have had the right to grow up surrounded by peace and love? What child deserves to be shot at age one?

What nation can allow genocide to continue?

What person can turn their back on the victims of such hatred?

When the genocide in Darfur has ended, what will you say you did to stop it?

A Note from
Gretchen Steidle Wallace

In June 2005, Brian and I returned to Africa to visit the Darfur refugee camps of eastern Chad, where hundreds of thousands have now fled. Brian hoped to reunite with any villagers who had escaped the same atrocities he had witnessed. I was on a journey to understand the impact of genocide on women and to help survivors launch their own ideas for improving their lives. We were also filming the first shoot for what would become an award-winning documentary on Darfur, also titled *The Devil Came on Horseback*.

Among the many refugees we met was Adam, an educated black Sudanese English teacher. Before genocide broke out in Darfur, he moved his family frequently to avoid the oppressive tactics of a government who disliked his democratic teachings to local, uneducated communities. Adam was living on the Chadian border in Tine, Sudan, when his village was first attacked. His family of eight—including his wife, seven months pregnant—escaped, with nothing but a few belongings, across the border to Chad hours before the Janjaweed militia arrived. Adam sold several of their blankets so that they could eat for the first three days, while he sought a better solution. Soon he was using his small cart to carry goods back and forth across the border for a few coins. It took months to earn the funds necessary to transport his family to a refugee camp. When they finally arrived, the camp was no longer registering refugees for the month, and so his family had to live in the bush for another three weeks. The family survived on the generous but meager food donations of other refugees before they were officially allowed to settle in the camp.

Adam has now lived displaced in Chad for over three years. Despite the hardship of daily life as a refugee, Adam is fiercely committed to sharing his knowledge with all who surround him. Most of the Darfurians in Adam's camp are rural farmers, many of whom have never attended school and have little understanding of their rights as refugees. Adam worked to obtain Arabic translations of UN documents on refugee rights to share with his peers. With no access to a meeting place of their own, they gather daily in the outdoor markets. Adam enlists the help of literate shop keepers to read the documents aloud while their customers sit and play cards. The result has been a growing dialogue, as displaced families discover what it means to be a refugee. Adam believes that his fellow Darfurians are eager to know more and that all they need now is a structure that can serve as a place of learning.

"We have many, many resources," he said to me, pointing out across thousands of dusty UNHCR-issued tents. "We have land, we have water. . . . If we are educated, we can make use of these resources to help ourselves with better living."

Adam's next step involves constructing a library center in the camp. He has carefully sketched a complete architectural diagram for the library and consulted a Chadian engineer to develop a line-item budget for his design. He envisions electric lights, satellite internet, and television to draw members in to hear educational lectures on issues of refugee law, women's rights, children's rights, and UN resolutions on Darfur. Adam also wants to address what he calls the "bad habits" of his culture impacting women, such as the practice of female circumcision and domestic abuse.

I have learned so much from those who seemingly have so little. The same has been true of the many Rwandan widows and orphans with whom I also now work through Global Grassroots. Women often bear the greatest burden of genocide. Our aim is to provide social entrepreneurship training and seed funding to help genocide survivors, like Adam, advance their own ideas for social change benefiting women.

The IDP and refugee camps are filled with families who have lost their fathers and husbands to the conflict. Most significantly, rape is used as a widespread tool of war. During attacks, girls as young as eight, women as old as seventy-eight, and even pregnant women have reported being gang raped by government officials and Arab militia members. Even after relocation to the supposed safe haven of the camps, women must reluctantly venture daily into the desert, facing the almost certain risk of rape in order to find firewood for cooking. Frequently, rape victims are ostracized. Others face unwanted pregnancies. When women report their rapes, they are often arrested for having sex out of marriage or experiencing an "illegal pregnancy." There are reports of the humiliation of virginity testing and further sexual assault within prison. When women are finally able to return home and rebuild their lives, many are abandoned by their parents or husbands with shame because they are now considered "tainted." Countless women are left to support themselves and their unwanted children alone.

The long-term impact of genocide can be just as difficult as the initial trauma. In Rwanda, where the UN estimates that between 250,000 and 500,000 women were raped during the 1994 genocide, many contracted HIV and now live as widows caring for their neighbors' orphans along with their own children. And yet, I have watched what these survivors have done with few resources and minimal education, struggling to earn enough to eat each day, and still at risk of persecution. These women are now transforming their communities.

Back here in the United States, I can't tell you how many times I've heard someone say, "But we're so *far* from Darfur. What can I possibly do?" How does one individual on the other side of the planet make any sort of dent in this issue or the next conflict? I know how easy it is to feel powerless or simply at a loss for any real answer. I wrestled with this same dilemma when I first began hearing my brother's stories. As I learned more about the unbearable consequences of rape used as a tool of war, there were times when I would embarrassingly burst into tears in the middle of social engagements that suddenly felt so meaningless.

When I work with marginalized victims of conflict, they often start with the same sense of powerlessness that we feel. As I begin a training program, gathered before me will be a group of survivors so battered by life's circumstances that they feel they have absolutely nothing to offer the world. Many have no house, no food, no job, no family, no hope. And then, together, we slowly begin the process of rediscovering and reclaiming their sense of self. By the end of our workshops, these survivors have designed their own initiatives to address illiteracy, violence, water scarcity, malnutrition, and many other issues facing women in their communities.

So, as *we* ask what we can do about this situation—the *We* that is likely relatively educated, well-fed, employed, safe, healthy, living in a system that aims to protect our rights, and with opportunity at our fingertips—I'd like to issue a challenge. We too each have a gift or capability that, I suggest, does not belong to us. It is our responsibility to nurture it and offer it back to the world. And there is no better time than right now. Whatever you have— a song, a work of art, a few dollars, a phone call, a day of service, some expertise, a few strong hands, an idea, some celebrity, the ability to listen, a recycled tool, a little extra time—find a place and a way to throw it into the pot of social change for the sake of those who have no choice, no voice, and no opportunity.

If a genocide survivor living the greatest hardship we can imagine has found a way to create possibility out of his or her circumstances, surely we can do so, too.

.   .   .

Writing this book with Brian has been an extraordinary experience. I am most grateful to my brother for trusting me with his stories and giving me the opportunity to help articulate them on paper. I thank you, Brian, for being such an inspiration and fierce supporter of my work with Global Grassroots. I thank our editor, Lindsay Jones, our publisher Susan Weinberg, our publicity and marketing team, Jaime Leifer and Lindsay Goodman, founder and editor-at-large, Peter Osnos, and the rest of PublicAffairs for believing in us and helping us through this first work. I thank my parents for their neverending emotional support and guidance that has anchored us throughout our involvement in this movement. I thank Jane Wells for her wisdom, encouragement, and friendship. I thank my good friends Jenny Holden and Cristina Ljungberg for joining me as warriors on this path and forgiving me when it sometimes eclipsed all else. I thank Annie Sundberg, Ricki Stern, Jane Wells, Leslie Thomas, and Andi Scull for putting their hearts into supporting Brian's story. I thank Alan Pesky, who remains an important mentor, and Jessica Dibb, my spiritual teacher. I honor the memory of Emmett Wallace and thank Karl Meyer and Nicholas Kristof— these three were responsible for helping us first find our voice. To the many individuals and groups who make up the Darfur movement, I acknowledge and thank you for your tireless passion. Most of all, I thank my husband, Andrew, who brings me the joy and unconditional love that fuels my every action.

.   .   .

To the people of Darfur and all genocide survivors, we humbly ask your forgiveness for our collective inability to act swiftly to protect your lives, your freedom, and your basic human rights.

BRIAN STEIDLE, a former captain in the Marine Corps, worked for the African Union where he served in Darfur. He has made several return trips to Africa and now works with his sister, Gretchen, to raise awareness about the genocide in Sudan and lobby for international support.

GRETCHEN STEIDLE WALLACE, the founder of Global Grassroots, has a BA in foreign affairs from the University of Virginia and an MBA from the Tuck School at Dartmouth College. In 2007 she was chosen by *World Business* magazine as one of the 35 most influential women in business under the age of 35. She was a producer of the documentary film *The Devil Came on Horseback*.

Brian and Gretchen live in California and New Hampshire, respectively.

Visit them at www.globalgrassroots.org and www.hopeartists.org.